JUST A GROCER'S SON

A Century of Family, Community, and a Neighborhood
Grocery

By

Daniel L. Frizzi, Jr.

McGilligan Publishing
3707 Cypress Creek Pkwy Ste 310 #505
Houston, TX 77068
www.mcgilliganpublishing.com

ISBN

Hardcover: 979-8-90190-333-9

Paperback: 979-8-90190-332-2

This book is dedicated
to my Grandmother Philomena DeSimone Frizzi,
my Mother Nancy Robinson Frizzi,
and my Aunt Kathryn Frizzi Regoli,
since the success of
any family business
is dependent upon the sacrifice
of wives,
and daughters
too!

About the Author

Daniel L. Frizzi Jr. is a practicing attorney in Bellaire, Ohio, where he has engaged in the private law practice for nearly 50 years. He was born in Bellaire in 1952, attended the Bellaire Public Schools graduating from high school in 1970. He is a graduate of Ohio University from the College of Business Administration in 1974 and later graduated from the Ohio Northern University Pettit College of Law in 1977.

The author has been an Adjunct Professor of business law at Ohio University Eastern Campus and Wheeling Jesuit University, while maintaining an active private general practice of law in his hometown. Mr. Frizzi has always held a keen interest in history and has published books on local history topics, as well as being a lecturer throughout the Ohio Valley to historical societies and libraries. He is the past chair and founding member of the Great Stone Viaduct Historical Education Society, and has made numerous contributions to the Winter Lecture Series sponsored by the Bellaire Public Library for the past 14 years.

Frizzi has also served 14 years on the board of trustees of the Bellaire Public Library and is currently a trustee of the Belmont County Tourism Council. His civic membership has included the Bellaire High School Alumni Association and the Ohio University Alumni Association. When not practicing law, the author enjoys golf, photography, and railroad history as he approaches retirement after 49 years of private legal practice. He has been married to his high school sweetheart, Penny Jo, since 1975, and has been blessed with three adult children and six wonderful grandchildren.

Acknowledgment

The pages of this book are filled with the memories of so many persons who assisted me with their own personal recollections of the past. While many of the pages discuss what I remember, I would be remiss if I did not acknowledge those other persons who contributed to my work by recalling their own memories. This book has been a collective effort, where I have been the scrivener to record the tales that appear herein. Some of my sources are living, while others have gone on ahead, leaving only their stories that can still be recalled today.

My Grandfather, Abe and my father, Danny, told me stories when I was a little boy that I have never forgotten. Names and places that they often spoke about, I still recall today. My attempts to document those names, places, and events during my research have been a rewarding and reassuring experience. To my Grandmother, Philomena, whom I have only known through photographs and the recorded memories of others, I was able to reconstruct many of the events and the stories that appear in this book. This has been made possible because of her preservation of documents and photographs of her life, and the keeping of those by her children. My mother, Nancy, who was an avid collector of family memories as seen through the lens of a camera, provided so many opportunities for recalling the past just by leafing through those old black & whites and color snapshots of our family. Without these important people in my life and their stories, photographs, and recorded memories, this book would have been seriously lacking in content.

Those family members with whom I have corresponded are also to be recognized for giving me a more detailed explanation of the people and events recorded on these pages. My aunt Kathryn Frizzi Regoli and my cousins Steve and Kathi helped to recall the wonderful times in the 1950s when we were all living on Washington Street as small children. My aunt Kathryn, however, was so helpful in recalling her own experiences as a young girl growing up on Washington Street. In reading her own recorded memories, I realize how similar our impressions of the little grocery store actually are, even though they were separated by more than 20 years. Tommy Ostasiewski, my father's cousin, was intimately familiar with the DeSimone family and was able to give me much information about this important Italian family of Bellaire. Clara Presutti and Robert Cicogna, also my father's cousins, provided me with personal remembrances of those days as a small child in the Cicogna family. Clara recalled intimate details of my Grandparents, Abe and Minnie. Former residents of Washington Street, like Minnie Nardo Taffe, Richard Massa, and Dean Giacometti, helped to provide me with confirmation of many facts necessary for accurately telling those stories that appear in this book. Robert Berher helped to piece together the final days of the Associated Grocers Warehouse and the formation of the Grocer's Development Corporation. My brother Dick, with whom I shared so many of the experiences about which I have written, helped to recall with me our past life together in those early years of our family living on Washington Street. The Bauknecht Altmeyer Funeral Home was helpful in supplying me with dates of death, spellings, and information that would have taken many days to otherwise compile. The Bellaire Public Library staff has also been helpful when I was unable to get into the library for information contained in the local history section. There are countless others who, just in passing conversation, helped me recall events, names, and dates. Trish Trigg, Lynn Steele, Vincent Kolenich, and so many others were helpful in my search for accuracy. My friend, Paul Cramer, whose critical advice on a cover design brought to life the title I had chosen for this book.

I have written within these pages about many different people who were customers of our store. Others mentioned are co-workers, friends, and fellow classmates during my school days. To each of them, I am grateful for the times we shared together and the memories we made when I was a young man. They have truly given me the inspiration for writing this book. I have attempted within these pages to remember them as they were when I was just a grocer's son working in the family store.

Contents

This book is written in remembrance of others now long gone. My father and Grandfather, with whom I worked side by side as a young boy. My mother, who gave me encouragement as a young boy when working in the family business, often seemed unfair. The many customers from whom I learned lifelong lessons during the 1950s, 60s, and 70s, each with different personalities and varying stations in life. Each of these people, in different ways, helped to mold me into who I am today. Their interaction with me then helped to create those memories that I treasure now more than ever as I grow older.

I will attempt to record my own memories throughout these pages, although in some ways they will be shared memories also held by my younger brothers. My purpose is not to supplant theirs with my own, but to explain what I remember of those wonderful days of my youth growing up as just a grocer's son working in the small family business. They will certainly remember and treasure their own experiences. By committing to paper my own memories, to the extent I am best able, the hope I have is that all will better understand the history of our family. Because I am the eldest among us, there are memories that are uniquely my own, and sharing them is important for a full appreciation of our family history.

My writing hopefully will explain how our Grandfather Abe and Grandmother Minnie operated a small family grocery store and raised our father, Danny, and his sister, Kathryn. The memories they shared are an integral part of the history of our family. They faced different times and circumstances during the 1930s and 40s, and their lives were shaped by those times. Who we are is in large part dictated by that period when we grew up and the influences to which we were exposed. I consider myself exceedingly fortunate to have known life growing up behind a counter in a little family grocery store. Things were not always easy, and sometimes things did not always seem fair, living in a family operating a small business. Yet, the lessons learned behind that store counter at an early age helped to shape so many of the better qualities I recognize today, some sixty years later. Self-employed for the past 49 years as a practicing lawyer, I often reflect on the experiences of my own childhood, working for my father and Grandfather in the family grocery business. My service is now of a different kind. No longer behind a counter, but now I have served from behind a desk or a courtroom podium for most of my adult life. Yet, what I learned from behind that store counter, in that little grocery store, continues to spring forth in me today as a lawyer. As I grow older, I realize that I am still just a grocer's son who now dresses in a suit and tie instead of a store apron.

Many of the things that will appear in these pages are not from my own memory, but from the collective memory of my father, Danny, and my Grandfather, Abramo. My aunt Kathryn and cousins Don and Kathi also have wonderful memories that they have shared with me. The Cicogna history was compiled through conversations with Clara Presutti and Robert Cicogna, cousins of my father. My brother Dick has also attempted to assist me where my own memory has been elusive or in doubt. Much of what is written in these pages will be stories and family history from our collective recollection of the past. Also recorded herein will be a local history that I have become familiar with over the past 73 years of living and working in the community. This recollection of memories, combined with my own, will hopefully provide an accurate picture of family experiences as operators of a small neighborhood grocery store for more than 100 years, commencing early in the 20th century. Sadly, the small neighborhood grocery stores in most small communities have disappeared. I hope to provide readers with an understanding of what it was like growing up during that time as a grocer's son in this type of business. Even more unique will be the experience of operating the business with Italian immigrant roots.

I find enormous enjoyment today from interaction with teens and young adults who are learning the meaning of service to others at their places of employment. Whether they are behind a counter, or in a shopping aisle, or waiting tables, or dipping ice cream, or flipping burgers, I revisit in them my own childhood memories. Some of these young people wear aprons, just as I did. Most of them operate what we termed a cash register in my day, handling the money of the customers that is tendered to their employer's business. Many of them willingly offer up advice to me as a senior citizen responding to my questions at an electronics or hardware store. Some serve as my guide, directing me through the jungle of aisles of Walmart or Lowe's, searching for something I simply cannot find on my own. Most react enthusiastically when I make inquiries about their school, their future, and their families. Most try to be helpful and respectful to this older man who was once in their place as a stock boy in a small grocery store long before they were born.

I am wiser today, however, and have learned over many years what they have yet to learn. They do not realize that the experience they are getting in minimum wage and inconvenient hourly part-time jobs will shape who they are, what they will become, and the cognitive ways they will approach life for years to come. Their experiences will become lessons on life and living to be carried with them into their first real job after graduation from high school or college. Qualities like responsibility, reliability, honesty, punctuality, personal appearance, frugality, respect, decisiveness, communication, and an overall work ethic are shaped in these types of jobs. Such jobs teach the meaning of sacrifice, because there are many 'fun things' that will be missed due to maintaining a work schedule. Hard work for meager earnings will often generate a desire to quit. Hopefully, they will understand that one day a better job will be found, if only they keep pace and patiently do their job now until that better job comes. Learning the trade and the skills of their bosses and managers, which comes from listening and watching, is an education that can make them a better employee and, in fact, a better person. The interpersonal relationships and communication with the public help to shape their skills at dealing with difficult situations and different personalities. They will be presented with many different choices, and learning to make decisions is an important part of these workplace experiences. Some decisions will be in error, but nonetheless, they will be learning experiences experienced in the school of 'hard knocks.'

Growing up behind the counter in a small family-owned business taught me so many things that I would have found nowhere else. As a young boy, I saw the sacrifice of the family fathers and mothers in making the business successful. I can remember many of those successes and the disappointments that simply come with the territory of being self-employed. The struggles of my parents to make ends meet financially are worth recalling, since, contrary to popular belief, you do not get rich just because you own your own business. I grew up in an environment where these experiences actually occurred. How fortunate I was to be able to do so. Sadly, so many young people today will never have that opportunity.

Yes, there are still other types of family businesses operated today by small business entrepreneurs. Because many are conducted over the internet in an electronic age, however, the close personal interaction between patrons and providers has been lost. Our conversations today are much different than those I had with my parents and Grandparents as a boy. Just try to eat dinner with your grandchildren today without an electronic device competing with you for attention. Or try to talk to the same person twice when making an inquiry about your credit card account balance and purchases, or renewing your internet radio service. That close personal contact that I grew up with has been substituted for an impersonal, faceless, and nameless contact when doing business. Do not misunderstand my point. I could never go back to mechanical typewriters and dictation by shorthand in my law practice. I have many computer applications for my office that make doing business so much easier for both me, as an attorney, and for the benefit of my clients. Of course, the electronic age has been a tremendous benefit to all of us, from which no one, including me, ever wants to retreat. Yet, despite the benefits that we all recognize, there has been a cost. Face-to-face interaction at an early age is important to a newborn baby's early childhood development. This same kind of contact in our early 'school year jobs' is also essential in preparing one for any career.

I am hopeful that young people will find within these pages lessons on why their jobs are important to their employers, their customers, and the patrons they serve. If they take away anything from these pages, my sincere hope is that they remember the people they are dealing with are real individuals who need a product or service. These individuals depend upon them. My greatest hope, however, is that these pages will reveal to them the hidden value of their early employment opportunities to their own future success and development.

For adults, these words are written with the hope that they will rekindle their own memories of a wonderful time when growing up was at a slower pace. For the younger person, presenting them with a view of the past they will never have experienced is my goal. If they learn anything from the collective memories set forth in these pages, then an even higher goal has been attained. For my grandchildren, my hope is that they will revisit my past while giving them an opportunity to learn more about their own.

My own father was a grocer's son, and as my father was, so too am I. This book records our collective thoughts and memories of growing up on West Washington Street in Bellaire, Ohio, in that little grocery store.

Abramo Frizzi The Grocer

1891-1967

(Frizzi Collection)

Chapter One

A Kindergarten Inquiry

What Does Your Father Do?

My kindergarten experience in 1957 was the first opportunity to reflect upon who I was as a person. Admittedly, I knew my name and that I lived at 2783 Washington Street in Bellaire, Ohio. I knew my telephone number. I knew that I had three younger brothers and a loving dad and mom. Yet, I was not really thinking about my family outside of our little upstairs residence. A classroom full of boys and girls growing up in a small town assembled in Miss Kirkland's classroom on the first floor of West Bellaire School. I remember meeting and making friends with kindergarten students that I did not know until that first day of class. Each had a different story to tell.

The school was built of brick in 1927 on several acres of grassy land fronting on the pike known as the Bellaire-Neff Road. This replaced the older one-room school used by children living in Klee Town in earlier days. The new schoolhouse was constructed with a basement housing a lunchroom, small gymnasium, furnace room, and janitor's room where the janitor, Mr. Adams, could be found. The first floor had restrooms on either side, which separated classrooms on the front and rear of the building. The second floor was similarly situated, making a total of eight classrooms in all. A long flight of steps in the front allowed access to reach the elevated first-floor classrooms. In the rear, entry was made from the playground. The classroom floors were made of hardwood maple. Chalkboards and troughs lined the walls. A coatroom was located immediately inside the door of each classroom. Some of the older teachers referred to this as the 'cloakroom.' Open at each end, the wall forming this room separated it from the classroom. This wall was also lined with a chalkboard facing the classroom. Along the outside wall facing the front or rear of the classrooms were windows that could be opened during the heat of early fall and late spring. During the holidays, these windows were beautifully decorated with artwork prepared by the older students.

Outside of the classrooms was a large common area where students would line up for school activities, lunch, and recess and at the end of the day to await their bus to transport them home. This common area had durable and decorative flooring and stairways. Here, in the common area, was a rope that went into a pipe dropping down from the ceiling. This rope, we soon learned, was used to keep students on time. At the side of the rope was a brass gong with a mechanical hammer and levers that also went into the ceiling to the second floor. Also used for keeping time, it served as the warning bell in case of an emergency, such as a fire.

Now, attached to the rope was a school bell located on the roof of the school. As was customary in the earliest days of schoolhouses and public education, the bell would ring out each morning and at lunchtime to signal when we should be in class. Mr. Adams, the janitor, was assigned the duty of being the timekeeper. West Bellaire was a growing community of homes during the 1950s, and there were many children living within walking distance of the schoolhouse. These students could walk to school and back home for lunch. Both sets of my Grandparents lived in West Bellaire; however, I lived on Washington Street about half a mile from the schoolhouse. There were no sidewalks all the way to West Bellaire, so I rode a bus to and from school. The convenience of local Grandparents, however, made it possible for me to eat lunch at either Grandparent's home, just like the other kids living in West Bellaire. The school bell, easily heard throughout this little community, was our timepiece to prevent us from being tardy. The First bell would signal you had ten minutes to get back to school before the second bell would ring, which made you tardy.

The schoolroom in kindergarten was on the first floor, in the front of the building. Immediately across the common area was the 1st grade class of Miss DeVendra, who I remember was quite the disciplinarian. She had what she called a 'Papa Paddle,' which was just a ping pong paddle to which a rubber ball was usually attached by a rubber band. Miss DeVendra, however, did not use this for recreation, as the ball had long been taken off, and now it was used for corporal reasons when a first grader was unruly. We could often hear Miss DeVendra exclaim that she was 'going to get the Papa-Paddle out' if her class did not settle down. The 2nd-grade classroom of Mrs. Frantz was on the back side of the schoolhouse overlooking the playground and the monkey bars. I remember her once telling us that there were clams in the ocean that were as big as 'the West Bellaire Schoolhouse.' My dad assured me that although there are big things living in the ocean, I need not worry about schoolhouse-sized clams.

Immediately across the common area from the 2nd grade was the classroom of the principal of the school, Martha P. Dick. Mrs. Dick taught 3rd grade. She was a kind lady, but one who also subscribed to the rule, 'Spare the rod and spoil the child.' Hers, however, was a quieter and gentler exercise of authority over unruly students. She commanded discipline in a reserved way that demanded respect for her authority. She would often read to bus students during lunchtime, and some of my best memories are of her ability to mesmerize her listeners with the story she was reading. In just reading these stories with such emotion, she brought to life those written words on the pages of the book.

The 4th, 5th, 6th, and 7th grades were upstairs. Although I came to pass through each of those classrooms in later years, kindergarten students were not permitted to go upstairs where the older students were attending class. Mrs. Penn was the 4th-grade teacher who made her students write each spelling word five times every day of the week. Miss Galloway taught 5th-grade students. She was a larger lady who, for some reason, had an affinity for polka-dot dresses, sometimes blue and sometimes green. She always had a hanky, which she kept inside her bosom, which was always a curious place, we thought, to keep it hidden from view. Mrs. Scott was the 6th-grade teacher, and she was at the rear of the 2nd floor overlooking the playground. My 7th-grade teacher was Richard Mehl; however, he began teaching after I was a Kindergarten student in 1957.

The kindergarten classroom was simple. There was a trunk with musical noise makers like cymbals, whistles, horns, and blocks that could be struck with a wooden rod to keep time. We would all get one of these crude instruments as Miss Kirkland would play a song from a record placed on the record player. This was our first school exposure to the world of music as five-year-old students.

We painted pictures, sometimes with a brush and sometimes with our fingers. Every student had to bring to school a plastic apron to wear so that our clothing was protected from the blue, red, green, and yellow colors that were supposed to go on our art paper. There were little scissors with rounded tips so that we would not be injured when using them. We had a box of crayons that we brought from home. These were the jumbo size that came with just the basic colors of the rainbow. We had wooden building blocks, and in groups of 2 or 3, we would build houses, buildings, and skyscrapers. One of the first boys I met was Don Cetorelli during one of these building sessions. Training our voices was important, of course, and so we learned new songs. Sometimes, all boys and girls would sing together before switching off with only the boys or only the girls. 'This Old Man' and 'Row Your Boat' are two songs that come to mind, among many others.

Every morning, we got a milk break. The milk came in little glass half-pint bottles sealed at the top with a foil lid. The teacher used a round metal plunger the same size as the lid, which was used to poke a tiny hole into the foil just large enough for a straw to be inserted into the bottle. And then it came time to take a nap. We all brought throw rugs from home so that we could take that nap mid-morning. Mine was an olive-green rug, with some sort of pattern embroidered into it. Everyone stretched out their rugs on the floor, each of us vying for a spot next to our newly discovered friends. We all lay down for the stated purpose of taking a nap, but it was really nothing more than just a quiet time for Miss Kirkland and for us.

Recess was always something that we looked forward to as youngsters full of energy. The school had a playground with seesaws, monkey bars, and swings suspended from a high metal crossbar held in place by metal poles. A basketball court with metal poles holding backboards and hoops was also behind the school on the playground. Few of us were strong enough at five and six years of age to shoot the ball high enough to make a basket. Most of the time, we just passed the ball back and forth, trying to catch it. We sometimes would have races and play tag, along with all those other schoolyard games to entertain us for fifteen minutes of recess. West Bellaire School had a large grassy schoolyard that surrounded the school itself, but for some reason, we were not permitted to play ball in the grass. Now after school hours, when all the teachers were gone, the rules were relaxed a bit, and the green spaces became more of a recreational area for the students living in the neighborhood.

One thing that I remember about kindergarten is that no matter who I met and befriended, my parents seemed to know who I was speaking of. When I talked about Rita, my mother instantly knew who I was talking about. If I spoke of Orphy, Don, or Johnny, my parents knew immediately who they were and everything about them, like where they lived and who their parents were. When I talked about Nancy, Judy, and Janis, my mother and father could always fill in the details about them that I may have missed. I would learn at the dinner table from my parents that these new friends of mine were really the offspring of parents who had gone to school with them when they were my age. Rita's and Terri's moms turned out to have been best friends of my own mother during their school days. Don's father and Nicolette's dad had been in the United States Navy during WWII, just like my dad. All of this was so reassuring for me, who was embarking on making his own friendships. Each of us had common threads that ran through our families, and this made us feel as though everyone was just an extension of our own family. We began to share those families together as we ventured home at lunchtime with a new boy or girl, or got permission to visit them after school. We expanded our knowledge about each other during these interactions, and our friendships blossomed. Perhaps, the best way of describing it is with the word 'community.' This was the magical and comforting characteristic of living in a small town during the explosion of births that became known as the 'baby boom.' All of us were a community of people sharing a wonderful time growing up with one another. All seemed content during the 1950s when 'IKE' was president, the nation was at peace, and everyone who wanted to be employed found work.

There are really two important experiences that I remember about kindergarten. One was at the end of the year when our class ventured to Neffs to catch the morning train to Bellaire. The other experience, however, came early that year when we were all getting to know our classmates better. This was the day Miss Kirkland asked each of us a question that we perhaps had never really thought about before. The question would certainly be considered 'sexist' today and definitely 'politically incorrect.' Yet at the time in 1957, it seemed to an ungroomed five-year-old, and Miss Kirkland, to be a perfectly sensible question to ask us. Miss Kirkland posed the question without any political motivation or desire to minimize the importance of our mother's role in the family. The question was simply, 'What kind of work does your father do?' The class had a variety of answers, and if one were able to ask this same question today, one would find out exactly how much has changed in the past sixty years. Johnny told the class that his dad 'built houses,' since his father owned a small construction company. Orphy's answer provoked the most laughter when he responded that his dad 'sells beer.' Jake his father owned and operated a local bar and restaurant called the Lincoln Restaurant on Belmont Street. Sandy told us that her dad 'delivered movies' to movie theaters. Dom delivered film to all the movie theaters operating in every small community that had a theater. He also operated a local taxi-cab service. Michael told us that his dad 'made firecrackers,' which was part of a family business owned by his Grandfather that manufactured and sold commercial fireworks displays. There were insurance salesmen, steel workers, coal miners, glass factory workers, auto repairmen and salesmen, teachers, railroad workers, bus drivers, and every other kind of blue-collar job that supported a family. Some fathers worked for someone other than themself, but many of my classmates were supported by fathers who owned their own small businesses. Some were family businesses that had been established by their grandfathers. This was my situation exactly!

So when it came my turn to respond to Miss Kirkland's simple question, I answered it without hesitation. My answer, however, was different from each of the others when I told my classmates that my dad 'sells groceries.' This he did in a small family-owned grocery store on West Washington Street about halfway between downtown Bellaire and West Bellaire. He worked in this grocery store with his father, Abramo Frizzi. This simple question presented by Miss Kirkland was most certainly the first time I had given any thought about who I was in relation to my father's work. I was a grocer's son. I was just like all the other kids in my kindergarten class whose fathers were supporting their own families in a multitude of small family businesses that made up the community. None of us was much different, nor were we particularly remarkable or special. I was just a grocer's son, like my own father was. He grew up a grocer's son during the 1930s and 40s, while I was similarly growing up in the

1950s and 60s. But the story of being a grocer's son must first begin with my Grandfather, Abramo, who began the grocery business as a young Italian immigrant, and who laid the foundation for my response to the class. Without my Grandfather, I would never have been able to answer Miss Kirkland's question as I did, if at all. This story begins with my Grandfather, Abe.

West Bellaire Schoolhouse 1970. Miss Kirkland's room is on the 1st Floor, right of the steps, where the question posed was "What does your father do"? (Frizzi Collection 1970)

The author, Danny Jr., third of the grocer's sons, with a lunch sack on the way to kindergarten in the fall of 1957. (Frizzi Collection 1957)

Two young cousins, Danny Jr. (left) and Michael Presutti (right), at the Neffs train station, awaiting a ride on the morning train to Wheeling to end the kindergarten school year. Danny is the grandson of Abramo Frizzi and Michael of Olimpia Frizzi Cicogna. (Frizzi Collection 1958)

The ancient city of Perugia from a postcard. Piccione was outside of Perugia in the hill country, and this is where the story of my family begins.

Chapter Two

The Beginning:
A Brief Family History

Coming to America

I am descended from Italian immigrant farmers from the Province of Umbria in central Italy. My Grandfather, Abramo Frizzi, was born on February 8, 1891, in the small town of Piccione. At 16 years of age, he had boarded a steamship in the Lloyd Italiano Steamship Company line named 'Florida,' which departed Genoa harbor on October 26, 1907, and began the voyage to America. This trip would require twelve to fourteen days on the Atlantic Ocean before he would see that grand lady at the entrance to New York Harbor greeting new arrivals. It was there that he first saw the Statue of Liberty. He arrived at Ellis Island on November 11, 1907. When he entered the immigration building, records reveal he had $15.00 in his pockets and no ticket to reach his final destination at Piney Fork, Ohio, where he was to join his brother Artemio. Artemio had arrived in America two years earlier in June 1905, and he found employment in the coal fields of eastern Ohio. This news of steady employment was communicated by letter to his younger brother, Abramo, in Piccione, and this communication served as encouragement prompting his voyage to America. Once he had arrived, his representations to his mother that he would attend school once in America were soon forgotten.

Although the records do not indicate, my Grandfather often recalled that he had contracted jaundice while aboard the steamship 'Florida.' The whites of his eyes turned yellow, and he was sent to the hospital to be treated before leaving quarantine on the island. Upon examination by medical doctors at Ellis Island, he was treated, but was not permitted to leave the island hospital until his condition had been resolved. He was a shorter young man at 5'2" tall. Records state he had a dark complexion and possessed a full head of chestnut colored hair. He was 16 years of age in a strange new land. He could read, write, and speak only in his native Italian tongue.

After his treatment for the jaundice, and his condition had improved, he was dismissed from the Ellis Island infirmary, transported to New York City, where he boarded a train bound for Eastern Ohio. He was headed to a tiny mining town called Piney Fork located in southern Jefferson County, Ohio. At Piney Fork, he would join his brother Artemio as a coal miner. He saw value in immediately working for a wage that attending school could not provide. The mine at Piney Fork was on the branch line of the New York Central Railroad, servicing the coal mine. In later years, a large mine of the Hanna Coal Company thrived in this small mining community. When he arrived, my Grandfather Abramo began boarding with what he always referred to as 'a French Lady,' living in this small mining town. He and his brother Artemio had meager possessions and were not fluent in the English language. However, they were accustomed to hard work and times. Both were unafraid to face what misfortunes their futures might hold as they began their quest for prosperity. They sought opportunity, and they took advantage of it in this small mining town. The Pittsburgh vein, or seam No. 8 of Eastern Ohio coal, was a six-foot vein which was vigorously sought by mining companies at the turn of the 20th century, and extracting this black rock from the ground became their chance to earn a living.

In many places in eastern Ohio, the coal was found outcropping from the sides of the hills, making it unnecessary to drive a shaft to reach the seam. These outcropped coal seams led to the opening of drift mines, where the seam could be easily followed underground. Dirty, dusty, and dangerous can best describe these early mining jobs. The hazards of coal mining made the work always dangerous, and often injurious to the health and safety of the miners. Work was plentiful in the Ohio Valley, and there was always a ready supply of new workers if you decided you did not want to dig coal as a miner. Coal mines, glass factories, railroads, and many other small industries that required coal as a fuel source gave eastern Ohio coal miners continued opportunities for work. Mining coal became my Grandfather's first source of income in America.

Just two years prior to my Grandfather coming to America, his older sister, Olimpia, had arrived in Ohio to join her husband, Abele Cicogna. She was accompanied by her older brother, Alberico. Together they traveled aboard the Princess Irene, which departed Naples on July 1, 1904, and arrived in New York harbor on July 13, after 12 days at sea.

The manifest indicated that her husband, Abele, was the person she would be joining in America. Olimpia's passage was paid by her husband, Abele, while her brother Alberico had paid his own. The record of this passage indicates that neither Alberico nor Olimpia had ever been to America.

Abele Cicogna met Olimpia on a mail route in rural Italy. He delivered mail to the Frizzi home in Piccione, and most of the time, he was greeted by one of the Frizzi brothers. One day, however, daughter Olimpia came out to get the mail, and when she did, they met each other for the very first time. They were married on February 17, 1900. At this time, my Grandfather Abramo was nine 9 years old. Sister Olympia was 17.

At the time of her arrival, Olimpia and Abele had a small child who was born to them in Ripa, Perugia. His name was Sam. Still a small child, Sam was left behind with Abele's mother, Marina, who feared that she would never see the boy or her son Abele if she permitted all to leave Perugia together. To assure their return, it was agreed that young Sam would stay behind with Marina to ensure that the young couple would one day return to Italy. Just over one year after their arrival, Abele and Olimpia welcomed their second child, a daughter named Ida, who was born May 28, 1905, in Scranton, Pennsylvania. Able worked as a coal miner, as did both of Olimpia's younger brothers, Abramo and Artemio. This work was easy to find, and because it was manual labor, language was not a barrier to earning a paycheck. Olimpia and her husband moved their family to the Ohio Valley, closer to her younger brothers, Artemio and my Grandfather Abramo.

A Final Goodbye to Italy for Abramo

With this coal mining employment, my Grandfather Abramo saved money to return to his native country one last time. His visit was to see his parents for the last time before returning to America. While there, he closed his affairs in Italy, then bid his Italian family goodbye. Although it is not known when he returned to Italy, his stay was of very short duration because he arrived back in the United States aboard the steamship 'San Giovanni' sailing from Naples on November 18, 1910. He was now 19 years of age. He was bound for the city where he would eventually make his home. Bellaire, Ohio, was his final destination. My Grandfather never returned to his birth home in Italy ever again. Upon his arrival back in America, he was greeted with the news that he was Uncle Abramo once again, as his sister Olimpia had given birth to another son earlier that month. Columbo William Cicogna was born on November 5, 1910, in Bellaire, Ohio.

One curiosity remaining a mystery is the spelling of the surname, which he adopted here in the United States. Immigration records indicate that when he arrived in America, his surname was spelled 'Frizza.' The pronunciation would have sounded in English like 'Fritza.' 'Frizza' is the spelling still claimed by relatives living in Perugia. The former spelling was abandoned and not used once he arrived back in the United States on a permanent basis. For unknown reasons, the spelling became 'Frizzi.' Changes in the spelling of immigrant names was not uncommon because of the recording of those names upon entry, where two different languages were trying to understand the information being recorded. Sometimes, what immigration officials heard was what was written down on official paperwork, whether it was correct or not. In my Grandfather's case, however, that name was correct when he entered, but appears to have been voluntarily changed by my Grandfather once he was here on a permanent basis. Local records indicate that as early as 1919, the name was clearly spelled and signed by my Grandfather as 'Frizzi.'

When entering the United States, most Italians were not greeted with open arms by English-speaking Americans. As with that unfortunate scheme often befalling all human beings, difference and diversity is not always welcomed. There is always discrimination by some toward anyone who is different. Clearly, the young brothers were different due to their language and culture that followed them to America. To those prone to discriminate on race and culture came slang references which my Grandfather detested. Slang words such as 'Dagoes,' were often applied to the new arrivals from the Mediterranean region of Europe. The term was applied based on the manual work performed by the Italians, Spanish, and Portuguese upon entry into the United States. Such work in the Ohio Valley was in the coal mines that employed my Grandfather and his brother Artemio. The term was derived from the phrase that these men were paid 'as the day goes.' My Grandfather was very sensitive to this word, which he considered to be a slur upon the good value and reputation of their native home, their heritage, and their worth as human beings. Even worse, however, young Italians were not spared from this general term applied to the Mediterranean people. Italians were also called 'wop' or 'guinea,' referring specifically to Italians. Often used against them with the intention to be derogatory and insulting, the young brothers had to withstand such discrimination and prejudice that came with being newcomers to this land of opportunity.

The language barrier created in the eyes of many Americans, and other foreigners as well, a terrible misconception that somehow a person speaking another language was not as intelligent as they might be. A person digging coal without any formal education and not understanding the English language was faced with many instances of discriminatory treatment. An unfair advantage could often be attempted and taken against someone who did not speak the dominant English language. Thus, the struggle could only be won by those who could withstand this prejudice, the insults, and be resilient in demonstrating their innate abilities and worth. Those who were ignorant of the centuries of civilization of the Italian culture would never fully understand how much they were underestimating the worth and value of the Italian people.

My Grandfather once told me that those derogatory words were used in a hateful way, and must never be spoken. This conversation arose because of a boy about my age, whose parents were Italian, and who had been given the nickname of 'Dago.' All the other kids called him this name, but he never seemed to mind being called this slang term. I told my Grandfather in passing about the name given to this boy. He told me that the term was an insult and was a put-down to the boy's Italian heritage. My Grandfather told me that the boy should be offended as an Italian being called such a name. Therefore, from an early age, this word was erased from my vocabulary. While not commonly heard today, I do cringe whenever someone uses it in my presence to describe the Italian people from whom I am descended.

My Grandfather, Abe, once told me a fictionalized story of the building of the famous Tower of Pisa that leans, instead of standing erect. The point of his story was that Italian people were intelligent builders, painters, and sculptors, who were deserving of respect from all people. The story he told me was about a father who asked each of his two sons to build something magnificent to bring honor to him. One son built a magnificent church, with beautiful spires, columns, and arches. The other son built the Tower of Pisa. The Father congratulated the son who built the magnificent church, and then turned to his son who built the Tower of Pisa. My Grandfather's story continued with the father stating, "This tower is beautiful my son, but you have failed to honor me because it obviously leans to one side." The son looked at his father, and with all sense of indignation replied, "My father, any damned fool can build the tower straight, but only a true genius can design it to lean, and yet still stand." My Grandfather believed that the greatness of the Italian people lies in their daring to do what others would not, and yet still succeed. Still leaning today, the moral of the story, and my Grandfather's point is proven! He believed that his Italian heritage should not be defamed by the insult of the slang words often used to describe Italian immigrants.

Co-Masonic Lodge and American Federation of Human Rights

My Grandmother Philomena's announcement of her own wedding in 1919 was written to announce not only her own wedding, but also the wedding of another young Italian couple. My Grandfather, Abe, had stood as the best man at the wedding of his friend Attillio D'Alessandro, who was to wed Mary Nardone. Attillio was a coal miner, just as my Grandfather and his brother Artemio were when they entered the United States. They would remain friends throughout the rest of their lives as they resided on Washington Street within a short distance of each other. That friendship was demonstrated in their Co-Masonic roots.

The Co-Masonic Lodge was a masonic order that was created by young immigrants to America in the first decade of the 20th Century. The first Co-Masonic Lodge in America was founded in Charleroi, Pennsylvania, on October 25, 1903. The Lodge was designated Alpha No. 301 of Charleroi. The man who was primarily responsible for founding this Lodge was a French immigrant named Francois Louis Goaziou, who settled in western Pennsylvania, where he also found work as a coal miner. Many of those who were attracted to the ideals of this lodge were other coal miners who immigrated to Pennsylvania and Eastern Ohio. Most Italians worshipped in the Roman Catholic faith, and this made them unacceptable in other forms of the Masonic Orders then existing. In fact, Pennsylvania passed legislation attempting to prohibit any Masonic Lodges that were not sanctioned by the state, as a way of discriminating against Alpha No. 301 of Charleroi, and others being established.

During the 1920s, the Co-Masonic Lodge grew in popularity and spread throughout Eastern Ohio and Western Pennsylvania, where immigrants of many nationalities with blue-collar occupations lived and worked. Immigrants not readily accepted into other Masonic Lodges of the day, because of their immigration, religious, or blue-collar status, found a home in the Co-Masonic Order. The lodge was referred to as The American Federation of Human Rights in 1908, and the International Order of Co-Freemasonry 'LE DROIT HUMAIN.' The French immigrant coal miner, Goaziou, from Charleroi, was named as the first President of the Co-Masonic Order. To some, Goaziou was looked upon as an anarchist because he was actively recruiting members to 'LE DROIT HUMAN.' He was also active in attempting to organize coal miners as union members who needed protection for health, safety, and welfare against the harsh reality of the coal mining industry. He was also a progressive activist who fought for the human rights espoused by the Lodge, opposing discrimination that immigrants often encountered.

The idea espoused by the American Federation of 'LE DROIT HUMAIN' masonic order was the concept that all human beings are equal, regardless of their differences based upon race, gender, creed, or nationality. It opposed attempts to restrict membership based on any of these conditions. To adhere to this philosophy, the Order accepted women to be admitted as freely as men without discrimination on the basis of gender. A belief in a Supreme Being was deeply rooted in Freemasonry; however, there was no single method or manner prescribed by which one might exercise their belief. The goal was to develop in members a yearning to be free of ignorance in thought, to be educated in the important truths of morality, and thereby foster a relationship with the Creator of the universe, and with their fellow men and women on equal footing. The Order sought young progressives like many of the Italian immigrants who often found discrimination and prejudice in their pursuits. The National movement to grant women the right to vote aided membership in the American Federation of Human Rights, which recognized women into the Order. The Co-Masonic Order increased its members and lodges during this movement in 1920, and the adoption of the 19th Amendment. Once the Depression struck the nation, however, the Co-Masonic movement's growth was slowed. Many members' employment was lost due to the economic setback in the nation. Only the most successful Lodges were able to survive.

In 1918, my Grandfather's brother, Artemio, joined the Human Rights Lodge No. 503 located in Bridgeport, Ohio. My Grandfather, Abramo, joined him in Lodge membership. Attillio D'Alessandro, my Grandfather's friend, would become a 32nd degree masonic member of this organization and help to found Unison Lodge No. 542 in Bellaire, Ohio. My Grandfather, Abe, also became a member of this Lodge. Attillio would rise to become the Deputy of the District of Eastern Ohio and Western Pennsylvania of the International Co-Masonry, The American Federation of Human Rights. Mike DiClemente, another of my Grandfather's friends and members of the local Lodge, would also assume that same post. Consisting largely of all Italian members, and most of whom were practicing the Catholic faith, this Lodge became known locally as the 'Italian Masons.' These men and women found a home in a Masonic Order that accepted them as an equal.

The First Grocery Store

At some point upon rejoining his brother Artemio in America, the two young men arranged for a trip west to Colorado, where they worked in the mining industry seeking silver, gold, and fortune. They traveled to Silver Plume, a popular mining town inhabited by many young Italian immigrants. Deep in the mountains, a railroad provided connections to Denver. My Grandfather found very little prosperity in Silver Plume, and so after working in the silver mines, he and Artemio decided to return to the Ohio Valley. Some have said that they were broke and had to prevail upon their sister, Olimpia, living in Bellaire, to wire money for the return trip. Their adventures in the Old West, however, provided them with a look at the beauty of the American West.

Upon returning to Bellaire and with no desire to return to the coal mines of Eastern Ohio, they devised a plan to open a small neighborhood grocery store. It would be located in a section of town where many Italian families were residing in the Rose Hill section of the community of Bellaire, Ohio. Rose Hill was named by an early settler of the community who built the first house on the bluff overlooking the town of Bellaire. The name which he gave to this new home was 'Rose Hill,' and when the hillside was platted into building lots, it became known as Sullivan's Rose Hill Addition. My Grandfather and his brother's first store and residence was established along Hamilton Street just below Rose Hill. It was located where the abutment of the beautiful stone viaduct railroad bridge, passing above the streets of Bellaire, struck the hillside. This store was located so close to the railroad tracks and the approach to the bridge that one standing on the back porch of the store building could almost touch the passing trains. Here, my Grandfather Abramo and his Brother Artemio lived together with their cousin, Henry Frizzi. Here on Hamilton Street is where they opened their first neighborhood grocery store.

While engaged in the grocery business, my Grandfather met a beautiful young Italian-American girl named Filomena DeSimone. Some confusion as to the spelling of her given name exists in the records, where it appears as 'Filomena,' which would be an entirely appropriate spelling in Italian. 'Philomena' is the spelling used on naturalized citizenship papers and marriage records; therefore, this appears to be her true legal name. Philomena is the Americanized version of 'Filomena,' which would have been adopted once she began to attend school. Her father, Donato, and mother Irene had moved to Bellaire from San Toy in Morgan County, Ohio, where she was born August 10, 1903. The DeSimone family first resided on 31st Street below the sandstone arches of the railroad viaduct between Belmont and Union Streets. A laundry was situated below the residence at this location. Their family relocated to Hamilton Street to make a new home in a small house about 1912. This new home was directly across Hamilton Street from the western abutment of the stone viaduct, which served the Baltimore and Ohio Railroad. The grocery store of my Grandfather was, therefore, very close to the DeSimone home. My Grandmother Philomena was the oldest of the children in the DeSimone family. She attended St. John's Catholic Grade School that was located on Guernsey Street. She obtained early employment at a laundry at some point since she had membership in the International Laundry Workers Union Local 41. She soon began to work at the grocery store, which was closer to her home on Hamilton Street. Soon, a courtship ensued with my Grandfather Abramo. Living just across the street from the Frizzi Brothers Grocery, there is little doubt that this was the nexus for the relationship between them. She was able to work at the grocery store, in close proximity to her own home and family. Abramo, however, was 11 years older than my Grandmother Philomena. When marriage was proposed, the difference in age was apparently not considered an impediment to their marriage by Donato DeSimone, Philomena's father. Donato was an Italian businessman just like my Grandfather. He was interested in being a partner in the Roma Theater. This movie theater was built on Belmont Street and incorporated under the name of Bellaire Star Amusement Company. His co-owners of this company were also Italian immigrants, and together they built this theater and oversaw its operation. My Grandfather, Abramo, demonstrated similar qualities in business acumen as a young grocer. Donato certainly believed his eldest daughter's relationship with Abramo was a good one and consented to the courtship.

An Italian Hero: Giuseppe Maria Garibaldi

As with most Italians, their faith was Roman Catholic, which they brought with them to America from their native homeland. My Grandfather, although raised by his family as a Roman Catholic in Italy, had during his time there become disaffected with the Catholic Church. A mystery surrounds his reasons. He never fully disclosed what caused his lack of loyalty to the Church; however, his views were shaped by his interactions with the Church while still a boy in Italy. Other reasons, however, he often made known. His primary belief was that business and government should be free from the dominance of organized religion, of any faith. The historical domination of the Catholic Church in Europe in government and business was viewed by many young Italian progressives, as was my Grandfather, to be an uninvited intrusion into their lives. Church hierarchy had always been most influential in the role of provincial governments of each region of Italy, and dominated the ownership of property and wealth. Many young Italian men of that day were seeking freedom and prosperity, which was often stifled by Church dominion over civil as well as religious matters. Although my own family had often struggled with my Grandfather's unwillingness to reconcile his beliefs with his prior religious faith and upbringing, his philosophy and reasoning had been deeply rooted in him as a boy long before he reached this shore. While most Italians retained their religious faith as

Roman Catholics, my Grandfather did not, and openly disavowed it. His upbringing and education in Italy as a boy made him very familiar with the Catholic faith and its traditions, but he voluntarily elected not to be bound by them. He was also familiar with the recent Italian history, which had occurred just a quarter century before he journeyed to America. That history was the tumultuous time when the Italian Peninsula struggled to form a united Italy, free of the influence and domination of France, Austria, and Spain.

The great Italian statesman and general, Giuseppe Maria Garibaldi, was my Grandfather's true inspirational hero as a boy growing up in Italy. Garibaldi was wildly popular throughout Europe. Italian progressives of his time followed and supported his cause in leading uprisings in support of the creation of an Italian Republic. His efforts at unification of the many regions and provincial governments to form a united Italy placed him at odds with the Catholic Church. To accomplish this goal of unification, Garibaldi would necessarily voice great opposition to the dominance of the Catholic Church, supported and militarily defended by outside influencers during the last half of the 19th century. Many of these influencers were supportive of the Vatican and Papal headquarters in Rome, and the domination of the Church over the regions of Papal Rule. My Grandfather's secular views were that religion should play no part in governing the people, and that religious views should be relegated to church activities, spiritual beliefs, and customs, without the force of law imposed by church hierarchy made up of mortal men. He would often voice objection to men confessing to men, and seeking absolution through papal representatives called 'Father.' My Grandfather believed that no man should have such control over another mortal being.

My Grandfather would often tell my father, and to me as a younger teen, that 'Garibaldi was a great man.' He would end this sentence with the further explanation that 'To bring unification to Italy, Garibaldi had to fight the Pope.' Garibaldi was, in fact, considered to be anti-Catholic because of his belief that any organized religion, and its dominance in government, business, and property of the people, should be eradicated. Garibaldi's main thesis was that a Church should be supreme in the salvation of souls, but separate from the secular governance of the people. Garibaldi also joined the Italian Masonic Order of Free-Masonry, as further evidence of this view. Garibaldi, and his 'Red Shirts' as they were called, were viewed by many Italians as 'liberationists.' History records him as a man of the people who sought freedom from what he viewed as the ritualistic and 'secret society' of the organized Catholic Church. Known throughout Europe as a liberator. Garibaldi was recognized by Abraham Lincoln when the former supported the Union during the Civil War. Garibaldi was widely acclaimed for his liberationist ideals. He died just nine years before my Grandfather was born, and there is little doubt that my Grandfather became familiar with his teachings and the movement which he created among many Italians of that day. The exploits of Garibaldi continued in the hearts and minds of many Italians in those years that followed his death, and to a small boy like my Grandfather, he was heroic. Much of what influenced my Grandfather as a boy would come from his parents who lived through the tumultuous time of Italian unification. This influence on my Grandfather's early education, and the folklore that surrounded Garibaldi, helped to shape my Grandfather's views of the Church, which he carried with him to America.

On October 16, 1919, Abramo, who was 27, and Philomena, who was just 16, both appeared with Donato DeSimone in open court before Judge John C. Nichols, Probate Judge of Belmont County. Donato gave consent to the marriage in open court, and it was expected that the Rev. Jos. Wittman would solemnize the marriage. He was the Priest serving St. John's Catholic Church in Bellaire, attended by the DeSimone family. Donato was willing to consent to this marriage because he believed that the groom was already established in business. He must have seen Abramo Frizzi as a respected young Italian merchant in the community. Just as Donato had already established himself, this consent was given in the belief that my Grandfather Abramo would follow him.

In anticipation of her marriage, my Grandmother wrote on paper to announce that 'prominent young people are wedded today, November 2, 1919.' Her handwritten description stated not one, but 'two marriages of interest in local Italian Circles' had taken place. One of those marriages was of Attillio D'Alessandro and Mary Nardone. My Grandfather, listed as Abramo, was the best man for his friend Attillio. In the other marriage, my Grandmother, Miss Philomena DeSimone, was to marry Abraham Frizzi, who was an 'Italian merchant.' This announcement states that the wedding took place at St. John's Church on Sunday afternoon at 2 o'clock. Obviously, this announcement was made by my Grandmother to memorialize this momentous day.

The proposed marriage to my Grandmother, Philomena, brought forth those feelings about the church as the day of matrimony drew closer. Abramo refused to be married in the sanctuary of the Catholic Church by the priest. Instead, rather than submit to a ceremony sanctioned by the Church, he was willing to submit to a compromise. The marriage ceremony could be held in the parlor of the church rectory, with a reception to follow at the home of the bride. Any marriage at all by the Priest was most likely only possible with the influence of Donato, my Grandmother's father. The Priest, Joseph Wittman, who officiated the ceremony, signed the certification of marriage after the nuptials had taken place. The newlyweds were married on November 2, 1919, as the announcement stated, and they were married in the church, even if not in the sanctuary at the altar. Celebrations followed on Hamilton Street that same day, across from the groom's grocery store. They became Mr. and Mrs. Abramo Frizzi. Records of the local church reveal no record of the marriage having taken place that day, so in all probability, the marriage was a purely civil ceremony that could not be church sanctioned.

The well wishes for the nuptials were given by sister Olimpia, and her husband, Abele, in a beautiful colorized wedding card inscribed in Italian, which stated *'Felicita Eterna e'l' augurio che Abele e Olimpia dal fondo del cuore fa agli.'* The translation is, 'eternal happiness is the wish that Abele and Olimpia, from the bottom of the heart, make to the newlyweds.' Olimpia's youngest brother was now wed.

Also present was brother Artemio, who was at that time not yet married. At this moment, Artemio, Abramo, and Olimpia, all from the small town of Piccione, were now in America, and they had joined together for this celebration. Each had become a part of the Italian community in Bellaire. The Cicogna family had returned to Italy and brought their firstborn son, Sam, to America with them. He had been originally left behind. Sam would now find employment with his uncles, Abramo and Artemio, in the grocery business, and Abele would continue to work in the coal fields to earn the steerage passage for the rest of his family. By 1921, the Cicogna family was growing with many mouths to feed. Bruno was born in Ripa, but his sisters Marie, Manuel, Fred, and Lelia were all born in the Ohio

Valley. The family made numerous trips back to Italy, and were never fully united together again until a final voyage in 1934.

This marriage of Philomena to my Grandfather, Abramo, had the unfortunate effect of an unintended consequence. This was the renunciation of the lawful citizenship of my Grandmother by the marriage to my Grandfather, who was not yet naturalized as a U.S. citizen. She had been born in San Toy, Morgan County, Ohio, on August 9, 1903. Having been born in the United States, she had immediately become a citizen of the United States by her birth under the U.S. Constitution. By marrying my Grandfather, Abramo, who was not yet a citizen, she lost her citizenship that had been acquired as her birthright. This was the law of immigration and naturalization at the time, with the many immigrants coming to America.

My Grandfather, Abramo, filed his Declaration for United States citizenship on February 28, 1924, and he was examined before Judge Warren W. Cowen of the Belmont County Common Pleas Court in St. Clairsville on April 14, 1927. His certificate of naturalization was issued to him on that day. My Grandmother Philomena filed her Petition for Naturalization some years later in the same court on June 23, 1937, and was examined that same day. The delay in making the application was most likely due to the discovery that she had lost her citizenship in 1919 when she had married my Grandfather, who was at that time an Italian citizen. She thereafter regained her status as an American citizen in 1937, which her marriage to my Grandfather had nullified eighteen years earlier.

A Second Store on Union Street

For a short time, the newlyweds lived at the store on Hamilton Street, with brother Artemio (sometimes called Arturo) and cousin Henry. Arturo was also soon wed to a young lady named Tilda Roman, and a similar consequence upon the marriage of Artemio Frizzi to his new bride was the loss of her citizenship as a native born American. She encountered the same fate as my Grandmother, and had to reapply in order to regain her citizenship as well. It was agreed that both brothers should move the store to the bustling downtown section of the city of Bellaire. Union Street was selected largely because of the recently constructed bank building of the Farmers and Merchants National Bank, and the traffic between the train stations of the Baltimore and Ohio Railroad and the Pennsylvania Railroad. Also nearby was the passenger and freight station of the Ohio River and Western narrow gauge railroad that traveled through the hills of Belmont County en route to Zanesville, Ohio. Here, along Union Street, were hotels, restaurants, confectionery shops, and dry goods stores. There were also many pubs and saloons. Clearly, this was a better business location because of the constant flow of traffic. The street was paved and was in better condition than the winding road known as Hamilton Street, where the first store was located. Although less than a quarter mile from the old business location, it was not so far that Italian patrons on Hamilton Street would not be able to continue to patronize the business.

Finding suitable accommodations in a building with a storefront on the sidewalk, and apartments above, both brothers and their wives set up Frizzi Brothers Grocery at 3175 Union Street. They opened to the busy trade of Union Street, selling fresh fruits, vegetables, and a variety of grocery items. The paper grocery bags printed for this new business stressed that the brothers only sold 'Fresh Fruits, Vegetables, and Groceries.' The store was modern enough to have a telephone where orders were placed by calling 672-M to be answered by wives Tilda or Philomena, or the brothers Artemio and Abramo. Deliveries were common for a small neighborhood business, and this was part of the service that could be provided to their customers. This delivery service continued into the 1950s and 1960s, when I, too, would venture to the homes of customers with bags and boxes of groceries.

Union Street was a busy place in 1919. Because of the two train stations and a public wharf on the Ohio River nearby, there was a constant movement of people and commerce. In 1919, the nearby B & O Railroad station at the end of the 3100 block produced four westbound trains daily from Baltimore en route to Cincinnati, St. Louis, or Chicago. The Pennsylvania Railroad also had a depot two blocks away, and it connected Union Street to Pittsburgh, Cleveland, and the entire Pennsylvania Railroad system to New York City. The depot was serviced by the five-story Windsor Hotel. Each of these trains produced pedestrian traffic between the Windsor and the famous Globe House Hotel next door to the new Grocery Store.

Therefore, on any given day, passing on the sidewalk in front of the new grocery store were people traveling from the largest metropolitan cities of the eastern United States. There abounded many different nationalities, many different languages, many different ideas and beliefs, and many different political and religious viewpoints. In this melting pot of people, the shingle of Frizzi Brothers Grocery was set out at the new business location.

The two brothers soon needed help at this store and enlisted their nephew, Samuel Cicogna, who was the eldest son of their sister, Olimpia. Sam was now a young man, about 18 years of age, and did not want to leave America to return to Italy. His father, Abele, continued working as a coal miner, but his young son Sam would learn the grocery business from his Uncles, Artemio and Abramo. Sam would take this knowledge with him to open his own grocery store in the oldest part of the town of Bellaire. In this early employment, however, Sam would take on the duties of stocking merchandise and making deliveries to customers, along with whatever else was required in the operation of the store. I was fortunate to remember Sam from an early age because he would often visit my Grandfather, Abramo, at our grocery store on Washington Street. A pleasant gentleman, he would always tell me when observing me working at our store, "I worked for your Grandfather Abe when I was a young man, just like you." His comments, and his friendly demeanor toward me as a boy, is the reason I remember him yet today.

The building at 3175 Union Street was a typical brick store building of the early 20th century. The building was no more than 33' wide at the sidewalk, since that was the lot size on which the building was built. It had a second and third floor, and this was used as residence space for the brothers and their wives, as well as additional warehouse space for inventory. The building was constructed of brick, with high decorative tin ceilings at least 10 to 12 feet above the floor, and a coal-burning pot-belly stove near the center of the room. The stove pipe from the pot belly stove stretched upward toward the ceiling and into a wall. The main storeroom was open in the middle to accommodate the traffic of customers, and along the walls were the shelves and cases holding goods for sale. Soon after establishing the Union Street store, there was talk of building a bridge for motor vehicle and streetcar traffic connecting Bellaire to Benwood, West Virginia. This bridge, if built, would substantially increase the motor traffic and pedestrians along Union Street. My Grandfather believed it to be a public improvement that would only increase the business of this store, and he subscribed for stock in the bridge company. He also served as a promoter for the company, encouraging others to join this venture.

A son was soon born to Artemio and Tilda, whom they named Louis. He was born in the upstairs apartment over the storeroom. My Grandfather, Abramo, and my Grandmother, Philomena, would not give birth to my Father, Daniel, until after the operation of this store came to a close in the late 1920s. Artemio, Tilda, and their son Louis decided to pack up and leave for California, leaving my Grandfather alone in the business. Arthur, as known by his Americanized name, had somewhat poor health and breathing problems, which could have been a result of his earlier work in mining. Contributing to his decline in health was the industrial environment. Bellaire was thriving with industry. The Carnegie steel factory, many glass houses, and train locomotives all belched smoke from the burning of coal. In addition, the coal furnaces of residences of that day burned coal and made the air hazy and unhealthy if inhaled. Artemio believed that by moving to a hotter and drier climate, where the air was healthier, his breathing would improve. The move ended the partnership between the two brothers in the grocery business in Bellaire, Ohio. They had traveled across the Atlantic to find fortune, worked together at Piney Fork, and traveled west into mining country. They were coal miners, gold and silver miners, grocers, and travelers in an expanding nation that was unknown to the small farming home they had left behind in Piccione. But now, they too would part and seek to make a home for their wives and their respective families. Artemio turned his eyes to the west, but my Grandfather Abramo remained a part of the community where he had met his bride, Philomena. This story of the grocery business must necessarily begin with my Grandfather Abramo.

Abramo Frizzi at the curb of West Washington Street store with His REO Speedwagon circa 1923 (Frizzi Collection)

Piney Fork in Jefferson County, Ohio, where both Artemio (standing front) and Abramo (behind mine car in dark jacket/white shirt) worked in the Jefferson Coal Company mine. (Frizzi Collection circa 1910)

Young Italian Americans offering a toast at the first Frizzi Brothers store on Hamilton Street. From left are Abramo Frizzi, Innocenzo Ragni. From right are cousin Henry Frizzi and Artemio Frizzi. Other young men are unknown. (Frizzi Collection circa 1914)

Philomena DeSimone Frizzi standing on Hamilton Street outside the first Frizzi Brothers Grocery Store shown at right. The arcade shown behind is the B & O bridge approach to the Ohio River. (Frizzi Collection circa 1920)

Interior of the second Frizzi Brothers Grocery store at 3175 Union Street. Standing from left are Sam Cicogna, eldest son of Olimpia, Tilda Roman Frizzi and husband Artemio Frizzi. The building is now occupied by the famous Roosevelt Restaurant. (Linda Frizzi Collection circa 1921)

Exterior view of the building housing the second Frizzi Brothers store with Nicholas Massa, owner and operator of the Roosevelt Restaurant, waving his hat. (Massa Collection circa 1939)

A grocery sack of Frizzi Brothers Grocery store advertising the location and phone number. (Frizzi Collection circa 1921)

Abramo Frizzi and Philomena DeSimone's wedding photograph. The age difference was 11 years as Philomena was only 16 at the time of the wedding. She had been educated at the St. John's Catholic grade school, and her maturity was an asset to the store business and her husband, Abramo. (Frizzi Collection 1919)

Chapter Three

Washington Street
Abraham Frizzi

Groceries of Quality

While still engaged in the business at Union Street, my Grandfather Abramo was making plans for his own grocery store. He summoned a contractor to prepare and deliver to him plans for the erection of a new store on West Washington Street. This third store would be closer to the customers in the Rose Hill section of town, where the original store had been operated on Hamilton Street with his brother Artemio. The new store of Abraham Frizzi, by which he was commonly known, would be located at 2783 Washington Street.

In March of 1923, my Grandfather purchased Outlot 414 in the Linwood Addition and implemented the plans for the construction of a new storeroom, garage, and dwelling. The specifications were prepared with precise detail and specificity. The first-floor entrance to the storeroom was to be two elevated steps off the sidewalk. The foundation walls were glazed tile building block (8"x8"x16"), and the rear wall was to consist of a poured concrete wall one foot thick. This thickness was intended to act as a retaining wall against the hillside, and was constructed to a height of nearly ten feet against the sloping hillside lot. The garage was to adjoin the storeroom so that a delivery truck could be parked inside and off the street. The upstairs apartment would be accessed by a stairway from the storeroom. The second floor home would have a living room, two bedrooms, a dining room and kitchen area, along with a bathroom. The living room would have a scratch brick fireplace with a wooden mantel and a tile hearth. The specifications also included an elevated porch from the second floor extending over the sidewalk below for use during hot summer evenings when heat and humidity drove dwellers outside. This became the home and grocery store that Abraham Frizzi, as he was known by his customers, had planned for his wife and family. This would become the home where my Father was born on June 28, 1926. He joined with a younger sister, Kathryn, at this residence, born 4 years later in 1930. This is also the store and the home that I came to know upon my birth on September 15, 1952, and it is this place where I began my own childhood as a grocer's son.

This third store location was a short distance from where the first Frizzi store was located on Hamilton Street. Washington Street paralleled Hamilton Street but was higher up the hillside overlooking the downtown. It joined Hamilton Street just a few hundred yards west of where the first store was located, and a short distance east of the new store. The place where this intersection of the two streets merged left only Washington Street remaining to points further west. From this merger of the two streets it became known as West Washington Street. This helped to distinguish it from what others referred to as 'Back Washington Street' which was narrower and more crowded. West Washington became the Bellaire-Neffs road, and it was wider and better maintained as the main highway to West Bellaire and Neffs. Later, this road would become State Route 149 on the state highway system.

To his customers who were English-speaking, my Grandfather was usually referred to as 'Abe.' Although his Italian name of 'Abramo' was still used by the Italian community of friends and customers, it became Americanized through the adoption of the name of our 16th President, 'Abraham.' The delivery truck used in the grocery business during the 1930s clearly calls my Grandfather Abraham Frizzi, and declares that he sells 'Groceries of Quality.' Shortened into 'Abe,' he and my Grandmother Philomena set up shop in their new store. My Grandmother's name would also change with time from Philomena to 'Minnie.' This couple were obviously fluent as young adults in their native tongue of Italian, however, they were learning the English language quite well. My Grandmother had attended the St. John's Catholic grade school on Guernsey Street and had formal training in speaking the English language. She would provide the discourse in English whenever my Grandfather would have difficulty with speech or understanding. They would continue to speak to each other in Italian and remained fluent while becoming bilingual. This fostered a relationship with so many of the Italian families living in Bellaire along West Washington Street. When my father, Danny, was born in 1926, he learned to speak Italian as a matter of course by listening to his mother and father. His sister, Kathryn, would arrive four years later in

1930. They both adopted the name 'Pabby' as the name they would call their father.

My Grandfather had an abundance of customers to whom he delivered groceries throughout the community. He needed a good delivery truck to make those deliveries.   Now I listened to the musical group REO Speedwagon during the 1970s, but I never realized until lately that my Grandfather actually had one 50 years earlier. An early photograph of both of my Grandparents in front of the truck reveals the insignia of the REO Motor Car Company. Grandfather Abe acquired his first truck from this company for use in the grocery business. So popular was this motor vehicle by REO, a pioneer in pickup trucks, that other manufacturers began to copy it. The REO Motor Car Company advertised its vehicle with the slogan, "If It Isn't a REO, It Isn't a 'Speed Wagon'." The truck had spoked wheels and a roof that covered both the cab and the truck bed. The bed was open air but could be enclosed with canvas drapery to protect the load from the weather. REO advertised the truck as having 'Speed, Power and Durability,' and was popular during the 1920s with farmers and those businesses needing a reliable delivery vehicle. In 1921, these so-called 'Speed Wagons' sold for $1,575.00, which was not in those days an insignificant expenditure. Yet, with deliveries constituting an important part of the grocery business, my Grandfather made the investment. This truck he drove to all parts of the community, making deliveries to his customers both in the city and the country. He returned with the supplies needed to restock his shelves at West Washington Street. With his new set of wheels, and with the 1920s roaring, I guess you could say my Grandfather was ready to 'Roll With the Changes' that were sweeping America.

The Noble Experiment called "Prohibition."

Abraham Frizzi Grocery opened during the first few years of the 'Noble Experiment,' which was the prohibition of the manufacture, sale, or transport of alcohol. This had a direct impact on communities such as Bellaire, which had long been a very wet town from its earliest days. The community had many mills, mines, and factories with hundreds of blue-collar workers who were immigrants from Europe. They were accustomed to the drinking of beer and alcohol. When the first Petition was filed in the 1850s to incorporate the town, one of the reasons given to support town government was that there had been an 'influx of Foreigners,' and among them 'drunkenness, rioting and gambling.' The Petition further stated that the community had upwards of thirty grog shops and drinking saloons, equating 'one grog shop to every twenty persons' residing in the town. Bellaire had always been a wide-open town where restrictions on alcohol would most likely be opposed. Some immigrants would secretly ignore laws passed, even though the 18th Amendment to the U.S. Constitution and the Volstead Act, made it the law. In Bellaire, where so many saloons dotted the main streets, a complete ban on alcohol would have been intolerable, and so the manufacture, sale, or transport of alcohol went underground.

The 18th Amendment was enacted due to persistent pressure over many years from those reformers and religious organizations that promoted the temperance movement. The Volstead Act was enacted by Congress to enforce temperance. Viewed by church congregations and organized religious movements, intemperance was viewed as sinful conduct and a social evil. This movement had begun in the late 19th Century and continued in earnest after the end of World War I, which brought home American soldiers from the European battlefields. Temperance was also a period of time when Germany was placed under the harshest of treaty terms and reparations for its role in instigating the Great War. German immigrants, accustomed to beer and ale, were to be punished by these groups, and Prohibition was a way of doing it. Many large breweries were owned by the familiar foreign names of Pabst, Schlitz, and Blatz. This German connection to the brewing industry was used by reformers, at the end of World War I, as a reason to support the prohibition of alcohol.

The Women's Christian Temperance Union, or WCTU, was instrumental in seeking passage of the law, along with the Anti-Saloon League. Both groups had noble goals of preventing alcoholism and the devastating effects that alcohol often had on families. My Grandfather, Abe, was not particularly a religious man, and the arguments of the sober citizen, social reformer, and church organizations were not persuasive to him on the issue of alcohol. He did not subscribe to the belief that the portrayal of those who enjoyed alcohol were flawed. Nor did he believe it was fair to hardworking blue collar Americans, who were his friends, customers and neighbors. He viewed the sale of alcohol from a purely business standpoint. Alcohol was a commodity like other goods, which he offered to the public for sale, and he believed that limitations on its sale could not be accepted by them. He did not, of course, subscribe to the abuse of alcohol, and other than an occasional glass of wine with dinner, or amaretto or whiskey in a hot cup of coffee, his personal interest in using alcohol ended there. I do not ever remember seeing my Grandfather drink a bottle of beer, and never hard liquor except with a cup of coffee. From a business point of view, however, he believed that the system was corrupt because it allowed some to use alcohol, but unreasonably restricted others from doing so.

The use of alcohol under the Volstead Act was not completely prohibited during prohibition. Only the manufacture, sale, and transport of liquor was in violation of the law. Therefore, if you could get it legally, you could consume it. Examples of where alcohol was lawful to be used abounded. Doctors could write prescriptions for alcohol as having medicinal benefits for ailments such as toothaches, pain, and other conditions where the stimulative effect of alcohol might offer some relief. Thus, drugstores wishing to dispense medicinal alcohol flourished and sought licensing to be able to dispense it on the order of a physician. Walgreens increased its drugstore locations during the 1920s, seeking to distribute medicinal alcohol. Any alcohol that was already purchased before the passage of the Volstead Act, and on stock in your own home, was also legal to drink after Prohibition. Wealthy families stocked up before the law went into effect so that they had alcohol to consume during the prohibition imposed by the law. They could entertain a party of friends at home, and liberally drink as much alcohol as could be tolerated, and there would be no offense to the law. Wine was also exempted for religious sacrament, which made it readily available to priests, rabbis, ministers, and other clergy for use in communion and 'official religious services.' Each of these 'exempted' individuals was viewed by blue-collar America to be privileged under a law that did not afford them the same privilege.

Saloons and bars would be the hardest hit since they could not buy alcohol once manufacturing was prohibited, and even if they had it on hand, they were not permitted to sell it. Those who were well-connected saloon and bar owners, however, through graft, bribery, corrupted politicians, and law enforcement, found ways around the law by limiting access to their establishments, through operating quietly, as a so-called 'speakeasy,' many continued operation of their establishments without drawing attention to their activities. Enforcement against the well-connected, who could pay for their privilege, was often overlooked.

Italian-Americans, German-Americans, Irish-Americans, and many native born Americans found the law burdensome, unfair, and violating what had historically been permissible in their native homelands. Many believed the prohibition should be ignored. The saloons and bars operating as speakeasies, where alcohol flowed more quietly for those who could be admitted as a club member, or who could pay the price for an illegal drink, flourished for the affluent. But blue-collar immigrants did not have the ability to join in this consumption with the high rollers of the roaring twenties. The church affiliated organizations that had pushed for Prohibition were able to still get wine for sacrament, and many found this hypocritical as imposing on their parishioners abstinence with church clergy being exempt. The American Medical Association even insisted that the law should not interfere with the ability of a physician to 'prescribe' for their patients alcohol, when, in the opinion of the physician, alcohol was medically suitable as a remedy.

Because the system of Prohibition was prone to corruption, many citizens began to quietly produce wine and beer outside the eyes of the law. One family member of my Grandfather's sister, Olimpia, explained that her dad brewed his liquor quietly in the basement and then sold drinks by the glass in the kitchen for a quarter.

My Grandfather Abe had built a large two-story storeroom, with a garage on the street, and with an apartment on the second floor. This building was constructed in 1931, across Washington Street from the grocery store. When it was constructed, a large copper tank was installed in the basement under the floor, where alcohol could be stored and manufactured. The apartment upstairs was occupied by Philomena's younger sister, Adeline, and her husband, Marion. Abe gave permission to Marion to occupy the storeroom below the apartment for a small eatery called 'Washington Street Lunch,' and soon Marion began to serve food and build a clientele. He had many regular patrons at this little eatery. One particular management-level employee at the nearby Imperial Glass factory would often dine in the lunchroom. I do not know today what beverages were served with the meals. Abe's copper tank, however, was placed there under the floor for a reason, and probably supplied a prohibited beverage containing alcohol. My Father Dan and my Aunt Kathryn remembered that on many occasions, when an order was filled, a bottle of brew from the storeroom would often show up in the grocery boxes of favored customers. Many residents of West Washington Street decided that their own brew or wine would be worth the risk if done privately and discreetly. And Many did. Grapes became a popular commodity in this little grocery store, all heading for private grape presses. Italians and other immigrants grew wonderful gardens, and a grape arbor was always a part of it. Grape juice for the children, as one might profess, was actually for the fermentation tanks.

Liquor violations occurred all the time at small grocery stores where clientele were the working class of the community. Less serious violations usually went to the Mayor's Court, where fines would be imposed as high as $300.00. Repeat offenders, or those engaged in the manufacture and transport, would face even stiffer penalties. One of Abe's closest friends and neighbors would be arrested, charged, and convicted of violations. Innocenzo Ragni, a fellow grocer, Italian immigrant, and neighbor of my Grandfather, was arrested and brought before Mayor Wyatt and fined $300.00 on liquor violations. The Ragni home was next door to my Grandfather's storeroom. Both families recall stories of how the basement of both buildings became a place about which everyone spoke quietly. All were good, working Americans, technically violating a well-intentioned but poorly conceived law. They believed the law was unfair to those who could not afford the luxury that exemption, privilege, privacy, corruption, or influence afforded to others. Prohibition failed to recognize that immigrants were deprived of an acceptable social tradition and way of life. The political influences on this issue became apparent in the presidential election of 1928.

The Election of 1928 and Alcohol

At a family gathering at the home of the DeSimone Family on Hamilton Street in 1928, there was a hotly discussed topic. This was the Presidential race in which Herbert Hoover was named as the Republican candidate after President Calvin Coolidge suddenly declined to seek another term. Facing him would be the Democrat Al Smith, the popular governor of New York State. My Grandfather and Grandmother, Abe and Minnie, were at the family gathering with their young son, Danny, who related to me an incident. All were discussing the upcoming election, and their hope that Al Smith, the Democrat, would be victorious since he strongly opposed the 18th Amendment and the Volstead Act. The consensus of the DeSimone and Frizzi families, and friends at the gathering, was that a victory for Al Smith would finally be the death of Prohibition. This was a desire that all present shared. But my Grandfather believed that Al Smith had a problem, which he vocally pointed out to the group. He said that Al Smith, even though he supported their position on Prohibition, could not win the election because he was a Catholic. At this time in United States history, there had not been any President ever elected who was Catholic.

Many years later, my Father remembered this gathering, and that the discussion was loud and argumentative, as any discussion between Italians can sometimes be. But my Grandfather, Abe, refused to retreat from his belief that Smith would not win. He said that Al Smith would be doomed in the eyes of voters because of his religious faith, and that too many Protestant voters would oppose him. My father, Danny, remembered how intense the discussion became as a young child. He told me that he 'was holding his mother's hand' as they abruptly left the DeSimone home, and 'walked quickly up the sidewalk along Hamilton Street.' The pace was fast for a little child, and my father recalled 'being tugged along' as his father Abe and mother Minnie returned to their Washington Street home. As it eventually turned out, my Grandfather accurately predicted the results of the election. Al Smith lost, and a significant reason was that Protestant voters cast ballots against him simply because of his religious faith. The hope that Prohibition might end with an Al Smith presidency was dashed by the results. Candidate Smith was also damaged by unwarranted attacks against him as an alcoholic because he opposed Prohibition. His opponents had claimed he enjoyed drinking alcohol from his own pre-Prohibition inventory. The following year, however, the national economy would change the nation forever and begin to erode the 'Noble Experiment.'

The Great Depression

Just a year after Herbert Hoover became President, the stock market crashed, and the Great American Depression settled upon the country. Unemployment soared, as thousands of Americans lost the jobs which supported their families and paid their bills. This affected the Abraham Frizzi grocery store. Abe and Minnie had to monitor the credit purchases of customers to ensure that no one got behind in payment. The circumstances of each customer also had to be considered, since creditworthiness could be affected by death, divorce, gambling, or unemployment. While credit was usually extended to the customers of the store as a way of promoting business, it was always a business risk that required close supervision. When the stock market crashed, Abe and Minnie faced an even more daunting task. The depressed economy brought hardship to customers and the Abraham Frizzi Grocery, which extended credit. When families struggled without work and were not able to pay their grocery bills, no matter how frugal they might have been, the little grocery store faced a terrible dilemma. How will the grocery store manage to pay its own creditors, yet be supportive of the plight of its customers?

My Grandfather kept a metal account book listing the separate accounts of each customer. The metal book had double-sided pages fitted with spring clips under which order booklet pages for each customer. Every booklet page contained the name 'Abraham Frizzi-Groceries of Quality' as the banner at the top of the page. Below the banner was a line for entering the name of the customer, an address, and descending rows where a description of the purchased groceries could be written. At the right margin, a column appeared for entering the price of each item being purchased. The total of all purchases would appear at the bottom of the page, and each page would be placed under the spring clip for that customer. The white booklet pages held a yellow carbon copy underneath that was delivered to the customer at the time of purchase. All customer accounts were arranged in the metal account book alphabetically for easy reference.

Payments were expected from a customer on payday. When payday did not come, the little grocery store suffered a loss along with its customers and the community. This metal account book carried many customers on credit for years, accepting only what the customer's family could pay, but limiting new purchases so that the outstanding balance would always be reduced, or at least remain the same, with each payment.

Even today, examination of the metal account book finds account statements from the 1930s that went unpaid, totaling hundreds of dollars. Some contain letters written by the customers expressing the hardships that they faced, their regrets for failing to pay, and reassuring their commitment to honor the credit obligation that Abe and Minnie had extended to them. One reads on an account total of $4.12:

"Dear Mrs. Frizzi [Philomena], I am sorry we haven't sent this money sooner, but things out here don't move very fast, so we have done the best we could. . . Mrs. Butler."

And yet another from a lady named only as 'Lizzie' owing $14.60 reads: "I cannot pay on my store bill this time. My Bills are all so big from having to move, I had to pay rent for the house I am living in and a half months rent for the old house. . . . You don't need to be afraid, for I will pay you every cent I owe you. I am very sorry. From Lizzie."

These customers were not living extravagantly. On the contrary, the purchase order slips indicate their purchases were for basic staples that one would expect to use to prepare daily meals. Bread, milk, potatoes, and flour are all needed to supply the daily bread for their tables and families. Thousands of Americans, who just months before had been gainfully employed, were now facing 'breadlines' to receive an allotment of cheese and other staples for their family tables. Unemployed individuals stood in line for possible employment opportunities whenever a company was able to seek workers. Unfortunately, most were not able to find employment to support their families.

Richard Massa was a small boy growing up on West Washington Street with his parents, Clarence and Rose, during World War II, long after the Depression had ended. He often visited the Abraham Frizzi Grocery for his parents, who dealt with my Grandfather. Richard asked his father one day, "Why do we always have to deal with Frizzi's Grocery? Why can't we go to the M & K or A & P?" His father's answer was direct and went back to the days of the Depression. Clarence told his son Richard, "People respect Abe Frizzi because when families didn't have jobs, and didn't have money to feed their families, Abe Frizzi carried them on his books. That is the reason." Nearly 70 years later, Richard still remembered his own father's words, and he repeated them to me.

During the Depression and wartime, my Grandfather was one of the few places to purchase olive oil and roman cheese. He bought directly from contacts that he had in Italy to be able to have these products shipped to America. These products were essential to the Italian diet and cuisine. The Romano Cheese came in large wooden crates in a round wheel of cheese about 3 feet in diameter, and weighing about 50 pounds. The crates were marked with the address of 'Abraham Frizzi, Bellaire, Ohio, USA.' This wheel of Romano had to be broken down into more manageable sizes. Once this was done, smaller cheese pieces were placed on a wire cutting table. A thin wire was cranked down onto the cheese and pulled through the block to cut the larger piece into two smaller chunks. Pecorino Romano is a salty cheese that dates back to early Roman history and is made primarily in Sardinia. Made from the milk of sheep or cows, this cheese is dried for at least 5 to 6 months to produce a harder texture that would be suitable for grating. Romano is distinctive because of the smell it produces, and is often referred to as the 'smelly cheese.' Olive Oil, another staple of Italian cuisine, was also imported through New York. The Santuzza Oil company, an importer located in New York City, distributed olive oil under the brand name 'Mamma Mia.' This was 100% pure Italian olive oil, which my Grandfather purchased for his customers. Being able to provide these products made the little grocery store a popular place with many Italians in the Ohio Valley.

Small neighborhood grocery stores could not compete with the Atlantic Tea Company, and later the Atlantic & Pacific stores, perhaps the best-known chain of stores during the Depression. Small independent neighborhood grocery stores were plentiful and were within a short walking distance of each other. The economic downturn beginning in 1929, and competition from major chains operating supermarkets, caused many neighborhood stores to close their doors. The only way small grocery stores like Abraham Frizzi Grocery could survive was through joining an association of grocers, which together could buy at better wholesale prices with more reliable distribution of product. Bellaire had a Retail Grocers Association whose members together could be more competitive with larger grocery chains. The small stores in Bellaire, as elsewhere, turned to such membership in an association of grocers where they were better able to compete and succeed by joining together with other small neighborhood grocery stores. The Associated Grocers Association (AG) and Independent Grocers Association (IGA) were two early examples of associations joined by small neighborhood stores for survival. Abraham Frizzi Grocery joined the local Bellaire association of retail grocers and later the Associated Grocers, which was headquartered in Chicago. Together with other local grocery stores, a local chapter of AG was created, and warehouse buildings first in Martins Ferry, then in Benwood, West Virginia, and finally in South Wheeling, became the supplier of groceries to the little stores like my Grandfather's. Abraham Frizzi Grocery became Frizzi's AG Food Center, and together with other local neighborhood grocery stores, they operated a warehouse to supply them with grocery items at more competitive prices and reliable delivery. This would allow them to survive the disadvantages that all small neighborhood grocery stores in the community were experiencing.

The Public Works Administration in Bellaire

The government also attempted to contribute to a solution to the high unemployment of so many Americans through funding of public works projects. Under President Franklin Delano Roosevelt, the Works Progress Administration gave employment to those who were unemployed so that they were able to sustain a minimal existence through the wages funded by government programs. Public work projects were begun in Bellaire. The public swimming pool was built under the WPA beginning in 1939, as was the visitors' stands at Nelson Field, where Bellaire High School entertained visiting schools on the gridiron. Many streets were lined with brick pavers, and in Pulteney Township, many public road projects were undertaken, either opening new public roads or improving existing ones. This work gave the unemployed hope that better days were ahead by allowing them to work instead of accepting handouts. Unemployed workers who were customers of the grocery store were able to sign up and be hired as workers under these construction projects, and receive compensation from the government program. The goal was to allow them to purchase the basic needs, like groceries, for their families. These projects also assisted the small neighborhood grocery stores by placing money into the hands of the unemployed residents who now had purchasing power. Not everyone, however, could secure work in these projects which required travel to St. Clairsville for enrollment. William Newell, in a letter to the director of the WPA program, wrote about not being enrolled in the program:

"I live in Bellaire, Ohio, and at the present time am not working. I haven't had any work for over two months. I have a wife and two children and am staying with my father-in-law and mother-in-law. They have 9 in their own family, and my family makes 13."

"I have been to St. Clairsville twice, and they won't sign me up for the Works Progress Administration, and I can't even get any direct relief until I get signed up . . . I haven't any clothes for my two babies and ourselves, and half the time not enough to eat." 'William Newell'

The small neighborhood grocer heard these same kinds of requests for help, only those in need were standing in front of them across their store counters. These were the friends and neighbors of the neighborhood grocer, like my Grandparents, Abe and Minnie.

In 1933, Prohibition ended with the passage of the 21st Amendment to the United States Constitution. This finally terminated the social experiment, which had utterly failed during the 13 years it existed. One can cite many reasons for the ultimate repeal. The state of the economy was one of the primary reasons to end the prohibition of the manufacture, sale, and transport of alcohol. The brewing industry was an employer of many workers who were thrown into unemployment in the 1920s when the law was passed. Small communities throughout America had breweries that were forced to close during the time of prohibition. In addition to these workers, however, were those engaged in the retail sale and distribution of alcohol who were also affected. This, coupled with the massive unemployment in 1929, left so many without work in what had previously been a thriving industry.

The most important factor in ending prohibition was the failure of the general public to accept it. Good Americans simply chose to ignore the laws and engaged in bootlegging. Home brewing and distilling became popular so that beer, wine, and alcohol were brewed and distilled for consumption. Some was undoubtedly sold quietly. Saloons continued to find ways to evade the law, and the exceptions for medicinal and sacramental uses were abused. What the law did was to make ordinary citizens criminals because they preferred beverages with alcoholic content, even though they were not abusers of the drink.

Another important reason was that a black market was able to thrive through those who were prone to breaking the law, and resorted to violence because of the heavy profits that could be reaped by bootlegging. This was not the average person violating the law for their own consumption, but the organized groups who sought control of vast black markets created by the huge profits from dealing in volume. These profits were only possible because of the illicit trade, which developed in the underworld trade of alcohol. When violence erupted over territory, and the government realized how much in tax dollars was lost to the bootlegging industry, it was finally decided that regulation, and not prohibition, would better assist the failed economy.

Abraham Frizzi Groceries, already advertised and known for 'Groceries of Quality,' could now once again offer beer, wine, and other legal alcoholic products as a beverage to its customers.

Abramo and Philomena DeSimone Frizzi stand in the yard of the DeSimone home along Hamilton Street just behind the fence. (Frizzi Collection circa 1920)

The third grocery store built by Abramo Frizzi at 2783 Washington Street where his wife stands in the doorway. The rear end of the REO Speedwagon is visible at left near the sidewalk ready for loading. (Frizzi Collection circa 1924)

Abe Frizzi with unknown friend stand together on the sidewalk outside the third store next to the delivery truck. The woman standing behind is Adeline DeSimone, younger sister of Philomena, who often worked as a clerk in the store. The overhead porch of the DeBlasis family is visible in the background. (Frizzi Collection circa 1926)

The first grocer, Abramo, standing with wife Philomena and the very first grocer's son, Daniel Louis Frizzi, posing for a family photograph. Philomena had suffered miscarriages, and Danny was not born until some 7 years after the marriage on June 28, 1926. (Frizzi Collection circa 1929)

Children of Abramo and Philomena, Kathryn, born in 1930, and Danny, born in 1926, pose for the camera. (Frizzi Collection 1930)

Sister Kathryn and brother Danny Frizzi pose with a new bicycle outside the store on West Washington Street, with the storeroom and 2nd floor apartment across the street and behind them. (Frizzi Collection circa 1935)

Abe and Minnie stand on the sidewalk along West Washington Street beside their grocery store. The steep hillside along the left is retained by large sandstone walls. (Frizzi Collection circa 1935)

Abramo and son Danny as a Boy Scout. (Frizzi Collection 1938)

Chapter Four

My Father's Memories

The Stories that He Told

My father, Daniel Louis Frizzi, was born on June 28, 1926, and 4 years later, he was joined by a sister named Kathryn. Although similar to the name of his maternal Grandfather, Donato, it is known in Italian as 'Daniele.' My father Daniel was the first male grandchild of Donato DeSimone.

Dad related how he walked to the schoolhouse on Rose Hill once he began school at 5 years old. He had difficulty in his early years, partly because he was fluent in Italian, which he often heard his parents speak. When he began school, however, he could no longer use his Italian parlance to respond and had to read, write, and speak only in English. This set him back in 1st grade. As time progressed, he was able to advance with less dependence on Italian in favor of English. Those early years of being fluent in the native tongue of his father, Abe, and mother, Minnie, gave him the ability to speak Italian for many years thereafter, to customers and friends of his parents, despite this early setback.

Both my father and my aunt worked as youngsters in the Abraham Frizzi Grocery during those tumultuous years of the Great Depression and World War II. They grew up together with the other children of West Washington Street in a neighborhood not more than half a mile from downtown Bellaire. In walking to town, they would pass other small grocery stores, such as that of the Busack family on Hamilton Street. Just below the Busack store operated by Joseph Busack was the home of the DeSimone family, where their aunt and uncle, Alphonse, lived. Further down the street, they would pass Fornia's Grocery and barber shop just before they reached 32nd Street. This street led into the center of downtown Bellaire.

Both my Father Danny, and my Aunt Kathryn, knew the grocery store from an early age. They instructed that when their parents, Abe and

Minnie, were busy with a customer, they should ask waiting customers, "Can I help you?"

Some customers were willing to accept the help of a youngster who knew the store well in spite of being of tender years. But some customers were not willing to let a child wait on them. My father told me that on one occasion, when he was working with his mother and father, a man came into the store. My father described him as a generally unsociable type, with an abrupt manner. Dad said as he approached him with the usual greeting, "Can I help you, Sir?"

The man apparently made comments about not wanting a kid to wait on him in the presence of the other customers and stated he would wait for Abe or Minnie. My father told me how embarrassed and humiliated he was by this incident. He said to me, "I went back into the back of the store and cried because he hurt my feelings and embarrassed me." This incident left an impression that my father could still recall many years later. He related to me this incident of his own youth when I, too would be old enough to work in the store. He wanted me to know that not everyone would find a child acceptable as a clerk, even if the child was capable of rendering good service.

Because the family lived upstairs over the store, the stairway leading downstairs gave them ready access to the work of their parents. They were able to learn at an early age about the store business by observing their parents. Because Mother Minnie worked alongside my Grandfather, they were often at her side during their younger years. As they grew older, their responsibilities increased, which made them important employees of the little grocery store. This also gave them the opportunity for interaction with the customers and their families, which became a learning experience.

When not working in the store, there were opportunities for being outside and with friends on the sidewalk, or close by at a neighbor's house. The boys of my father's age all had nicknames. My father was called 'Puste,' a nickname given to him by his gang of friends. He was also known as 'Paba.' His neighbor and friend, Dominic Presutti, was 'Buzz.' Another friend, Dom Tuccio, was called 'Banjo.' The boy up the street, Armand Fana, was known as 'Cobb.' The oldest Ragni son, Frank, was known on the street as 'Hippo.' Well into adulthood, they still used those names from time to time when together at outings, which preserved their long-held friendships. I never did get the true origin of the name given to my father, but he was often called that by his friends after becoming an adult. This gang of friends from West Washington Street created lifelong friendships and memories together. To many living along West Washington Street, these boys were always called by their nicknames and would not be known if you referred to them using their given names.   Throughout school and World War II, they would remain close. Photographs of those days present a scene that was a typical Depression era imagery that could have been taken in any small town neighborhood in the 30's.

My Father's Life as a Grocer's Son

When Dad was 7 years old, he was treated to a birthday party sponsored by his parents and hosted by his mother, Minnie, at the family home on Washington Street. This was during the Great Depression, and was a welcome event for his friends in attendance. His neighborhood friends, Columbo 'Jitters' Tellitocci, Pete 'Smokey' Andriano, Dom 'Buzz' Presutti, Victor 'Vic' Ragni, Jack 'Barrel' Schwartz, Jimmie 'Clutch' Clutter, Vincent 'Vince' Tedeschi, and Edward 'Eddie' Potter were all in attendance.   Many parents of these children, and DeSimone's aunts, were also in attendance, including his 3-year-old sister Kathryn. In all respects, his early life was that of the typical child during the Depression. Those whose parents could afford to invite friends did so in the home where the celebration was held, and this event was recorded in the social news of the local newspaper.

My father engaged in the normal activities of that day for a boy growing up in the economic depression facing the country. Boy Scouts of America, an organization in which every red-blooded American boy wanted to participate, was organized in Bellaire. The Bellaire Christian Church sponsored the local Troop 115 for boys in the community, and they came from all parts of the town. These scouts came from all backgrounds. Kelley Archer was the son of a prominent attorney in the community. Walter Bauknecht was the son of a local mortician who was engaged in the Grafton-Mellott-Bauknecht Funeral Home. Many in the troop were sons of mill workers and other blue-collar workers. Together, they bonded as the young men of Scout Troop 115. In joining this local scout troop, they earned the customary badges awarded through merit and projects.

Dad drew up maps of hikes he participated in and kept a journal of where their hiking took him, his Troop leader, and fellow Scouts. One hike was listed by Dad as a 'Fourteen-mile Hike', which began at the Christian Church in Bellaire and proceeded west. He recalled in the journal being with 'Junior' Po. Together they found along the way what Dad called a 'milky ball tree'. From his description, this was undoubtedly a common hedge apple tree that produces a round, bumpy fruit and secretes a white, sticky sap. Dad recorded that he and his fellow scouts "rolled the balls down the hill at a horse" that was running in a field. When the scouts reached the halfway point of their hike, they came to a church somewhere in the hills of Pulteney Township.   The journal records that they camped here, building a fire to cook dinner. On their way back the next day, they came upon a road sign that said 'six miles to Bellaire.' The journal reports that they 'finally reached home' back at their starting place at the church.

Another popular activity associated with Scouting that Dad talked about was camping at Camp Agaming on Wheeling Creek near Elm Grove, West Virginia. Here, their Troop would pitch their tents for a week of camping in the great outdoors. This Scout Camp was a popular campground where the boys could fish, swim, and enjoy the collegial atmosphere with other scouts. When my Dad left for camp, his younger sister Kathryn told me how she cried in the car because he didn't come home with them. "I cried myself to sleep," she continued, missing her older brother even before they got home to Bellaire. Philomena comforted her, telling, "He will be coming home soon!"

On Friday evenings during Camp Week, family members would join them at this camp, where the scouts participated in campfire programs for their parents and siblings. Mother Minnie would join with mothers of the other scouts to provide ice cream and cake at the conclusion of the outdoor program.

Dad also signed up for the local running of the All-American Soap Box Derby, which was first begun in the 1930's. Local competitors vied for the right to compete at Akron, Ohio, where Derby Downs was located as a Depression era public works project through the Works Progress Administration. Chevrolet became a sponsor of the annual racing event.

Many of the Bellaire youth joined in the local competition with the hope of winning the right to compete at Derby Downs in the national competition. McGraw Chevrolet, a local dealer, helped to sponsor the local events along with the Times-Leader newspaper. My Dad told how payment of the entry fee earned a set of racing wheels on which your car was to be constructed. In the 1930's, girls could not join the soapbox derby as contestants, and the competition was strictly for boys. The passage of time has changed all that today.

Sometimes, business establishments sponsored the local racer, and my Dad was racing his car under the sponsorship of the local newspaper. He set out constructing his race car without adult help, and to the best of his abilities, a young teen would have. Dad said his father Abe was busy with the store business, and so Dad said he built the car himself. He remembered that some of the other boys had pretty professional-looking racing cars, but his was crude and simple. The racers assembled on Hanover Street in Martins Ferry, where the racing cars and drivers were to gather for their race heat against another local boy. My Dad recalled that his car was placed into position for the start of his heat. Soon he was heading east on Hanover Street, and he began to pick up speed. The racing wheels were made of solid, hard rubber tires on large metal wheels fitted with bearings that allowed for easy rotation. All cars, according to the rule book, had to have the ability to steer and to brake. My Dad recalled that when he passed the finish line, "I [he] put on the brakes, but the car started to come apart!" The brake was a hand-pulled lever that dropped down to drag on the pavement, but it could not withstand the strain on the car. He crashed the car and took a tumble that made the newspaper. He had built the racer himself, and although he won no trophy that day, he had gained the experience of having raced in a competition as a boy that would prepare him for life. My Dad salvaged the wheels of that race car after that day and stored them at his home on Washington Street. Some 30 years later, they would be found by his sons, and together they would build a primitive race car just like their father had done when he was a boy, to make their own memories riding those Soap Box Derby wheels from the 1930's.

Dad also took music lessons from an Italian accordion player from Bellaire who was an accomplished accordionist with the 'music box.' My Grandmother Minnie saw to it that when his interest peaked, he would have his own accordion with the name 'Danny' pressed into the face of the musical instrument. He learned all the wonderful polkas and practiced in the apartment above the Abraham Frizzi grocery store.   The houses were very close to one another on Washington Street, and without the air conditioning of today, windows were open in the hot summer months. When you practiced a musical instrument, not only did your family get to listen, but your neighbors were treated (if it could be called that) to a serenade. My father told me that when he was a small boy, his mother would often make him take an afternoon nap. Unfortunately, the DeBlasis family next door had a son who would often practice his own musical instrument at about that same time of the day. This practice usually woke my father from his sleep. My Grandmother Minnie asked the matriarch of the DeBlasis family if it was possible to have her son practice at a different time of the day. Rose DeBlasis remarked to my Grandmother, 'Philomena, che dorme, il Papa?' The English translation reveals that Rose had no intention of changing the time of her son's practice on his horn. Her response was 'Philomena, who is sleeping, the Pope?'

Some of the most wonderful memories that I still have from my own boyhood are my father getting out his accordion to play for the family. My brothers and I would often urge him to play for us after dinner, and on some occasions, he would accommodate. Usually a little rusty with the keyboard, and playing from memory, it would take a few minutes of remembering what his teacher had taught him in those lessons from the 1930's. Soon, however, he would break out into one of those wonderful polkas that he learned as a boy, and his sons would beam with excitement and joy as he played. As the 'Beer Barrel Polka' lyrics attest:
"Roll out the barrel, we'll have a barrel of fun
Roll out the barrel, we've got the blues on the run"
That we did whenever my father played the accordion!

One of the memories that Dad related to me about the Cicogna family was in 1934, when the entire family, Abele and Olimpia, and their 10 children were able to reunite in America. During the prior years, those family members who were living in Ohio sent back to Italy funds with which to be able to pay for the 2nd class steerage fare to America. Abele and his three oldest sons, Sam, Columbo, and Bruno, were living and working in Ohio. Still in Italy, however, were Olimpia and the remaining six children, being daughters Marie, Lelia, Clara, and Edda, along with their brothers Manuel and Fred. On July 28, 1934, the family boarded the Steamship Saturnia at Naples and sailed for America to be reunited for the first time in 30 years.

My Father recalled that the Cicogna family was to sail into New York harbor and there be met by two motor vehicles that would transport the family back to Ohio. Dad related how his father, Abe, agreed to supply one vehicle, and his nephew, Sam Cicogna, would supply the other. Together in a caravan, the long road trip to New York was undertaken. My Dad, together with his parents, Abe and Minnie, traveled together in one automobile, with Sam following closely behind in the other vehicle. Now these were not small cars and had to be big enough to carry all of the children. When they arrived in New York City, they went to the steamship company to be directed to the proper dock. The ship [Saturnia] was still at sea and would be a day late getting into port in New York. Dad related, "So we had to wait, and sleep in the car after our long road trip," he said.

At the time, Dad had just turned eight years old and did not recall much about New York City. When the ship finally arrived, the Cicogna family passed through immigration and then made their way to meet their American family. My Dad would meet his Italian cousins for the very first time.

Clara Cicogna Presutti related to me how when they arrived, the family divided up between the two vehicles, and began the long trip back to Ohio. "The ride was so long coming back to Ohio," she said, "and it was very uncomfortable". Some of the family was placed in rumble seats for parts of the ride home to allow more room inside the automobiles. She related how my Grandmother Philomena gave her a stick of chewing gum as a treat, "but I had never seen chewing gum before." Philomena told Clara, "masticare su di esso," trying to explain to her what she should do with it. "I did chew on it for a while, but then I got tired and spit it out," she remembered. This kindness of Philomena, which she showed to the Cicogna youngsters, also brought back other memories at Christmas time after the family moved to 29th Street in Bellaire. "Your Grandmother Philomena gave to me and Edda our first baby dolls one year ago for Christmas," she said. The family, upon arriving back in Ohio, lived in Martins Ferry for a time and then moved to 128-29th Street in Bellaire.

Clara recalled how Abe 'would deliver groceries to our house, and he would always have a sack of candy that he would give to us kids.'

Both Clara and Edda had been born in Italy and could not speak English. "It was difficult to learn a new language," she said. "I should have been in the 4th grade, but I was put back into the 3rd grade." The teachers would work with the girls after school to help them learn the language. Eventually, they were able to advance similarly as my Dad was able to overcome the difficulties associated with learning a new language.

A First Look at Death as a Small Boy

The headline in the Bellaire Daily Leader read 'Italians Mourn Man Who Aided Many Residents.' In the summer of 1935, my father was first introduced to the passing of a loved one. Philomena's father, Donato, fell ill after being in poor health for several years. He had undergone surgery on his stomach, and although he was not well, death was not expected when it finally came. Dad had related how his Grandfather Donato, had been a respected businessman in the community for many years as a co-operator of the Roma Theater on Belmont Street. He had been instrumental in assisting other Italian immigrants to become naturalized citizens. He also acted as a notary and an interpreter for the Italians living in Bellaire and the surrounding area. When he fell ill, my father recalled going to his Grandfather's home on Hamilton Street with his Mother Minnie. My father told me, "It was hot outside, and the house was very hot. I sat by my Grandfather's bedside with a fan and fanned him to make him more comfortable." Death came on August 3, 1935.

Donato had a history similar to that of my Grandfather Abe. Both had come to America as young men to begin a new life. Like my Grandfather, he was a businessman and leader of the Italian community in Bellaire. He was a charter member of the Christoforo Columbus Society and a founding member of the Sons of Italy lodge in Bellaire. His funeral took place in his home on Hamilton Street, with a Requiem Mass read at St. John's Catholic Church one hour later. His body was taken by a funeral procession with family and friends trailing his coffin from his home on Hamilton Street to the Church, in the tradition of Italian burials. From there, his casket traveled by hearse to the Mt. Calvary Catholic Cemetery in Rock Hill. My father witnessed the first of his family to pass away with the death of his Grandfather Donato. My father was given the gold pocket watch carried by Donato throughout life as the firstborn grandson. Any photograph that I have ever seen of my Great Grandfather shows the chain of this timepiece stretching from his button hole to his vest pocket, where the watch was kept. My father kept it for years in a little pouch in remembrance of his Grandfather, Donato DeSimone. This pocket watch has now become a treasured possession that one day I will pass to my grandson.

Most children remember the passing of Grandparents. This is usually the first memory of death. My Dad had told me that when he was a little boy, he would often see Donato on the streets of Bellaire. "Whenever he saw me, he would summon me and take a dollar from his pocket, and place it into my hand," he remembered. Donato would be sorely missed by the DeSimone and Frizzi families.

The Little Rascals, Ice Cream, and Hillside Adventures

The entertainment that my father and aunt enjoyed on Washington Street was very much different from what I experienced as a boy, and light years distant from the kind that children in the 21st Century have today. Entertainment in the 1930's was enjoyed primarily at home in front of the radio. Most but the poorest homes had one, and this is how the family got the news. But it was used for weekly shows where the entire family gathered around their radio receiver to listen to 'Amos and Andy,' 'Little Orphan Annie, 'The Lone Ranger,' or 'The Lantern.' These shows didn't permit a discussion about what to listen to since the choice was limited by the tuning dial. The Kraft Music Hall brought musical entertainment into the homes of thousands of families. When the President spoke to the nation, it was by radio, and FDR was able to give hope and optimism to a suffering American Nation during the Depression through his Fireside Chats. During wartime, the President gave reassurance of victory in Europe and in the Pacific theaters of the war. The radio was a gathering place for the family. Instead of each family member being glued to their own electronic handheld device of today, all family members were seated together and shared the words coming from the speakers of the family radio. This was audible entertainment. Each listener used their own imagination to create their own picture painted by the words that they heard. There was no admission charge for this entertainment.

Movie theaters, however, became a place for visual entertainment in the form of serials that played weekly. Western adventures like the 'Lone Ranger' or futuristic science exploits of 'Flash Gordon' could be viewed at movie theaters. 'Jungle Jim' and 'Tarzan' portrayed adventures in deep, dark Africa, while 'Dick Tracy' was the detective crime fighter in a big city. Stars like Shirley Temple were born during this time period. Buckwheat, Alfalfa, Spanky, and Darla became childhood icons in episodes of 'Our Gang,' portraying the 'Little Rascals.' Children often went to matinee's at theaters in bustling downtown Bellaire. Not everyone could afford the price of admission, however, so kids had to come up with their own form of entertainment. If you ever watched the 'Our Gang' series of episodes, you realize that kids growing up during the depression had to use their own imagination and ingenuity to create their entertainment. For most kids, the movie houses were a luxury that many children simply could not afford.

The grandest of all the movie houses in the 1930's was the Temple Theater at the corner of 34th and Belmont Streets. Built to house the offices of the United Mine Workers of America upstairs, it served as a public movie theater built to serve the citizens, coalminers, and other residents of Bellaire. There was the Elk Grand Theater on Belmont Street, providing live acts during the 20's and 30's, to complement the movie houses. The Capitol Theater, on Belmont Street, although smaller than the Temple, provided movies and serials. There was the Columbia Theater on 33rd Street between Guernsey and Hamilton Streets. The Roma Theater, on Belmont Street, also served as a movie house providing serials and musical performances. The Roma, however, was less expensive than the larger movie houses like the Temple, Elk Grand, and Capitol Theaters, which made it more popular with the blue-collar families. While my father had spoken often about the theaters downtown, the one he seemed to speak about most fondly was the outdoor theater that was arranged from time to time on Washington Street by Abraham Frizzi Grocery.

Ice Cream had become a popular refreshment during Prohibition, when the use of alcohol was outlawed. Ice Cream continued to be a tasty treat during the Depression; however, it now had to compete with 10-cent beer that once again could be served legally. Ice cream manufacturers sought ways to bolster sales. Both Telling's Ice Cream and Seal-Test Ice Cream were sold during the depression at my Grandfather's store on Washington Street. Telling's Ice Cream had a local plant in North Wheeling, and distributed ice cream to Bellaire and other local communities. Seal-Test ice cream was also distributed locally by truck to the grocery store. Fairmont Imperial ice cream was also a popular brand. This company had plants throughout West Virginia, including one located in Parkersburg at 1019 Murdoch Avenue. Another location was in Grafton, West Virginia. The slogan for Imperial was 'Guaranteed to Satisfy.' On hot summer nights on West Washington Street during the 1930's and 40's, Seal-Test ice cream became the treat for outdoor movie nights.

The host for these movie nights was the neighborhood grocery store of my Grandparents, Abe and Minnie Frizzi, who arranged the event with the Seal-Test company. The refrigerated truck would come to Washington Street and park in front of the grocery store. A large projector was set up, and a movie screen was hoisted above the many children who gathered with their parents along the sidewalk. Families would soon arrive and set up their stools and chairs to get a good spot for the movies. In anticipation of the beginning of the show, ice cream was dipped and served by employees for the children and adults at 5 cents a cone. At dusk, when darkness had fallen, the shows would begin. These were similar to the movies shown in the theaters in downtown Bellaire, but this was a completely different kind of atmosphere because it was outdoors. Many families could not afford the cost of admission in the downtown movie theaters, and still had money left for refreshments for the children. This was entertainment that an entire family could enjoy at only the cost of the ice cream cones. The grocery store would also stock and sell ice cream all summer long at the price of a nickel, as a way of attracting customers who would purchase other items while there. My father related how sometimes, when these outdoor shows were in progress, so much ice cream was dipped that "your arm would begin to ache with each scoop of ice cream you dipped."

Old timers remember these hot summer evenings at the Abraham Frizzi Grocery store on West Washington Street. When movies and ice cream came together, the kids living on the street could not forget those wonderful times. There are a few now living who are old enough to remember. Dean Giacometti, now 100 years old, told me he could remember them in the 1930's. "We didn't have the money to get into the movie theaters downtown, but I remember these movie nights with ice cream well," he assured me. The Giacometti family lived just west of the store after moving from First Ward to Washington Street. They were grocery customers of my Grandfather Abe, while still living in the First Ward. Dean remembered that "Abe delivered groceries to our home even before we moved to Washington Street" during the 1930's.

Growing up on Washington Street along the steep hillside above the grocery store provided a countryside wilderness for youngsters to explore. High atop the hill lay the old Greenwood Cemetery, where many of the early inhabitants of Bellaire found their final resting place. Reading the headstones was akin to reading a history book of the first people establishing businesses in the community. The grave of Eliza Heatherington and her husband Jacob was at the crest where one could look east down upon Bellaire City and west into Kleetown, now known as West Bellaire. There were the graves of Civil War general Benjamin Rush Cowen, and the namesake of the Grand Army of the Republic Lodge in Bellaire, Captain Spengler. The Schick family plot was nearby, where the coal family members were laid to rest. Toward the south along the crest of the hill were the graves of the Tappan family, early photographers and stove manufacturers. This was the same family that became famous for the so-named 'Tappan Stove.' Further south, toward the 'point' where the hill narrowed, was the family plot of the Rodefers, who were early glass manufacturers in the community. Just below the hilltop to the east was a mausoleum built of the finest blocks of granite stone work with an interior lined with marble.

The hillside below the cemetery had a road leading to an old, run-down building that looked like a barracks that might be found in a military camp. This building was the old hospital built in the late 1800's for quarantining those who had contracted smallpox, and later tuberculosis. Everyone referred to it as the 'Pest House' since these early diseases were known to be pests in the community to the health and safety of all residents. No longer used for that purpose, it had become a dilapidated structure along the road. The hillside was terraced in several areas where quarrying of stone was evident for building purposes. There were abundant springs that flowed from the hillsides, and the residents of Washington Street used the land near them for hillside gardens behind their homes. The hillside was clear of trees in the 1920's, but would gradually become forested over time with more trees. Into the trees would grow what children called 'monkey vines.' These were actually grape vines that had grown high up into the tree branches. My father, just as I and my brothers would enjoy years later, loved to play along this hillside, camp, and enjoy the great outdoors. From high atop this hillside, you could see the buildings in downtown Bellaire, the great sandstone arcade which was the approach to the railroad bridge spanning the Ohio River, the Interstate Bridge stretching toward Benwood, and the boats working their tow on the River. Smoke from the Imperial Glass factory's tall stacks, and any other glass factories, as well as the steam locomotives working the local delivery of freight and passengers into town, drifted skyward. These hillside adventures and views provided hours of fun for a youngster named 'Puste,' my father, Danny, and his gang of friends.

Dad and his friends often traveled the hillside above Rose Hill. They found an old log structure that sat high above the city streets below, and would gather at this spot. Central Avenue divided Rose Hill as it climbed the steep hillside toward the ridge. To the left was the Greenwood Cemetery, and to the right, higher still, was the Mt. Calvary Cemetery. The old log structure was on this hillside overlooking Indian Run below them. The old Carnegie Mill was then a memory, but other concerns had taken over the site. It was clearly in view. The elevated railroad trestle separated this industrial area from the residences along Noble Street. There was a constant passage of railroad traffic transporting coal to Holloway, Ohio. The old donkey field behind the St. John's Catholic Church was all plainly visible to them. Someone living nearby used this area for pasture, and cows roamed this hillside together with them.

The gang from West Washington Street lived in homes that were on the hillside above the street and below it. Any grassy yard that existed at any of their homes was sloping land, not suitable for playing ball. The only flat area on which to play ball was the level street between the homes. The street surface was brick pavers, and was not a completely smooth surface, but it was level enough for a better playing surface than a hillside. The brick-paved Washington Street would survive into the early

1950's before asphalt paving covered over the playground of the depression era gang. During the depression, the street became the ballfield, and all would gather to pick sides on the street. Whether it was stickball or football, the street between the curbs formed the boundary of play. Now, there were occasional interruptions when a passing vehicle was grudgingly given the right of way to pass by. My Mother once told me that she remembered as a little girl being in her own father's car, and watching the looks of all the boys who parted so the family car could pass. Mom said that "The boys looked like they were annoyed that their game was being interrupted by the intrusion of a car using the road." Nonetheless, traffic always passed, and the games soon resumed. The only other flat area was down by McMahon's Creek at the old Columbia Ballfield, which even I remember as a small boy living on Washington Street. This field sat below the grade of 26th Street in the flood plain of McMahon Creek. It had a set of goal posts and a small set of bleachers, and as I recall, it was more of a football field. Some football teams practiced here, and pickup games also used the field. Yet, Washington Street was closer to home and more convenient for kids, and so the street was the place where athletic skills were developed.

When my father was in his early teens, he would often drive the delivery truck to make deliveries to customers. When the deliveries had been completed, he often took his friends with him in the truck for a so-called 'frolic and detour.' By now, the REO Speed Wagon had been replaced with a late-model Chevrolet panel truck. On the side was painted Abraham Frizzi Groceries of Quality. Clearly, my father had to be careful not to get into mischief since the panels of the truck advertised whose truck it belonged to. He and several friends would often use the Chevrolet Truck for camping or going to their favorite swimming hole west of town at McClainsville. The clay pit of the Standard Stone & Brick Company was deep and held cool, clear water that accumulated when the brickyard was not in operation. This was a popular swimming hole frequented by my father with his friends and the Chevy panel truck.

My father had obtained a 22 caliber short pump rifle that the boys took with them on many of their adventures. This rifle became an oft-photographed companion of my Dad and his friends. The rifle, however, was not kept at his home, perhaps because his mother, Philomena, would object. Many years later, the rifle was discovered at the DeSimone home.   It is the same rifle seen in the photographs of my Dad posing in the woods.   My father's happiness in these boyhood jaunts is evident from his smile in the photographs.   It was a similar happiness that I, too, and my brothers would come to know when one day we also would live on Washington Street.

My Father's Love of Football

Of all the stories that I remember from my father, most related to his love of football, and playing for the local Bellaire 'Big Reds.' Football had long been a tradition in Bellaire, begun when the local team would play Saturday afternoon games at the old Riverview Stadium, north of the town near 53rd Street. When my father was 8 years old, a new stadium was built along 26th Street south of the downtown business district.   The stadium was on a low-lying plot of ground that had, in prior years, been used as a brick yard and slaughterhouse. The site was prone to flooding when the Ohio River caused backwater to creep into the McMahon Creek Valley. This new stadium would become known as Nelson Field, named for the long-standing and beloved Superintendent of Schools, J. V. Nelson. This stadium was close to the grocery store on West Washington Street and was within easy earshot of the roar of the partisan hometown crowd in the grandstands during home football games. My father was attracted to the lure of football and the grand heritage of playing for the 'Big Reds.'

Shortly after the field was inaugurated, the Works Progress Administration began construction of a new concrete structure for a visitor's stand. This side of the field would actually be better than the home field grandstands, built with the old bleachers that had been relocated from the Riverview Stadium. Once all were completed, the Nelson Field could seat approximately 5,000 hometown and visiting partisans for a football game. Bellaire football, with the new stadium, was becoming a premier program in the Ohio Valley.

My father told me that his father, 'Pabby,' did not attend the football games since he was always tending to the grocery store. His mother, Minnie, and sister Kathryn, however, did attend the games. Both were fans of their son and brother, Danny. Only when he was a senior did his father, Abraham, come to see him play in the game in honor of Senior players. He never expressed any anger that his father did not attend games to watch him play football, and instead said that his father was busy with the store business. Dad seemed to understand that his father's absence should be excused, and he accepted this.

Dad was not a big boy to play the game, but then, in the late 1930's and 1940's, boys did not have weight training programs as they do today. He began participating in the football program when in the 8th grade, and continued to get better as a player as each year passed. By the time he was a Junior, he had grown to 5'10" tall and weighed in at 157 pounds. His high school coach in his Sophomore year was John 'Butch' Nemiec. He had come to Bellaire to coach after playing under the legendary Knute Rockne at the University of Notre Dame. My father would play for him during the 1942 football season when Bellaire mustered just two victories, although Dad earned his first varsity letter. His final two seasons as a Junior and Senior were played under a new coach, James Foti. Coach Foti would change the Notre Dame style of offense that had been employed by Nemiec in the previous seasons, opting to go with an Ohio State style of backfield. Dad's final season would be a disappointing one, and his teammates would achieve only 4 victories against 6 losses. After winning the first three games of the season against Shadyside, Linsly, and Union, the offense was shut out in the next 5 games. The highlight of the season came when Bellaire defeated a strong East Liverpool Potter team 14-6. The defense was a prominent part of the 'Big Red' team, and it was on defense that my Dad excelled in backing up the line.

When I returned to Belmont County from law school, I was just a young lawyer working in the recorder's office at the courthouse when a man approached me. He was well dressed, wore a bow tie, and always had a cigar. He was an attorney named Kelley Archer, who also practiced real estate law as I did. He was a graduate of Bellaire High School during the 1930's, and had attended Princeton University and Harvard Law School. I had never met him before this day, but I will never forget what he told me. "My name is Kelley Archer, and if you ever need to find something here in this office, why you just ask me, and I will be happy to help you." I thanked him for his courteous manner, and then he said to me, "You are Dan Frizzi's son, aren't you? I just want to tell you I watched him play football at Bellaire, and he was a superb player and 'hard hitter' on defense." Coming from Kelley Archer, that was a real compliment. He had watched the Bellaire teams for nearly 50 years without missing but just a handful of games. He could always be found, near the 40-yard line in the next-to-last row in the visitors' stands for every home game, cigar in mouth, and attentive to every play. What a great feeling Attorney Archer gave me that day with that compliment about my father Danny!

My Dad used to tell all his sons' stories about his days playing football. His position of linebacker on defense earned him laurels, but his offensive position at center was also an important part of the team. Football during the 40's required a very skilled player at the center position, because the offense was built around shifting backfields where the ball could be snapped to a quarterback, halfback, or fullback. The center had to be constantly aware of where each running back was located in the backfield when they snapped the ball. Each play was designed to snap the ball to a particular back, and not always the quarterback. Dad often recalled that "You had to snap the ball to the right back by knowing where they were, and then block the rush."
Always touching the ball on each play made the center an important position on offense.

My father was fortunate that he suffered no serious injury while playing football in those early years. He did have a scar on his eyelid that he had received when a power running teammate named Willie Ford charged through the line and caught him in the face with his shoe and metal cleats. This was a relatively minor but clearly visible injury that he carried with him for years. Dad used to say, "I threw a block and fell down on the ground when Willie stepped right on my face." Dad always continued, "there must have been a hole because Willie kept on going." In these days of the game, leather helmets without face masks gave little protection to a player's face. Dad had the scar to prove it.

Another story my father used to tell was about Bellaire's loss to Steubenville Central in 1944 by a score of 6-0. This was wartime, and Bellaire players wore tattered and torn uniforms. He told us, "When Steubenville Central took the field, they had brand new jerseys, and we were wearing old, faded, and beat-up game jerseys." He intimated that seeing those bright colors worn by their opponents was "demoralizing" and "intimidating." The outcome of the game, however, would not be decided by Bellaire's dingy and faded jerseys. Once the game started, "their jerseys got dirty just like ours," Dad said. He related how the score was close throughout the game, but the 'Big Reds' lost by a 6-0 score to their well-dressed opponents from Jefferson County as the clock ran out.

The Linsly game that year also featured a real matchup. Not only were the teams comparable and able to win, but the special interest in this game for the Bellaire boys was that Mike Keane, who was from Bellaire, would be playing for the Cadets of Linsly. Dad and his teammates from Bellaire especially wanted to win this game to earn bragging rights against their fellow Bellaireans playing for an opposing school. Dad was named as the Acting Captain of the Bellaire team to face the 'Soldiers' of Linsly. Dad always remembered this game since the newspapers recorded his great defensive performance. After a Willie Ford fumble, Bellaire punted from the Red 1-yard line. Linsly got control of the Bellaire 16-yard line and was advancing their drive to the goal line. With only 7 yards to cross the goal line, and 4th down, the newspaper reported the runner was stopped when 'Frizzi dumped him for a two-yard loss, and Bellaire took possession at the nine."

I once asked Dad as a kid if he had ever scored a touchdown, and his thoughts came back to this game. He told me how, on defense against the Cadets, he was dropping back to cover a pass, before leaping up to make a one-handed interception of the ball in front of the home grandstands. The ball was thrown by Mike Keane, a Bellaire native attending Linsly. "I thought that I could race toward the goal line to score, but after catching that ball, I started to run, and someone caught me from behind just after a few steps forward," he related. Bragging rights in this game went to the Big Reds as they defeated Linsly 14-6. Against Union High School, the following week, newspapers reported that "Frizzi, Bellaire center, made a swell 'iron claw' tackle of a Union back" who was attempting to run back a punt. Playing both on offense and defense, there is no doubt that his play on defense from the linebacker position was what would earn him gridiron laurels. When Shadyside picked their 'All-Opponent Team,' Dad was selected by the Shadyside players as one of the toughest players they faced.

As a Senior, my father was 170 pounds. He wore number 20 on his uniform. He earned personal honors as First Team All-Eastern Ohio by the Times-Leader, and First Team All-Valley by WWVA Radio. The Times-Leader remarked that he was a 'Pepper Pot of Bellaire High's team." The paper continued that "whether the Big Reds were up or they were down, Frizzi was in there giving all he had." Dad received, for his All-Eastern Ohio honors, a coveted gold-engraved football as a 'symbol of his fine efforts' on the gridiron.

One of the defeats Dad remembered as a Senior was his last game wearing the 'Red & Black' of what would soon become his alma mater. The final game would be played at the Wheeling Island Stadium against Wheeling High School. This was a traditional Thanksgiving holiday game. Dad's team lost that close game 6-0 to end his final season at Bellaire. I asked my father once, as an adult, what he remembered about playing football for Bellaire High School at Nelson Field. His answer led him back to this final game. He didn't tell me about the game, or about his performance on the field. He didn't tell me about a particular tackle, or a hard-hitting block for his backfield. I am sure that he could have told me more stories relating to this game and others, but instead, he gave an answer to my question that I will never forget. He told me that he had walked from Nelson Field after his final practice for the Wheeling game. There was no locker room at Nelson Field, so players had to walk back to the high school to shower and dress. As he approached the gate at the field to leave, he stopped and turned around to gaze on Nelson Field, and the grandstands just one last time.

He said, "I stood and watched as a fog was settling over the field from McMahon's creek. I watched it move in and blanket the field until I couldn't see the goal posts at the south end of the field. They had completely disappeared." I was at first puzzled that this was the memory that he chose to share with me. Looking back on what he told me, however, I think I understand why this memory stuck with him. He was drafted before football season had begun and was to report for duty and service in the final year of World War II. He had written to the draft board and asked them to defer his date of report until after the football season had ended so that he could finish his Senior year playing football. The request was granted, and this game against Wheeling would mark the end of that deferment. He also knew that his mother, Philomena, had been diagnosed with cancer, and despite radiation treatments, her condition and health had not improved. There was much about which to be uncertain at this moment in his life.

I asked him to tell me what he was thinking as he stood there. He paused as he drifted back to that day. He then told me, "I was thinking about where I would be going after this game, and about my mother while I would be gone." Of all the stories that my father told me about playing football, this story has become by far the most meaningful to me. With this story that he chose to tell me, I realized, as he did then, that the fog settling over Nelson Field was hiding it from his view, just like his own future, which he could not see. While his story could have been about the events that had earned him football honors and laurels, instead, he chose to tell me a story not about a game, but about life, and the uncertainty that goes along with it. As much as my father loved the game of football, I believe this story he told me was his realization that football was still only a game to play. The score of course matters, and especially so to a young man. The score, however, is not necessarily the best yardstick to determine what the young man learns from the game. It will always be those intangibles that the young man learned along the way and took with them into the world after football. Those intangible qualities learned on the gridiron would always matter the most, no matter what the score may have been. They would prepare the young man to confront the uncertainties and sorrows of life.

World War II and the 'Housatonic'

World War II had been ablaze in Europe and the Pacific throughout my Dad's high school days. Commodities became scarce during this time because of the war effort. His father, Abe, had difficulty getting some of the products needed in the grocery business from Europe. He imported directly through many brokers in New York that handled much of what he required to meet the Italian customer demand. Scarcity became even more of a problem as the United States manufacturers were producing primarily to support the war effort. Many goods were not available to American consumers. The Office of Price Administration was created to help maintain a fair and equitable system for the distribution of many goods in the United States. To do this, a ration system was put into place, which limited the amount of grocery staples that any person or family could purchase within a given period of time. The goal was to limit the purchases to a specific time period so that more Americans could receive goods they needed to maintain some level of stability in their lives.

Many grocery items were subject to the rationing. Coffee, sugar, processed food, meat, and dairy products like milk and cheese all became subject to rationing. Ration books were given by the OPA to all families that were based on the number of members in the family. These coupons were exchanged at a grocery store and redeemed by paying the cash price of the item, provided that you had sufficient coupon points to make the purchase. Because the coupon denomination was usually in an amount greater than the number of points required for the purchase, a system of giving change to a customer was necessary. The OPA established a change system by creating tokens, both red and blue, equal to 1 point. If a good purchased costs 35 cents and 3 ration points, and you had a paper coupon worth 10 points, the grocer must return to you 7 points. This was done by using the red point and blue point tokens. A separate token tray was required to separate the tokens from the money held in the cash drawer. This system was the law, and grocers had to comply with it. The government coupon books contained this simple phrase:

"Give your whole support to rationing and thereby conserve our vital goods. If you don't need it, DON'T BUY IT."

All Americans were supporting the war effort at home, buying War Bonds and adapting to rationing, while so many young American sons and daughters were serving abroad. In 1942, after the Japanese Empire had struck the United States at Pearl Harbor in the horrific attack known as the 'day that will live in infamy,' U.S. forces retaliated in April of the following year. The 'Doolittle Raid' on Tokyo was payback in which Mitchell B-25 bombers took off from aircraft carriers with fuel to carry out their bombing mission, and then bailed out over mainland China. Some of the airman perished, and others were picked up by allied forces when their aircraft ran out of fuel after completing the bombing raid. Eight airmen were captured by Japan. They were incarcerated in concentration camps of the worst kind as prisoners of war. When three of the eight captured airmen were executed, my Grandfather Abe immediately went to the Farmers' and Merchants Bank in Bellaire and bought $3,000.00 of U.S. War Bonds, angered by the treachery perpetrated on these

American airmen.   Local papers quoted Abe as saying after he heard the news of the execution of the fliers:

"If they're going to do that to our boys, the least I can do is to buy more bonds NOW!"

Perhaps my Grandfather was motivated in part due to the knowledge that his own son would soon become an American sailor.

My father would now join that war effort in uniform. Dad left Bellaire on February 1, 1945, after posing with 29 other young men on the indoor steps of the Bellaire City Building. He was bound for the Great Lakes Naval Training Camp, where he would be in boot camp before departing for San Francisco. Upon his completion of boot camp, he returned home one last time to bid his family and his mother, Philomena, goodbye. Despite treatments at the Mayo Clinic in Minnesota to find a way to rid her of the cancer, the doctors finally told my Grandfather that there was nothing more that could be done. So Dad said goodbye to his mother for what would be the last time. My aunt Kathryn remained at her side throughout the terrible ordeal, facing it alone. Dad's transfer would be to the USS Housatonic, an AO-35 Tanker bound for the Pacific theater of the war against the Japanese Empire. He remembered how passing under the Golden Gate Bridge as the ship moved toward open sea and described how "terrible a feeling it was" to be leaving home.

My father often talked about his life aboard the ship and living with his shipmates. Dad once related how he was assigned to KP duty peeling potatoes and sifting through the flour to screen out the mealworms. Dad also told my brothers and me about getting put on report for going into a crowded head, and hollering 'Fall Out'! His object was to be able to find a vacant stall, which soon freed up as all the other sailors ran out, believing they were under a command to do so. He was reported for this infraction and sent to what he called 'Happy Hour' along with others who were found to violate rules. Each sailor given a rifle was ordered to stand at attention and then directed to use the rifle as a weight for punishment. Dad said that "The MP would order us to hold the rifle in a certain position for ten minutes, like outstretched arms," and then, "he would order us to hold the rifle with one arm out from our side." After 45 minutes of this kind of punishment, many were unable to continue. "Some," he said, "passed out with muscle fatigue and crashed down on the floor. We were all at attention, and not permitted to look at them, but we could hear them." He remembered that although he finished the punishment, it had not been a pleasant experience, and one he did not wish to revisit.

Life on board the ship below deck in the bunks, where it was hot and smelly, was another unpleasant experience. To avoid the heat and odor, Dad decided that he would get a hammock and go topside, where the air was fresher. He remembered that he tied the ends of the hammock between some pipes, took off his shoes, and placed them underneath. A tanker fully loaded with diesel and aviation fuel, however, sits low in the water, and thus the deck of the Housatonic was not high enough above the seas. That night, waves lapped up on the deck while he was sleeping, and when he awoke, his shoes were gone! He never explained how he got another pair.

Aboard the ship, my Father was assigned to General Quarters in a gun turret tub. General Quarters was the highest level of readiness for battle, and each sailor was assigned to their own battle station. He explained that "My job was to catch the spent shells from the gun when they were ejected after firing, and to throw them out of the tub." The shells were hot and hard to handle, but getting them outside the turret prevented anyone from tripping while reloading the gun. Repeated firing of the gun caused my Dad's hearing to suffer, and he always attributed his hearing loss to those days in the Navy. His stories were always of great interest to my brothers and me as we looked upon Dad as a real hero. "Board a tanker as he was, the ship was never in any active battles where life was lost. In fact, the one death that Dad related was a sailor who went missing while swimming when the ship was at anchor." Dad told us that when the ship was anchored, many on board would go swimming. Once in the water, "we would climb up the anchor chain and dive back into the water." One particular day, a sailor went missing while in the water, and his body was never recovered. "We didn't know what happened to him, and we presumed that he drowned," from some unknown cause. This was the only death that he ever related to us that had occurred while on board the Housatonnic. He did relate an injury that occurred to a shipmate when a cable snapped during refueling another ship. Apparently, the end of the cable whipped back and struck a sailor in the face, taking out his eye. Dad said, "I had to carry him cradled in my arms up the narrow steps to the next deck to get him to the medics on board."

Graduation and Sadness at Sea

Back home in Ohio, the class of 1945 was preparing to graduate. Although Dad had sufficient credits to join them, he would be absent from the ceremony and would not wear the traditional cap and gown. Instead, his sister Kathryn, only a freshman, accepted his diploma in his absence after the ceremony had ended. With each graduate who could not attend the ceremony, it was announced that they were serving their country in uniform. His Mother Philomena, was too ill to attend the graduation ceremony, ailing from uterine cancer.

News of Philomena's death was sent from home just 12 days before Dad's 19th birthday, while he was somewhere in the Pacific. A cable about his mother came to him in June of 1945, sent by his sister Kathryn, informing him of his mother's death on Saturday, June 16. Because of the logistical problem of getting news from home, the cable came late. He attempted to persuade his commanding officer to arrange for him to return to Ohio. My father said, "I explained to him that my father [Pabby] was from the 'old country', and would need help taking care of things at home. The CO did not like the fact that I referred to the 'old country,' and he denied my request." Germany had already surrendered in May, and Japan was under siege and soon would surrender in August of that year, so Dad believed that chances were good he could get leave to come home for the funeral. Dad once told me that, "he felt like the CO held the cable from me until it was too late to be able to return to Ohio," to prevent hope that he might get to return home for the funeral. His absence was particularly difficult for his younger sister Kathryn, who was now a teen of tender years. Without her older brother's support, she would bear the loss of their mother alone with their father, Abe.

My Grandmother Philomena was only 41 years of age. She was every bit the businesswoman as my Grandfather was a businessman. Philomena was a partner, not just in marriage to my Grandfather, but also in the operation of the grocery store. She took care of the books and the accounts, as well as clerking at the store. All the customers of the store knew Minnie as a kind and good woman. On the afternoon of the funeral, Washington Street was overflowing with the customers, friends, and neighbors of the Frizzi and DeSimone families as my Grandmother's casket was carried to the waiting hearse from the upstairs residence.

Burial took place in the mausoleum at the old Greenwood Cemetery high above the town of Bellaire. The Italian Co-Masonic Order of Bellaire performed services as she was laid to rest. The biblical phrase inscribed over the entrance of the mausoleum from the Book of Job reads, "Until the Day Break, and the Shadows Flee Away." When that day comes, I hope to finally meet my Grandmother Philomena, whom I have only known through the stories of my father and my Aunt Kathryn, and the many photographs picturing this beautiful lady.

My Father wrote letters to my Grandfather Abe and my Aunt Kathryn, attempting to express his grief over the loss of his mother. Particularly difficult was his inability to return. His mourning was endured alone at sea in the vast Pacific. He would remain shipboard and visit the defeated Japanese mainland after the bombing of both Hiroshima and Nagasaki, and the Japanese surrender to American forces. The Japanese, he said, appeared respectful in defeat, even though they had been brutal in war. "The police would salute us, and civilians would step aside on the city sidewalks permitting us passage," he said. He remembered that "All sailors were to carry canteens with drinking water, and were warned not to drink anything while on shore for fear of reprisals." The Housatonic carried him back to San Francisco after leaving Japan, and he once again saw that beautiful Golden Gate Bridge as he returned. In San Francisco, his ship was decommissioned and was destined for the mothball fleet. He was assigned to painting duty as the entire ship was painted gray and was readied to become a part of history. He was also placed on duty aboard the USS Antona II, another tanker that was also to be decommissioned and sent into the retired Navy fleet of ships.

He was honorably discharged in June 1946, with rank as a Machinist's Mate Third Class, having served aboard the USS Housatonic at sea, and the USS Antona in San Francisco. He returned to Bellaire by train from California and recalled the long, tiring trip home. "My Navy uniform was white when I left San Francisco, but it was gray with the soot and dirt from the long train trip home," he remembered. But home he was, and he walked from the Union Street train station out Hamilton Street, to his boyhood home on West Washington, a proud veteran of World War II.

He was now one of the 'Greatest Generation' to have lived in America. Although the war was over, it did leave scars. I remember showing my Dad, many years later, a new automobile that I had purchased. He took a ride with me, and said it was a pretty automobile and rode good. Then he said to me, "But I am sorry, but I would not own one." It was a Nissan Maxima. I chalked it up to my Dad's remembering the war, the attack on Pearl Harbor, and the Japanese treatment of American soldiers. He had not been able to forget those horrors of war, including his friend Armand Fana.

Dad was only one of many Veterans of Washington Street who returned home from the war. As the war was progressing, a local lumber company decided to erect a wooden marker in 1943 near the junction of West Washington Street and Hamilton Street, noting their service. As young men and women entered military service as volunteers or by draft, their names were painted onto the marker. With each name was written their boyhood nickname by which they had been known growing up on West Washington Street. One of those young friends, Armand 'Cobb' Fana, did not return, having been killed in France. Another friend, William 'Mose' Respole, was captured by Japanese soldiers and endured the 65-mile Batan Death March in the Philippines. He survived after more than three years of captivity in a brutal prisoner-of-war camp. After the conclusion of the war, the wooden marker was supplemented with a permanent concrete marker noting the supreme sacrifice of their fallen friend, Armand Fana. Similar to a tombstone, a plaque was mounted atop the concrete pedestal along the sidewalk, reading "In Memoriam Armand 'Cobb' Fana Who Made the Supreme Sacrifice." Their fallen friend, 'Cobb,' was never forgotten by his friends on West Washington Street. I know that my Dad never forgot him either.

Football at Chattanooga

Dad's love of playing football once again became a focus of his life. He was approached by Andrew Nardo, a man with local ties to West Washington Street, about playing for the University of Tennessee at Chattanooga.

Nardo had been a student at Chattanooga in the 1930's, and upon his graduation, became a well-known football and wrestling coach at the school. He was instrumental in finding local Ohio Valley talent for the team. Vincent Sarratore, a Martins Ferry boy nicknamed 'Stumpy,' was already on the Chattanooga team, and so my father decided to attempt to make the team as well. He registered with the help of Coach Nardo for the fall semester, before departing Wheeling Airport on a DC-3 bound for Chattanooga to play for the 'Moccasins' as they were known in 1946. That fall season, he moved to the position of right guard and played defense wearing No. 31 on his jersey. Dad was now 180 pounds and listed on the roster at 5'10' tall. He recalled games played against No. 8 Tennessee, No. 3 Georgia, and No. 12 Wake Forest. He did not get to play much during this season, and only when the 'Mocs' were hopelessly behind or safely ahead in the scoring. But it was the game played in Miami at Roddy Burdine Stadium, later to become the 'Orange Bowl,' which he recalled with the greatest enthusiasm. Dad had made the traveling team, and he often remembered how 'Getting to run out onto that big field with the team as the game was about to begin was an experience that I won't ever forget.' He remained injury-free during this season, except for an elbow to the mouth, which he sustained in one game. He explained, "I had blocked an opposing player low and to the stomach, and I heard him groan from the block. He got even when I took from him an elbow to the mouth." He remembered that his face and mouth were swollen from that retaliatory strike from his opponent.

One other story that my Dad told was an experience in Chattanooga related only indirectly to football. He remembered that once he was chastised by upperclassmen on the team because he was in friendly conversation with a Negro while off campus. This man had some connection to back home. Dad said his teammates "pulled me aside, and told me that I should stay away from the 'n**gers' if I wanted to play on this team." To my father, this came as a complete shock and the rude awakening that he was in the deep south. He had played with and attended class with African-Americans all throughout high school. The Bellaire School System had been integrated from the late 1800's. But Chattanooga in the 1940's was a part of the deep south, and prejudice against the Negro race, or 'colored people,' as they were then called, was still an unfortunate and ugly part of it. The state of Tennessee and its athletic programs would not be integrated for another 20 years. To my father, this incident left a mark. He was being educated by his teammates about rank and unrepentant prejudice. Back home in Bellaire, discrimination, while existing, was not as pronounced and severe as it was in the deep south.

Dad only played college football this one season at Chattanooga, and then returned home to Bellaire. He had seen limited playing time with the team, even though he had shown promise as just an underclassman. As the season was ending, he no longer had interest in continuing with classes at the University, and withdrew on November 6 with several games remaining. I asked my father once, "Why did you quit Dad?" He told me that he had been away from home during the war and missed being back home to be with his friends who were also returning from the military. He always told me that he was 'homesick,' and this was his reason for not continuing with his education. Dad told me once that he was studying to be a coach in the physical education program. He also had mathematics and English composition in addition. Dad had graduated in the general course of study at Bellaire High, and most likely found college work difficult. Dad was good at mathematics in high school, and he often told us as kids, "I had good grades in math and exempted trigonometry when I was a Senior." In college, however, this could prove to be a disadvantage in preparing to do college work. Yet, his transcript from Chattanooga indicates that when he withdrew, he could have continued his studies had he chosen. So before the football season had ended, Dad said goodbye to Chattanooga and turned in his jersey. He returned to his hometown to join up with his friends to enter the post-war work force.

When he returned to Bellaire, Dad did not immediately go into the store business. Instead, he found work driving a truck at a coal mine. His father, Abe, had a fractional ownership interest in a coal mine which was located in northern Belmont County, Ohio, on Nixon Run. His father was able to secure this employment with the coal company. Dad's job was to have coal loaded into a dump truck, which he would then drive to a tipple where it was dumped. On one occasion, he said, "I was backing up to the tipple and got too far back with my load, which was being dumped. The truck almost upset when the front end lifted off the ground." He said it was a frightful experience, but never did say if that 'experience' made him decide to seek other gainful employment.

In 1947, several years after the death of my Grandmother Philomena, my Grandfather Abe purchased a large, undeveloped plot of ground in the middle of West Bellaire. This was always called the 'Mystery Mound' by all the locals since it was a large and high hill resembling a haystack that was situated behind the West Bellaire School. Children living in Klee, and later West Bellaire, used this high hilltop for camping out during the summer, and sledding in the winter. This was really not a mound built by ancient Indian people, as many locals used to say. This was just a geological formation that, from the high hilltop, afforded a panoramic view of West Bellaire and the McMahon Valley. When my Grandfather decided to build a home on this hilltop, excavation revealed a seam of coal that had to be removed before construction could begin. This ended the mistaken belief that the mound was built by any ancient people.

My aunt Kathryn had still not recovered from the passing of her mother. The memory of Philomena and the funeral at home made it exceedingly difficult for her to stay in the residence upstairs over the grocery store. She spent most nights at the home of her 'Zsi,' or aunt Adeline, who was her mother's sister, and who lived over the store room across the street. Her cousin Eleanor was about her same age, and this provided her with female companionship that was lost when her mother died. Once the new home was built in West Bellaire, Aunt Kathryn moved with her father, Abe, and my Dad to West Bellaire.

One particular day, Aunt Kathryn, upon reporting for work at the store, was puzzled by the absence of 'Zsi.' She went to the apartment over the storeroom and found her unconscious. She frantically worked to find someone to help. Dad was called at the mine, and Adeline's sisters were found. My Father and Uncle Stanley Ostasiewski traveled to the mine to inform Mariano Raspa that his wife was seriously ill. She was transported to the hospital, and after weeks of recovery and rehabilitation, was finally able to return home. This close call had an effect on both my aunt Kathryn and my father. This was just another reminder to them about their mother's passing just a few years earlier, and so it frightened them.

Abraham Frizzi & Son Grocery

Not long after 'Zsi's' close call with death, Dad returned to the work that he knew best as a boy. He became engaged with his father, Abe, in running the Abraham Frizzi Grocery Store on West Washington Street. At some point, an agreement was reached that he and his father would join together to operate the store, and it became known as Abraham Frizzi & Son Grocery. The garage on the side of the storefront was eliminated so the interior of the store could be expanded. The stairway from the upstairs residence was closed, and this created more interior storage. The additional space provided would be used for produce, cereals, and more canned goods. The ice cream freezer could also be moved from the front window to behind the store counter now that the stairway to the upstairs had been eliminated. A second entry way was still available from the sidewalk by a narrow doorway and passage leading to the pop room and storage area.

By 1952, my father was married to my mother, Nancy Ann Robinson, and I soon came along on the 15th of September of that year. I was named Daniel Louis Frizzi, Jr., after my father. Because my Grandfather Abe had already built a new home in West Bellaire, the home above the store is where my Dad and Mom would set up housekeeping in 1952. To do so, the Massa family, which was renting this upstairs apartment were notified that they would need to find other housing. Just like Abe and Minnie had done 30 years earlier, 2783 Washington Street became the home of another Frizzi family. This is the home that spawns my earliest memories of being a grocer's son.

One of the first photographs taken of me in that upstairs residence was a few weeks after my birth. As was traditional, a nude baby photo was taken with me lying on my stomach on my parents' bed. My Father had placed a football next to me.

The stockroom and garage built by Abramo Frizzi to provide more room for the grocery store. The garage housed the delivery truck and the storeroom at the left was used as a small luncheon room known as Washington Street Lunch operated by Mariano Raspa who lived in the upstairs apartment with wife Adeline. (Frizzi Collection circa 1940)

Abe and Minnie pose together outside Washington Street Lunch which by now was used as a stock room. Behind them is the porch and home of Innocenzo and Gina Ragni.
(Frizzi Collection circa 1940)

Associated Grocers members at a meeting at the warehouse located on 23rd Street, Wheeling, West Virginia. Abe Frizzi sits first row first desk along with fellow rocers of the Belmont County and Wheeling areas. Included in front row are another Bellaire grocers Israel DeBlasis of Stadium AG to right of Abe, and Anthony Berher of Diamond AG fourth in row. (Frizzi Collection circa 1945)

A gathering of the Co-Masonic Lodge members at the picnic grounds located in West Bellaire. The women are members of the lodge which did not discriminate on gender. Abe Frizzi stands at left in white shirt and tie, with Innocenzo Ragni holding his hat at right. Attillio D'Allesandro stands behind him. (Frizzi Collection circa 1945)

"Big Reds" of Bellaire High School football team with Danny Frizzi at center, with the Imperial Glass Factory looming in the background. First row from left, Willie Ford, Tom Yadrick, Frizzi, Dom Liberati, Carl Johnson; second row from left Don Miller, Pittman, Homer Workman, and Bob St. John. (Frizzi Collection 1944)

The final photograph of Philomena with her son Danny at their home above the Washington Street store before he departed for active duty.

Induction photo into the U.S. Navy, and post war photograph of Danny in football uniform for the University of Tennessee at Chattanooga football team, the Moccasins. (Frizzi Collection 1946)

Danny Frizzi now back home on Washington Street at the Frizzi AG Food Center with Attillio D'Allesandro at right discussing the news of the day with an unknown man holding the newspaper. (Frizzi Collection circa 1950)

Chapter Five

My Childhood on West Washington Street

My Boyhood Memories

I was not old enough to begin working in the store until about seven or eight years old. So until that age, most of my time was spent at play in our backyard behind the store and the residence above it. This was the same yard where my father had played as a child, together with my aunt Kathryn. My earliest memories of Washington Street originate there, and with the many people who were our neighbors, customers, and friends. Most had been a part of Abraham Frizzi Grocery when my father was a boy growing up on Washington Street, and they now became a part of my life as well.

My first real memory at this upstairs residence was a traumatic one, yet it provided me with the opportunity to meet so many of my neighbors for the first time. Living above the store, the sidewalk was about fifteen concrete steps below the small 6-foot walkway that we used to access our back door. I was about three years old, and I had a little riding tractor with foot pedals that propelled it back and forth on the walkway. A gate was fastened to the side of the house and stretched to the concrete wall bordering the walkway. It was fastened so that I could not get down the steps when on foot. I would ride my little tractor back and forth in that narrow walkway, turning it around to complete the ride back.   One sunny morning, I was making my loop when, for some reason, I decided to take out that fence head-on. My next memory was hopping down those fifteen concrete steps, still riding the tractor all the way to the bottom. The tractor upset near the bottom of the ride, and landed me onto the sidewalk with the tractor coming to rest on top of me. I recall being scuffed up with beautiful road rash raspberries on my arms and legs, and laying on the sidewalk on my back. I was in a little pain, very frightened, and recall wailing loudly until help arrived. Fortunately, I sustained no serious injury. This is when I got to meet many of the people living in the neighborhood.

The first person to arrive was my aunt Adeline, or 'Zsi,' who lived across the street in the upstairs apartment over our storeroom. Her husband, uncle Mariano, was at work in the coal mine. Aunt Ad came running when she heard my screams. My Grandpa Frizzi and my Dad, working in the store, came out to see what had happened, and about that time, my Mom was racing down the steps to rescue her firstborn child. I remember looking up, and there were many older Italian ladies standing there looking down at me. "Poor little boy," I heard them say. Gina Ragni came running from across the street where she lived, and then Nora Andriano, who lived next door to us, appeared. Ida Pallisco, who lived next to Ragni's, joined these women, and before long, there was a real crowd. All of them were offering sympathetic words on observing the predicament in which I had placed myself with my reckless driving. When I was finally extricated from the wreckage and was in my mother's arms, I realized that the crowd had gathered to make sure I was not seriously injured. This was the way it was with the West Washington Street community.

My Aunt Ad always remembered this event, and would remind me of that day long after I had grown to be a man. She was a younger sister of my Grandmother Philomena, and she was very close to my Dad and my aunt Kathryn. When my Grandmother died, aunt Kathryn, was comforted by 'Zsi,' as she called her, and opened her home across the street. She had a pleasantly plump build and was always so happy to greet us as children. When she smiled, you would see the gold tooth that she had, which was always amusing to my brothers and me, since I had never seen such a tooth before. When she approached my brothers and I, her first instinct upon greeting us was to take hold of us by the cheek and pinch it between her forefinger and thumb, moving our cheek in a back-and-forth motion. This was her way of expressing her happiness to see us. That pinching of our cheeks was her trademark move whenever aunt Ad visited, and we always knew it was coming!

The Andriano Family

Many of my childhood memories of neighbors come from the Andriano family of Anthony and Rose. This large Italian family lived next door and was an important part of my Washington Street community. My father had grown up with the younger children of the Andriano Family that lived next door to the store. My aunt Kathryn, as a young girl, spent much time with this family. The Andriano's looked upon my dad and aunt as part of their family. Finer neighbors could not be found anywhere.

Anthony and Rose Andriano had raised a hard-working Italian-American family whose children were always kind to me and my brothers as little boys growing up next door. Nora was always there for our birthdays and watched out for us at play in the yard above our home. Bessie, another daughter, when not working at the Echo Restaurant in town, was also with us many times while at play. Just as she had been with my aunt Kathryn, time had not changed her with age. She would often bring her nieces, Nancy and Diane, over to play with us since we were all about the same age. Daughter Marie worked outside the home, I believe in Wheeling, and she was usually absent during the workday, but returned each afternoon after her workday had ended. Brother Tony was a barber by trade. Pete, who was Nancy and Diane's father, would often stop by to help with carrying groceries that his elderly mother and father needed. Josephine, one of the younger daughters, had poor health and was confined to the home. Joe Catina, Rose Andriano's brother, was also a friend to us as little boys.

The Andrianos were a deeply religious family raised in the Roman Catholic faith, and this entire family became friends with my Grandparents, Abe and Minnie. My parents and my aunt Kathryn always felt so comfortable when my brothers and cousins were visiting, knowing that the family next door would watch over them at play. There was a connection with this family that came from living in close proximity to them. It was a special relationship that fostered acts demonstrating a true neighborly love and friendship. I can remember as a small boy that our family was to travel to Maryland to attend a funeral and visit relatives of my mother, Nancy. Nora came to our home before we left on that trip. I can still recall her words expressing her concern about our traveling so far away. She reached into her pocket and pulled out a statue of St. Christopher, the patron saint and protector of safe travels of the Catholic faith. These types of statues were commonly found on the dashboard of automobiles owned by members of the Catholic faith during the 1940s and 50s. They often had a magnetic bottom, so that they could be attached to the metal dashboard of cars of this vintage. I recall as a boy listening to Nora's words spoken with the greatest sense of sincerity. I stood by my mother's side as Nora explained why she had come to our home. As she placed St. Christopher in my mother's hand, she said, "I know you are not Catholic, and you may not believe as we do in Saint Christopher, but we would feel so much better knowing that he is with you on your trip." My mother graciously took St. Christopher, hugged Nora warmly, and told her that we would gladly take Saint Christopher with us to Maryland, and so we did!

Nora said, "*You don't have to display St. Christopher on your dashboard, just keep him close.*" This was just one of the many kindnesses shown to us by the Andriano family. They were genuine in their concern for our welfare, and they truly loved our family as they loved their own

Another memory was our visits with "Josie," the daughter with poor health. Josephine was confined to an attic bedroom of the home during my childhood days. Except for our occasional visits to see her, we would not have known she even existed. I still recall climbing the narrow steps with my brother Dick to the attic bedroom where Josie would be found. This was a little eerie the first time, as a kid, when we climbed those steps to visit Josie. Upon entering her room, Josie was always in her bed, dressed in a nightgown, and propped up with pillows so that she could greet us. She was a pretty young woman, and we found it difficult to understand why she would be confined to bed. She did not look sick to us. On the wall behind her bed was a large crucifix with Jesus hanging from the cross for the Salvation of all sinners. I had not seen such a crucifix before at this early age, or the agony on the face of the man hanging upon it, named Jesus. I recall my young granddaughter's reaction to seeing a near life-size crucifix in Cincinnati at her sister's baptism, and pointing at the man and asking me, "Why is that man hanging there?"

Her question brought back my own memories of Josie's attic bedroom. Small votive candles were burning throughout the room in red-tinted glass. My brother and I were not accustomed to seeing a person ill and in bed, and the candles and the crucifix of our Lord gave us pause. Josie called us with an outstretched arm to her bedside, gave us a hug, and engaged us in dialogue that seemed to ease our fears. Josie also had a crucifix at her bedside, and she always held it to our lips and asked us in kindly and sincere words, "Kiss Jesus our Lord." Hesitant, of course, but reassured by her calm and kindly way, we did as she asked. Josie would visit with our mother, and we would look around this room, which was so different from the others we had seen. After a visit, we would depart, and Josie would bid us goodbye and remind us that we could always visit her again. We always did.

The Andriano home, although next door to our store, did not sit close to the sidewalk. It was built higher up on the hillside and, therefore, was accessed by a long, arduous set of concrete steps to reach the rear door of the home. Along the sidewalk below the home was a large sandstone wall that held back the front yard below the front porch of the house. The family had many visitors who walked those long set of concrete steps past our kitchen window as they climbed up the hill to the Andriano back door. We would often see Nuns from the local convent traveling the steps to visit the family. Priests were frequent visitors. As little boys, we often captured their attention and their warm greetings.

The kitchen at the rear of the Andriano home is where the concrete steps finally ended, and from that vantage point, Rose was able to look out her kitchen window into our backyard. Although we also had to climb a set of steps to get to our backyard from our house, it was not as long or difficult. The Andriano home towered above the roof of the store and our small house, giving them the ability to see us at play in our backyard.

Everyone had a shed behind their house. Mr. Andriano was an avid gardener, but to make the land usable for planting, he terraced the ground above the house and placed wooden catwalks perpendicular to the grade of the hill. These catwalks were used for tilling the soil for planting, watering the growing vegetable plants, and harvesting the crop. There was a long set of wooden steps climbing the hillside from which each catwalk could be accessed. The vegetable garden was full of tomato plants of a wide variety. There were pepper plants, lima beans, green beans, peas, radishes, and carrots. There was also an herb, spice, and seasoning garden where you would find rosemary, sage, basil, and spearmint. When accompanying one of the Andrianos along the terraced hillside, they would show us the plants, naming them for us and identifying the vegetables we could pick from the vines. Some we could bring home to our mother.

My favorite herb in the garden was spearmint, and I would always snap a sprig from the plant and chew on it to get that satisfying burst of flavor. Herbs were especially important to Italian cuisine for flavoring that made soups and dishes taste so much better.

At the very top of the wooden steps climbing the hill, was a smaller shed where Mr. Andriano kept his garden tools and implements. Here you would find tomato stakes, strips of denim for tying up the vines, water buckets and cans, rakes, shovels, hoes, and everything needed to produce a prolific vegetable garden. He even had large colored chalk, which my brother and I found particularly interesting. Above the shed, there was a path that ran a few hundred feet to an opening in the hillside that had been eroded over many years by a natural spring. The spring ran continuously throughout the year from a cast iron pipe that was driven into the hillside, and which emptied into a wooden barrel that sat below the pipe. The water was always crystal clear, ice cold, and offered us an invitation to drink from the barrel. We had been admonished by our parents not to do so. They always told us that, "The water is good for gardens, but not for you to drink!" We did so anyway despite the admonition from our parents. From this clear spring, many gardeners on Washington Street found bucket after bucket of water for their thriving vegetable gardens.

One of the springtime activities that I remember as a boy was the harvesting of 'chicorium,' a common weed-like plant with blue flowers growing from its taller stems. This plant is in the family of the common pest, the dandelion. Some people considered this plant to be just a weed that should be cut down and eradicated. We treat our lawns to be rid of this yellow flower that grows in early spring. The plant is common in the Mediterranean region of Europe, and Italians on Washington Street knew better that the plant had beneficial qualities. It could be harvested for its spring leaves to be used as edible greens, and larger plants with roots could be dried and ground up for a coffee or powder additive. My first experience with 'chicoria,' as my father called it, was one spring day when Rose DeBlasis came into our yard with a basket and a knife. Now, Rose was a little scary to me as a small boy. Her grayish-white hair was billowing in the wind in an unkempt way. Her housecoat was buttoned up the front, and often her hose were rolled down at her ankles. She was gruff and did not like my brothers or me scampering about in her yard. I once remember her yelling at us as kids for having crossed over from our yard into hers, and she scared the proverbial 'crap' out of us! We were so frightened that we immediately ran down the steps into our home and said to our Mother, "Rose is after us, Mom."

Rose, you will recall, is the mother whose son played his musical instrument when my father, as a boy, was taking his nap. Well, on this spring day, my brother Dick and I were in our back yard playing, and guess who showed up on our side of the property line to pick, "Chicoria?" Yes, it was Rose! She had apparently exhausted her supply in her own yard and was now trespassing on our turf. "Hi boys," she said as she bent over with her knife and began cutting the chickweed from the root. My brother and I naturally found this to be somewhat invasive, especially because she had been so territorial with her own yard. We raced down to let our Mother know what was going on, but when we returned, Rose was gone. Perhaps she knew that we intended to report to our mother that she was now in our yard and not her own!

Our Terraced Yard and Shanty

Our own backyard was also terraced in order to provide flat and usable space against the hillside. When my father was a boy, my Grandfather had built a 'shed,' or 'shanty,' as we called it, behind the house on the first terrace. This was a square wooden building with lap siding and a hip roof. Inside this shed were stored all kinds of contraptions that had been accumulated over the years by my Grandfather in operating a grocery store. There was a grinding wheel operated by a pedal for sharpening knives, meat cleavers, and other butcher tools. There was old store shelving and outdated equipment that was too valuable to just throw away. Glassware was abundant, since it was often given away as part of a promotional campaign for the sale of certain products. I recall that some of the glassware had the image of the childhood star Shirley Temple baked onto the side. Soap powder boxes often contained glassware, much like a prize could always be found by a kid in a Cracker Jack box.

One large piece of glassware that I recall was an umbrella stand. As a kid peering down into this tall glass stand, I found a poor little skeleton of an unfortunate field mouse that fell into what became his final resting place. Strange how that memory stuck with me after more than 65 years.

Another amusement was a deer antler that had been shed by a buck, and which someone hung up inside the shed. My father's Navy tote bag was inside, with some of his old Navy gear. An old Japanese Rifle that he had been given at the end of the war was inside that shed, which he showed to us. There were fishing poles, tackle boxes, and all kinds of 'stuff' that would fascinate any kid. Whenever my father unlocked the shed door and would go inside, we were right behind him, because entering that shanty was like entering P.T. Barnum's museum of oddities and curiosities.

Peering through the boxes of 'stuff' that many would consider junk, however memorable, could not compare to the set of red wheels on axles that had been kept by our father from his Soap Box Derby days. He explained, as we intently listened, how he built his own racer on those sets of wheels some 30 years before. He told us the story of racing on his racecar and wrecking as he attempted to brake. This old shed was probably the most fun place for a kid to explore, because everything in it was new to us, and even better, it had a story that accompanied it. The exterior of the shed, however, also created many fond memories of the backyard, which became part of my childhood. When my brother Dick and I were quite small, a litter of pups had been born in the crawl space under the shed. The momma was a stray dog, and she was taking care of her litter as best she could. We were concerned about them, and could hear those pups whimpering, so our parents were alerted. The pups had become active after a few weeks of being hidden from our view. My dad had to crawl into that narrow space under the shed to bring each pup out one by one. Together with their momma, we cared for them until we eventually were able to find permanent homes. I remember how we wanted to keep one for our own, but we were told that "they needed a home where they could run around away from a busy street," like the one in front of the store. "But Dad, you had a dog here in the back yard when you were little, didn't you?" we cried. We knew he did because he told us about his dog that he raised from a pup. This dog was tied, however, and served more as a watchdog than as a pet once it got older. We were disappointed, but we did understand about the street, since it was not uncommon to hear the screech of tires on the pavement and a corresponding wail of an injured stray dog or cat. So instead of a puppy, one Easter we got rabbits, and my father built a rabbit pen on the back of the shed. My rabbit was a copper brown color that I named 'Rusty,' and my brother Dick had a rabbit that was black on white, which he named 'Salt n Pepper.'   The rabbit pen was framed on the side of the shed wall, about six feet long and several feet deep. Wire mesh was wrapped on the exposed sides of the pen, and on the two doors for each side to access each pen. My rabbit 'Rusty' was in the left side pen, and brother Dick's rabbit was in the right side pen. We had to feed and water them daily, and clean up the mess that dropped to the ground underneath the pens. The rabbits were allowed out of the pens when we had enough adult supervision to corral them in the backyard; however, we had an abundance of clover and grass to keep them busy eating instead of running away. These rabbits really grew quickly, probably owing to the feed pellets that we fed to them and a lack of exercise. I don't recall how long we had these rabbits, although I do recall one day we found out they were both gone. Someone had agreed to take them, we were told, where there was 'more room for them to run around' without being cooped up in the pen.

The shed was also the home of several large black snakes, who occasionally would come out to lay on the stone wall that separated the first terrace from the upper terrace of the yard. We were afraid of snakes, and so was my poor Mom. One day, we had been playing with the clothesline props. We left them laying in the yard instead of placing them against the side of the shed as we had been told. Mom went up the next morning and was going to hang some clothes outside for drying in the open air, but needed to pick up the props that were still lying on the ground. When she picked up the first prop, it was heavier than it should be, and that is because a long black snake was stretched across it on the ground. Mom screamed bloody murder! A man whose identity I do not recall was next door at Andrianos' house, and came running. He went over and picked up the snake by the tail and, in a whipping motion, like you might do with a bull-whip, cracked the snake lifeless. Yes, that is probably not the most humane way of dealing with a snake that was minding its own business in the sun, but darn it, my poor Mom was scared to death. After that, we were always looking for black snakes whenever we were around the shed. Because we were so close to the woods above our yard, snakes were always sunning themselves in the warmth of the early morning sun. The last of the outdoor pets that I recall having were once again 'Resurrection Pets' that came to live with us during Easter. We always went to the five & dime store in downtown Bellaire during this time of year. Both W. T. Grant and G. C. Murphy stores were located side by side on Belmont Street, and we, as kids, loved to go see the colored chicks and ducks that were sold at Easter. The chicks were each tinted with a pastel color of pink, green, blue, or yellow, and they would scamper around in the small pens built to house them for easy customer viewing. A heat lamp over the pen would provide the warmth needed for the little guys and girls. The little ducklings had a natural yellow color, and with so many of them all running about, it was a treat for young and old alike to watch them. The little 'cheep, cheep, cheep' or 'quack, quack, quack' of these cute little creatures was a call that was interpreted by little boys, like us, to be saying "take me home!" And so we did. Four ducks for four brothers. They lived in boxes at first, which we got from the store below our home, and we watched them grow. As with all living things, however, the boxes needed to house them had to get larger and larger every week that passed as they grew bigger.

In order to properly house them, my dad decided that he would build a duck pen on the third terrace above our home. This third terrace was where dad had a vegetable garden, and he built the duck pen at one end. When we were very young, my father had built a wooden plank stairway from the second terrace to this garden area to easily access it. The duck pen was built of wooden slats, much like a picket fence, on all four sides about six feet high. An open space was between the slats so that you could peer into the pen. Because this enclosure was so close to the woods, the height was necessary to keep the ducks from becoming prey. A door allowed us to access the pen for feeding and cleaning, chores that we had to tend to weekly. We fed the ducks with whatever fruit and vegetables my Grandfather Abe would set aside as not suitable for selling in the grocery store to customers. We also had other bags of feed that Dad got from the feed store.

One day, I remember going to the duck pen for the morning chores, and was shocked by what was found. Lying there on the straw bedding of the pen was the largest egg that I had ever seen. At first, my brother and I thought someone had played a trick on us, but we raced with the egg tucked firmly in hand down the wooden plank steps, across the second terrace, down the stone steps to the first terrace, and then down the concrete steps to our back porch. Bursting into the kitchen, we exhibited what we had found. As I recall, even my Dad and Mom were a little shocked. Dad made a breakfast meal out of the first egg we picked from the pen. Day after day, we would go back to that pen and find another egg or two, and return them to our parents. I am not sure how long this went on before one day, we discovered that the ducks we had been raising were no longer in the pens. Now it was clear to us that they didn't escape from the duck pen, and so we asked where they went. As I recall, being the oldest brother and as an advocate for all, I felt as though there was a story behind the disappearance. I am not sure who found out first, but I learned that permission had been given to our next-door neighbors, the Andrianos, that they could have the ducks, so long as they made sure that we saw nothing that would upset us. I can remember once seeing Rose Andriano take two chickens by their necks and stretch them until their necks broke. Her brother Joe Catina then hung them by their feet under the porch. I thought about our ducks with their necks being stretched in the same way. But true to their word, my brothers and I never saw a thing! However, I think the ducks became a meal.

Being older now, my thoughts went back to 'Rusty,' my rabbit, and I wondered if his disappearance had a similar ending! The first and only indoor pet I remember having was a parakeet named 'Buddy Boy.' I know what happened to him, because he was found in his cage. He died of natural causes, and probably would not have been tasty anyway.

At Play

In those years before I began to work in the store, the backyard above our residence was where my brothers and I spent many hours playing together. We were often visited by my cousins, Steve, Kathi, and Gary, who lived on Washington Street about 300 yards from the store. Our yard was terraced behind and above the rooftop of the house. You could actually climb onto the roof from the hillside as it sloped down to the back porch roof. We were warned as kids not to go on that roof, and as an adult today with grandchildren of my own, I shudder when I think of how dangerous this roof was. The roof was a hip-type roof with sloped sides that came to a peak at the very top. There was a precipitous drop of nearly twenty-five feet from the edges of this roof above the sidewalk below. I do remember at least one time climbing that roof to the peak, and peering off toward the street side, before Nora or Bessie Andriano yelled for us to get back in the yard. Soon, my Mom was summoned, and we were punished for trespassing where we had been told not to go.

The first terrace was where our shanty was located. There was a large mulberry tree that grew on the sloped ground near the shed, and we would climb into that tree often. From that vantage point, we were high above the rooftop of our store and home. The mulberry tree grew those plump berries, which we were told as kids 'not to eat.' I never remember us harvesting the mulberries on the tree, and when they became ripe, they fell to the ground, making a slippery slope of mush when you walked over them. At the rear of this terrace was a stone wall that separated it from the second terrace of the backyard. On this second terrace was our swing set and teeter-totter, which occupied much of our time. This was an attraction for us. It was here that we entertained our Cousins Steve, Kathi, and Gary when they would visit us. We would spend hours talking and swinging. Sometimes we would climb trees, and the mulberry tree seemed to be a favorite. On the second terrace were some fruit trees. There was a large pear tree, and my Dad had planted an apple tree and a fig tree. My father had spoken to an older Italian man who was experienced in grafting one type of fruit tree to another. As I recall, he came to our house with a small tree branch, which he had clipped from an apple tree somewhere else. He then began the surgical process of grafting this branch to the apple tree in our yard. He took one of the sturdy branches on our apple tree and cut a V-shaped notch into the branch. Then he took the apple branch that he brought with him, sized its diameter, and cut it into the shape of a V that would fit neatly into the notch he made on our apple tree. After he placed it into position, he took paraffin and melted it over the surgical area to give it strength, carefully holding it in place until the paraffin hardened. With the assistance of my father, he then took old denim from a worn-out pair of overalls and cut a long strip about 8 inches wide, which he wrapped around the grafted area, leaving an opening above the graft. Loose dirt was then filled up inside the denim, and this was used to keep the branches moist while nature was taking time to grow the two different branches together. After several months of waiting, I remember that the branch sprouted leaves and grew along with the tree. We waited for apple blooms of a different kind than those produced by the rest of the tree, but I do not recall that we ever had two different kinds of apples grow on that tree.

The best tree for climbing was one near our property line with the DeBlasis family. This tree was tall and straight, and I recall that high up in it we found a hole that had been pecked out by a woodpecker who had long since abandoned it. The hole was filled with brown, stinky water that oozed out of the tree and dripped down the side of the bark below the hole. But this tree also had a bird nest that I have seen nowhere else since my boyhood days. This bird nest was built in the form of a hanging pouch that drooped down from the branch to which it was attached. The bird that frequented this nest was brightly colored in orange and black. Further inquiry with my parents led to the discovery that we had a Baltimore Oriole living in our tree. Perhaps it was the abundance of mulberries nearby that attracted it, since these birds thrive on both berries and insects. I have never seen since my boyhood days a similar nest inhabited by this beautiful bird. Crows were frequent visitors in the trees near the top of the hill just below Greenwood Cemetery, sometimes in numbers so large that you could not count them. They would congregate in the early morning, calling out with their 'caw-caw-caw,' before flying off to some distant place.Above this second terrace was another hillside, and it too was separated by a stone wall. From this wall, the wooden plank steps stretched to the garden and duck pen. Beyond this third terrace was nothing but an overgrowth of weeds, jagged bushes, grape vines, and a single tree of thorns. This thorn tree was particularly enticing because it had long thorns that were a brownish or deep maroon color. Each thorn grew as much as 3 to four inches long, and they were extremely sharp at the point. When we were a little older, we would cut some of these thorns from the tree, fasten them to the end of a hollowed-out dry weed stalk, and use them as a primitive type of spear. We believed that we could hunt the numerous rabbits scampering about the hillside, but they were always as elusive as the 'Road Runner' was to 'Wile E. Coyote' of Looney Tunes fame. We had fun throwing the spears, but we never struck any living thing.

When we matured to 8 or 9, we both got Daisy 'Red Rider' BB guns and our hunting tools became less primitive! Most of the shooting we did caused no damage to the life or limb of any living thing. We did a lot of shooting at old cans and bottles that had been discarded over the hill from the cemetery.

Our Dinner Table

We always ate dinner together as a family growing up in the 1950's. The family would wait while Mom prepared our final meal of the day in anticipation of Dad's arrival from work below in the store. Meals were always a time for discussion about the activities of our day. This was a time for learning, and each would get the chance to document our exploits. Mom taught us how to set the table and how to fold the napkins before placing the silverware. We helped set out the glasses and cups for drinking. We drank milk. Mom was a good cook, and she had learned much about Italian dining during these early years. My mother had the best spaghetti sauce whenever we ate pasta. She prepared it with pork cuts from the store, tomatoes, onion, and all the ingredients that would be simmered on the stove for much of the day into a thick sauce. One of the dishes that we were introduced to at an early age was what my Dad called 'Ceci.' This was a common dish on our table. Chick peas, or 'Ceci,' were also widely known as Garbonzo Beans, or when ground up into a paste, as Hummus. A type of legume, 'Ceci,' was always on our table as a healthy side dish.

My Dad would always arrive from the store so that we could eat the meal that my Mother had prepared for us. My Grandfather Abe would remain below us in the store, and he would close or wait until my father returned to relieve him. When Dad arrived, we would gather around the table and say grace before the meal. All heads bowed, hands clasped together, and all was quiet as one of the brothers was asked to give thanks to the Lord for the "food set before us. Bless us and keep us, in Jesus name, Amen." Only then would the meal begin.

The television was never on during dinnertime. All attention was focused on what each of us wished to offer in discussion at the table. We were especially intent on listening to our parents' stories about when they were little, as we were then. Sometimes my Mother would talk about stories in West Bellaire, where she had grown up. Mom had attended the same school where we were now going, and so she had interesting stories that we could relate to about our school. Dad would often tell us stories about living in the same house where we were eating dinner when he was a little boy our age. We listened intently to both our parents' tales because we could relate to what they were describing to us from our familiarity with the location. We especially enjoyed hearing my Dad tell us about the Navy and being on a ship in the ocean. He related to us many stories about growing up on West Washington Street when he was a boy. Because he grew up in the same house where we were now living, those stories came alive when he described his life within the walls of this little upstairs apartment over the store. The dinner meals were a real teaching experience for my four brothers and me. My Dad was fluent in the Italian language from the time of boyhood, and so he wanted his sons to have some exposure to Italian words. We had already started school, and the words he was teaching us would not interfere with speaking and writing in English. His instruction, however, would introduce us to the language of our Grandfather Abe and Grandmother Minnie.

Now, to hold the attention of four little boys, all under the age of eight, he had to make the class interesting. The first exercise that I remember was teaching us how to say the different parts of the body in Italian. He would point to each part as he said the words, and we would watch and listen. Then he would make it fun by only pointing and giving us the opportunity to pronounce the Italian word. 'Capelli,' as he pointed to his head of black hair. 'Orrechio' when he pointed to his ear. 'Braccio,' as he touched his muscular arms covered with 'capelli.' This would go on from 'Testa' [head] to 'Piedi' [feet] with all parts in between.

He would usually skip the parts that were the most fun to say, and perhaps not appropriate as table talk, but on occasion would refer to them. *"Siediti sul tuo Culo"* he would say when we were fidgeting and wanting to leave the table before dinner was over. I was much older when I asked him what you called every male child's pride and joy that made us boys. He must have considered me old enough to be told, and I learned the word 'pene!' These memories have stuck with me all those years ago, and I found myself emulating my Dad at the dinner table with my own children, in the hope that they too would have some appreciation of their Italian heritage.

One of the proudest moments of that heritage came to me years later in the eighth grade when I was a student in Mr. Griffin's home room class. He was telling the class that when you get to high school next year, you should take a language class. The options were either Latin, with Mrs. Vogt, or French, with Mrs. Berger. Italian was not an option. But Mr. Griffin was explaining to us how beautiful other languages can be, and why we should take advantage of learning them. He then looked at me and said, "Frizzi, do you speak Italian?" Now I did know some words, and I knew what 'pene' was, but I don't think that was something I should tell Mr. Griffin. He asked me further, "Do you know what the Italian word is for 'Springtime'?" I responded by saying, "I know that my Grandfather would know." Mr. Griffin immediately told me to go to the office and call my Grandfather to ask him how to say 'Springtime' in Italian. So I did.

I went to Mr. Griffin's desk in the office, as he was the Principal at Central. I dialed 676-6386 (also known as Orchard 6-6386), and soon I heard my Father's voice answering the phone with the greeting "Frizzi's AG Food Center." I asked my Dad if Grandpa Frizzi was at the store, and I could hear him call out. I explained why I was calling and what Mr. Griffin had instructed me to ask. Dad said, "Pabby, how do you say springtime in Italian?" After explaining why he wanted to know, Grandpa Frizzi's voice called out clearly so that I could hear his audible response over the phone. "You say 'Primavera," he said, which translated to English can mean 'First Life.' This is what always occurs with flora and fauna in the springtime season. I immediately returned to the classroom, and Mr. Griffin, who was waiting for my return, was there. I spoke those words to Mr. Griffin, *'Primavera,'* and he was elated as he explained to the class the beauty of that word and its meaning. I remember beaming with pride in my Italian heritage in that very moment in Mr. Griffin's classroom.

The Sites Along West Washington Street

The porches along West Washington Street were places of great social interaction during the 1950s and 60s. The street was not wide, perhaps just forty feet or so, and all of the houses on the side opposite our store were built near the sidewalk. Our store was on the opposite side, also on the sidewalk. A porch from our home projected out over the sidewalk from the second-story residence. All families spent time sitting on these porches in the late afternoon and early evening. On hot summer evenings, the outdoors seemed cooler. We could sit on our porch in the suspended swing, while others across the street did the same on their sidewalk porches.

Bill Clutter and his wife, Rhea, were directly across from our store. Bill was always there listening to the Cleveland Indians baseball games. His daughter, Florence Shaw, lived next door to Bill with her children, Billy, Bobby, Sheila, and Sue Ellen. My father's aunt Adeline and her husband Marion lived above the storeroom where the Washington Street Lunchroom had been, and they also had a porch which overhung the sidewalk. Next to them were the Ragni family and Pallisco family, who lived in a large duplex home. Christy and Steve Pallisco were our same ages, and schoolmates, and they would often be on their porch as well. Gina Ragni and her husband, Innocenzo, were good friends of my Grandfather, Abe. When my aunt Adeline and Uncle Marion moved from above the storeroom, that apartment was rented by my Grandfather to the Velegolla Family. Their children were older, except for Rossie, who was just a few years older than me.

Porches, being so close to one another, allowed us to carry on conversations with each other without ever leaving our porches. The sidewalks afforded the opportunity to visit with neighbors sitting on their porches as the afternoon turned into early evening. The traffic on Washington Street was usually brisk until 5 o'clock because many were on their way home to the west. But after 5, the traffic became more intermittent, and conversations could be better communicated from one side of the street to the other without the roar of a passing automobile. Our store was still open until 8 p.m., so there was always pedestrian traffic to and from our store, or to the Imbrosio store a hundred yards further down the street. One night, my mother had me and brother Dick sitting on the porch swing on our porch above the sidewalk and store below. We were swinging back and forth, enjoying the outside air, and having fun in this old porch swing. All of a sudden, one side of the swing dropped to the floor because of a worn-out chain link that was attached to the ceiling. Boom! Everyone heard us crash down and called out to us. This was an embarrassing event for my poor mother, although no one was actually hurt. I remember that my brother and I thought this was funny, and we laughed. I remember that my poor mom thought it was awful as we crawled through the door off the porch to our living room without being seen.

Many conversations were carried on from the sidewalk when we were kids. We were not allowed across the street except with permission, and neither were Steve nor Christy. So we would sit on our bottom steps, and they would sit on their porch, and we would carry on conversations with one another. One day, Steve was sitting across from us when a large rat came up through the walkway between the Clutter house and our storeroom. It scampered along the garage doors and up to the step where Steve was seated without him even seeing it. We kept trying to alert him, but he was oblivious to what we were trying to tell him. The rat must have seen Steve, made a U-turn, and run back down the entryway. The only thing that would have made this a more entertaining event would have been Steve's reaction had he seen the rat at his feet!

The traffic being so close to the sidewalks, the fire hydrant in front of the storeroom was often struck by passing cars. In summer, the mishaps were quenching, but in winter, they were more dangerous as the water made the road surface even more slippery. The water would shoot skyward, showering the street and sidewalk, before the city water department would come and shut off the water to West Washington Street to make the repairs. Watching the men dig up the hydrant and replace it was a learning experience and a way to pass the time. There was always a local contingent of West Washington Street onlookers who would stand and supervise the work of the city crew. In the 1950's, the city employed a water department employee who walked the town in the summertime to flush the hydrants, and this was a fun time. The water would shoot out from the opened hydrant into the street. Passing cars were often showered with the steady flow, splashing the water high into the air. Although we were never allowed to go out into the street to enjoy it, some of the kids on the street did, and we were entertained by their antics. Once that hydrant was finished being flushed, the worker would move another few hundred feet to the next hydrant, and the process would take place again. This regular maintenance assured that the hydrant would work perfectly in the event of a fire.

The traffic along Washington Street also provided an opportunity to see schoolmates passing by with their parents west toward West Bellaire. We would wave to them as they passed by, and sometimes they would have their parents honk their horn to alert us of their momentary presence. Sometimes during the day, we would hear the loud shouting of men, and look out to see the Busack Brothers, grocers from Hamilton Street, coming down Washington Street hawking produce. People would come out of their homes to see what was on the truck before purchasing. 'Hawking' occurs when a person travels about a neighborhood selling their goods by shouting, much like a person selling popcorn or beer at a baseball game. So the shouting was something like "Cantalopes here," or "Corn here!" Our store had both, so we never bought anything from the Busack truck that had invaded Washington Street from their store on Hamilton Street.

There was a bus service during the early 1950s between Bellaire and Neffs. Each day, it would take coal miners and workers to Neffs and return them at the end of the day. There was also a factory near Neffs, which everyone called the 'Slaughterhouse,' that processed dead animals and meat scraps for disposal. Farm animals and pets near the end of life were often brought to this place to be put out of their misery. If a farm animal died, they could be picked up from the farm and transported by truck to the slaughterhouse for disposal. The carcasses were then incinerated, producing a horrible smell. A dump truck used for hauling rotting meat and carcasses passed from time to time on its way to this factory for disposal. The smell of rotting flesh would fill the air as this truck passed by our store, and that rancid smell lasted long enough to chase everyone from their porches indoors. Doors closed, and windows were shut to keep the odor from getting inside your house. If you were lucky enough to see the truck coming, you could escape that terrible smell by ducking inside before it passed by.

Sometimes police cars raced by chasing someone or going to some emergency, or an ambulance to assist someone who was ill. At times, we would see the hearse of the funeral home removing a person who had passed. Sometimes there would be a drunk driver who would take out a row of parked vehicles. I once remember seeing a man who was so intoxicated from drinking at a local tavern in town. He was walking home in the middle of the street, clothes all disheveled, pants wet from incontinence, and talking loudly to himself. He was holding up traffic as he swayed from the westbound lane over the centerline to the eastbound lane of travel. I had never seen an intoxicated person before, and I thought he was just crazy. My Mother explained to me that he "had too much beer to drink." Many sober people walked to town in those days, and so there was always a steady stream of individuals walking on the sidewalks. I will always remember, however, that poor drunk guy in the street.

There was a United States Mailbox right in front of our store, and so most people on Washington Street would walk to our store to post letters. This mailbox did not sit on the ground and instead was supported from a concrete post about five feet tall above the sidewalk. This post was shaped like an obelisk you might see in Egypt. The mailbox was equipped with a weighted door at the top where the envelope was deposited. When you opened it to deposit a letter, it would automatically shut and deposit the envelope into the mail bin below. The mail would be picked up by our mailman, George Pyle, as he made his rounds carrying mail on his Washington Street route. George was always a happy guy and so friendly, even when he had to climb a few steps to deliver mail. He always called everyone by their first name and always greeted me and my brothers when passing by

We would see Bessie and Marie Andriano come home after work and begin that long climb up the steps to their house. There was 'Dale' who used to run to stay in shape. My Dad told me that he was training to be a boxer. There was Danny Busack from down the street, who was our paperboy making daily deliveries of the Times-Leader to our home. After Danny gave up the route, he turned it over to his brother Freddie, whose mode of delivering the paper was to toss it up on the front porch as he rode under it on his bicycle. Rudy Nardo would make his rounds for dry cleaning, and he would come to our house for my Dad's shirts and pants. He made stops at other homes along the street for similar pick-up and delivery. When someone was sick, we would often see Dr. Peter Lancione or Dr. Tom Ring making house calls to attend to them. Dr. Lancione was our doctor and had delivered me and all my brothers into the world. There was a poor old man who everyone called 'Buttermilk' who would often be seen riding his bicycle to and from town. He was dressed poorly, appeared to need a bath, and usually did odd jobs for money. A couple who lived on Trough Run routinely walked to town and back. The man was supposedly blind because he walked with a sightless person's cane, walking briskly, but always tapping as he went. He had a little mustache very similar to the one worn by Aldoph Hitler, and sadly, that is how many people referred to him. Watching the traffic on

Washington Street was like Forrest Gump's box of chocolates..... "You never know what you are going to get!" There was always something different to watch.

Adventures on the Hillside

As we grew a little older, maybe eight or nine, my brother Dick and I would explore the hill behind our home. We would climb to the top of the hill as far as the Greenwood Cemetery, and once we saw the tombstones, we dared not climb further. The cemetery was very old, and the graves reminded us of something that we might see on 'Chiller Theater,' a popular horror movie channel on WIIC TV in Pittsburgh. We were familiar with the cemetery because of the Mausoleum where my Grandmother Philomena was buried. My father would visit this site to place flowers below her burial vault on holidays. The view from the top of the hill facing east gave a panoramic view of downtown Bellaire. The cemetery to a young kid, however, was always a bit spooky.

Even more spooky and mysterious to us was the place everyone called 'the Pest House,' which was just below the cemetery. This old structure had been a part of the community since the 1860s, soon after the town had been incorporated under the name of 'Bellaire City.' This was the hospital-type barracks built to quarantine individuals who had contracted smallpox, and in later years, tuberculosis. In the years after the building of a city hospital, the importance of this place had come to an end, and it was abandoned. Poor unfortunates of the community found refuge living in 'the Pest House,' and permanently occupying the property. Part of the building had burned when I was a kid, and what remained was a dilapidated old structure. The given name 'Pest House,' and its proximity to the old Greenwood Cemetery, presented my brother and I an eerie place that was mysterious and somewhat frightening.

We used to creep up the hill to within just a few yards from the place, hiding in the weeds and grape vines, hoping to see the individuals who were living in this old abandoned structure. We called the man, the 'Pest Man,' and his female companion, the 'Pest Lady.' We were frightened of them as kids because of their appearance in old, tattered clothing, and this strange place with a history of former residents of the community being taken there to die. They were living in the very place where this occurred!

On one of our hillside adventures, my brother Dick and I got our chance to encounter the 'Pest Lady.' This is an experience that we talk about to this day, and we will never forget the adventure of that day. We had been walking along the 'main path,' as we called it, to the spring that flowed from the hillside. At this location, it was intersected by a path through the woods from the upper hillside. The spring was located in a depression or small opening in the hillside, which was surrounded by steep and damp mossy soil. We were standing at the spring, peering into the crystal clear water in the barrel below it. We were listening to the running water flowing from the iron pipe, splashing into the barrel. This sound was interrupted when we heard the noise of weeds being crushed beneath the feet of someone walking behind us. The path leading to the upper hill above the spring was where the sound of footsteps was coming from. We both turned to see the sight we had long imagined. It was the 'Pest Lady' standing before us! She stopped when she saw us at the spring, and she stared at us intently without a smile or a greeting. Brother Dick and I had nowhere to go to escape from this 'Pest Lady,' except to climb the steep mossy hillside that surrounded the spring. She was wearing an old dress just below her knees. An old sweater with buttons up the front and designed for a man was covering her shoulders and arms. Around her straggling hair was a scarf tied under her chin. Her shoes were old. She resembled, in the minds of small boys, the wicked old witch in the 'Snow White and the Seven Dwarfs' movie of Disney fame. And she stopped right in front of the spring, blocking our escape! We were petrified! She uttered not a word as she stood there, and we were too afraid to move. She drew from her sweater pocket a cigarette paper, and a pinch of tobacco, and rolled a cigarette in her fingers. We had seen our Grandfather Robinson do that a few times, but never a woman! She placed the cigarette in her lips, all the while watching us, and took a single match from her sweater pocket. She struck the match and lit her rolled cigarette. She took a long drag. This mysterious lady blew a puff of smoke into the air as it came from a chimney. She then turned away from us and continued down the hillside toward Washington Street without ever having said a word.

She never approached us in anger or in a threatening manner. This encounter was perhaps no more than 30 seconds long. Yet, we were so scared to death of this old lady. As she walked away, my brother and I ran all the way back to our home, stumbling in haste all along the hillside. We burst into the kitchen, proclaiming to our mother this experience with the 'Pest Lady,' now feeling secure that we were back home, where this scary old lady could not get us. I never knew her name, and looking back on this experience today as an adult, I realize that she was just a poor, unfortunate old soul living with her companion, the 'Pest Man.' Yet, because she lived in that old dilapidated structure called the 'Pest House,' her very presence was so frightening to us. This childhood memory, to boys of tender years of age, was a terrifying adventure which, now as adults, we can fondly and without fear recall today.

Brother Dick and I were several years older than our younger brothers, and they were not usually permitted to leave the backyard. There were a few children our age to accompany us on our adventures on the hill. There was, however, one boy who was several years older than us that we frequently encountered when we ventured into the woods. His name was Cyril Scott. He was older than us by at least two or three years, and my Dad and Mom did not really want us to be loafing with Cyril. He lived on Washington Street with his grandparents, and he was sometimes visited by his aunt. Cyril was the kind of kid who could always find trouble, and to some extent, he was downright dangerous. He had large eyes that seemed to bulge from his face. To my brother Dick and me, however, he was someone who was filled with the thrill of adventure, and we found him to be exciting.

Cyril would find us on the hill by taking a route other than through our backyard, and he would join us, despite warnings from our parents 'not to hang out' with him. He also liked the woods. He had a bow and arrow, and he had a BB Gun that was modeled after a .45 caliber pistol. Cyril enjoyed shooting things. Anything. Even us with his BB Gun. He would sometimes chase us and sting our legs and buttocks, even though we protested for him to stop. He would also terrorize other children on Washington Street in a similar way. Rossie Velegolla, who lived across the street from our store, was a boy about Cyril's age. Even he was the subject of target shooting by Cyril, before Rossie threatened to thump him. Cyril was not a belligerent fellow, just full of criminal mischief. He was a cross between 'Eddie Haskell' and 'Brutus.' Friendly but devious like Eddie, and dangerous and a bully like Brutus. He always seemed to find us, wherever we were, and trouble followed.

On another occasion, his penchant for mischief went a tad too far. Brother Dick and I were one day playing in our back yard on the first terrace behind our house. Suddenly, and without warning, we heard something strike the ground just above us on the second terrace about 10 yards away. When we looked to see what it was, there was an arrow sticking out of the ground. We scanned the hillside, but did not immediately see anyone, and soon a second arrow struck the ground. This time, Cyril stood up from a clump of weeds and raised his arms into the air over his head so as to say I am here. His pose reminded us of an Indian brave who was signaling his courage to onlookers. This was his dangerous side, and even we knew that this was a crazy thing for him to do. An errant arrow could have struck us, but Cyril appeared not to be concerned.

Another adventure that I will always remember, however, was not really dangerous, but could be classified as criminal. It involved television reception on West Washington Street. Before commercial cable companies, television reception was only possible with an antenna. 'Rabbit ears' were indoor antennas that only worked well if you were close to the station or had a direct, unblocked view. Rooftop antennas worked better, but were still only capable of getting reception where nothing was obstructing the signal. The hillside along West Washington Street blocked most signals, even the signals from WTRF in Wheeling. In order to get a good reception from Steubenville or Pittsburgh channels, you needed to have an antenna high up on the top of the hill. I knew this well, because our own television set was connected to a flat two-strand plastic-coated television wire that ran up the hillside several hundred yards to an antenna my Dad had placed into a tree in the Cemetery. This cable was always susceptible to falling limbs of trees and the wind blowing the antenna. From time to time, when the television would get fuzzy, Dad would climb the hill, checking the cable. When he arrived below the antenna, we would turn on the television set and wait for him to move the antenna to a position that gave the best reception. When that occurred, we would loudly yell to him "OK" hoping he would hear us down below. We could only get the Wheeling, Steubenville, and

Pittsburgh channels if the antenna was properly adjusted. This was a tedious and time-consuming requirement for television viewing in the 1950s and 60s.

Now Cyril, reckless as he was, now enters the story. We were once again on the hill trying to find a grapevine that was secure enough to a tree for a 'monkeyvine' as we called it. This would be used for swinging from an embankment, much like Tarzan of the Apes did in the movies. Unfortunately, we had no success in finding a suitable grapevine hanging from the branches of a sturdy tree. Cyril, however, came up with the bright idea that the plastic cable stretching from tree to tree up to the top of the hill might work just as well. He walked over to such a cable, which was cylindrical and about the diameter of a bean shooter. He suggested that if he cut this cable down, we could tie it around a tree branch for swinging in place of the grapevine. I remember protesting to him, "You can't cut that because it is someone's cable to their television antenna on top of the hill." But Cyril, unwilling to listen to a seven-year-old, pulled out his knife, sliced it in two pieces, and when he did, condensed water droplets ran out of the hollow center. Cyril said to us, "See, it isn't any good, it has water in it!" Now, brother Dick and I watched as Cyril cut down about 40 to 50 feet of this cable. He tied it to a tree and said we now had a 'monkeyvine' made of plastic.

The next day, my father came up from the store below the residence and questioned my brother Dick and me about this cable. We told Dad what had happened and that we were there when Cyril cut the cable. Dad explained that the cable television belonged to Mr. Presutti, who lived a few houses west of our store. He had come to the store and was informing my Grandfather Abe that *"Some SOB cut down my cable television!"* I am not sure how Dad and my Grandfather dealt with the situation, but neither Dick nor I were punished, only told that we "should stay away from Cyril, because he is trouble!" This incident made it clear that if I wanted to stay out of trouble, I would need to avoid Cyril.

Some years later, my Dad told us that someone had come to the store to visit, and it was none other than that mischievous kid, Cyril Scott. Dad said he was wearing a military uniform and wanted to show people on Washington Street that he was now a changed young man. Somehow, I can not imagine wanting to be in a foxhole with Cyril! Maybe the military had made him a good soldier with a real .45 caliber pistol strapped to his side! I hope that it had, for the sake of whoever was going to be his bunkmate!

Another person that we would encounter on the hill was John Iadanza, a young man from Italy, who had come to live with an older Italian woman on Washington Street. John was a gardener and liked the outdoors as much as my brother and I did. John could hardly speak a word of English when I was a boy. We had no way of understanding him, and I remember him resorting to sign language of sorts. The only time that I remember venturing into the cemetery was one day with John. He was older, and we were confident he would keep us from any harm. We walked west toward the point where the crest of the hill narrowed. We stood and looked down on West Bellaire and back toward town. The Ohio River was clearly visible, stretching southward on its journey to the sea. John was a short man, maybe just 5 feet tall, but he had strong, muscular arms and chest beneath his white T-shirt. Overalls, or blue jeans, were all that I ever saw him wear. John's English got better with age after he had been in this country for several years. I remember him as a hard worker and always a friendly person. He walked wherever he went, and I would often see him at the grocery store where his lady friend had an account. Over time, his English got better, but he still enjoyed talking to my Grandfather Abe, who was fluent in Italian.

The Masonic Order and Bellaire Elks Lodge

The Masonic Lodge that my Grandfather Abe and his brother Artemio had joined as young men was still active during the 1950s. My father, Danny, had followed them into this Co-Masonic Lodge in 1947. Dad entered the Unison Lodge 542 in Bellaire. He was passed in 1948 to membership and was raised on March 20, 1949. At some point, he was affiliated with the Alpha Areopagus No. 41 Lodge, Camp of Bridgeport, and was perfected on February 11, 1962. I can remember my father practicing the readings of the rituals and teachings as he proceeded to study for higher degrees in the Lodge. He rose to the 30th degree in 1965. Through dad, I became familiar with so many of the names of the members of these Lodges that had served with my Grandfather Abe.

These Lodges acquired in the name of Attillio D'Alessandro, as Trustee, 7 acres of real estate located in a wooded section of land west of Bellaire just after the conclusion of WWII. A building was erected and became a meeting hall, and it would be known commonly as the 'picnic grounds.' This property was used frequently by the Lodges in Bellaire and Bridgeport. The real estate was not taken in the name of the Unison Lodge No. 542 in Bellaire, or the Alpha Areopagus Lodge 41 in Bridgeport, but was held by Attillio D'Alessandro as Trustee of the Eastern Ohio Fraternal Association. The membership also established a subsidiary association known as the Eastern Ohio Mutual Benefit Association, which was operated to support the payment of sick benefits to injured or ill members. Virtually all of the members of the organization were Italian-Americans, and most of the minutes of their meetings were recorded in Italian. My Grandfather Abraham, and his Italian friends were original members of these Lodges and subsidiary organizations. When my Father joined the Order in 1947, he became Secretary of these subsidiary Associations, and kept the minutes of their meetings

As a small boy, I recall attending Lodge Picnics at this location, which we called the 'Picnic Grounds.' There were bocce courts built under the building. The men played this bocce game, long associated with Italians, all day. As children, we would watch the contestants as they tossed the bocce balls down the long corridors of the court, hoping to gain a favorite position to score points. Their opponents would seek to use their tosses to strike and move the balls outside of scoring position. Other men were shouting loudly as they played another favorite game called 'morra.' This was a hand game where both contestants would shout a number in Italian, while throwing a set number of fingers on their throwing hand. The goal was to have your fingers, when added to the fingers thrown by your opponent, add up to the number you had shouted. For example, shouting 'sette [7]' and throwing three fingers would give you a win over your opponent, throwing four fingers and shouting 'cinque [5]!' Morra sometimes was frightening to a little kid as the shouting and hand-throwing got louder and faster, almost as though the players were angry at each other. There was a kitchen on the lower level of the hall above, and there were picnic tables for use at meal time. Upstairs in the hall would be a gathering place if the weather were rainy. This outdoor summertime atmosphere was a great place for kids to run around and play. The running brook below the hall was a great place to explore with the other children who attended these events.

This Co-Masonic group of men and women of Unison Lodge 542 and Bridgeport Lodge 41 produced many Italians from Bellaire who were well known in the Grand Lodge Order of Co-Masonry. Mike DiClemente, John Boido, and Attillio D'Alessandro were members who rose in degrees toward the 33rd and highest, and were well known in the national American Federation Lodge. However, the depression in the 1930s and war during the 1940s, and the death of many of these old timers, without new blood to replace them, brought the Lodge of Co-Masons into decline. My Grandfather Abe's friends were growing older by the 1950's, and my Father Danny, according to the minutes of the organization, was the youngest man to join. In 1958, my Grandfather's friend, Attillio, died after a month-long illness. Dad, acting as Secretary in a meeting on August 31, 1958, recorded in the minutes that "the death of A. D'Allesandro would be a great loss to them and the association." His wife, Marie, was paid sick benefits calculated at 34 days. In 1959, the Eastern Ohio Fraternal Association sold 'the picnic grounds' to the West Bellaire Community, and it became known as the Forest Hills Community Association, consisting of West Bellaire residents. The Lodge then moved the meeting location to 316-33rd Street on the second floor in the old downtown Carroll Building.

At a meeting on September 1, 1963, President DeLuca suggested that the auxiliary Eastern Ohio Fraternal Association should consider dissolving due to "lack of membership" and because "90% of our remaining membership are over 65 years of age and ranging up to the oldest 82 years." The organization had only 13 members who were paying their dues to the Lodges and the Blue Lodge. A motion and vote resulted in a decision to dissolve. All agreed to temporarily suspend the meeting until September 5. At this meeting, dissolution was again discussed. Eleven of the thirteen members were present. The minutes record the comments of the members who attended. Only my Dad and his Uncle Mariano Raspa voted against dissolution. By a vote of 9-2, the subsidiary organizations of the Lodges were officially dissolved. Thereafter, all meetings were held at the meeting hall at 316-33rd Street in the Carroll Building in Bellaire. On September 26, 1963, a special meeting was held, and it was agreed to transfer remaining funds held by the organizations to the Blue Lodge and to pay rent on the meeting hall.

I remember once climbing the stairs to the 3rd Floor of this 33rd Street Lodge Hall following one of the meetings held in 1965. My Mom had driven downtown to pick up my Dad to return home for dinner, and I was there to let him know we were waiting in the car. When I was in the large hall, Italian men were standing about speaking to each other in post-meeting conversation. I told Dad that "dinner was waiting." He invited Orazio Pica, a 32nd Degree Co-Mason and Grand Master of the Lodge. He was known to us by his American name, Horace. He was a quiet man, soft-spoken, but pleasant. Because he did not drive, we drove him home after dinner to Stewartsville. We would often see Mr. Pica walking back from town, usually dressed in a suit, and whenever we did, we offered him a ride home so that he would not have to walk the five or six miles from town to Stewartsville.

These events, which I remember as a boy of my father's participation in Lodge affairs, and the gatherings at the 'picnic grounds,' could never be what they had been when my Grandfather Abe was an active member. My memories are limited to the days of the declining membership in the Lodges. Were it not for my father having joined this Co-Masonic Order, I would have no memories of this Lodge at all. These will always be great childhood memories and times growing up in the 1950s and 60s.

My father was also an active member of Bellaire Elks Lodge No. 419, located in the old Elk Grand Theater Building. This Lodge was chartered by the Grand Lodge and Grand Exalted Ruler John Galvin on May 12, 1898. The original lodge hall was located in the Carroll Building when the Elks contracted to have a third story added to this building at the corner of 33rd Street and Belmont. The Lodge then took a lease for 5 years on the third floor of the newly constructed Lodge Hall addition to the building. This first Lodge Hall was dedicated on January 29, 1902. After it was furnished at a cost of $4,500.00, it was by far the finest Elks Lodge Hall in the state of Ohio. Ironically, this 3rd floor hall would become the same hall occupied by the Co-Masonic Unison Lodge No. 542 to which my father also belonged as a member.

Membership continued to increase during the next few years, and the third-floor Lodge Hall in the Carroll Building demanded more room. So the Lodge members issued stock subscriptions of $50.00 per share to be purchased by the membership. The result was the construction of the magnificent new home of Lodge No. 419 on Belmont Street, which housed the Elk Grand Theater, an event hall known as the Pine Room, and the third-floor Lodge Hall for official ceremonies. Lodge No. 419 in these early years had a band consisting of Elk members, which won numerous awards.

The Elk Grand Building, during my Dad's tenure with the Lodge during the 1950's, produced many wonderful memories for me as a boy. I was always impressed by the large head of an Elk that adorned the 2nd-floor front of the building. I remember many weddings and dances that were held on the 2nd floor, where the Pine Room was located. My Dad and Mom often went to the Pine Room to attend dances and other social events. The walls were all lined with beautifully finished pinewood, which gave this room its name. Downstairs on the first floor was the Club Room and bar, and in the back was the 'Stag Bar' where only men were permitted.

My Dad, in the 1950s, went through the chairs to become the Exalted Ruler of this lodge. As a boy, I remember Dad's trip away from home to attend the Grand Lodge Convention in Chicago in 1956. This was the first time that he would be away from the family for any extended period. We stood behind the fence at the Wheeling, Ohio County Airport as he walked to the waiting airplane that would take him to Pittsburgh for connections to the 'Windy City' of Chicago. He stayed at the Conrad Hilton Hotel. He wrote to my mother on CHH stationery telling her that "a couple of times I thought my insides were coming up" and that at landing "the wind just tossed the plane around so." The trip was '1 hour 35 minutes from Pittsburgh to Chicago.' His letter inquired about me and brother Dick. He asked, "How are the boys? I could see them waving bye when the plane was taking off." He closed the letter to my Mom with "All My Love, Danny."

Dad's participation in the Elks Lodge gave him the opportunity to meet so many other fine members and make professional contacts. The Elks Lodge participated in so many events. There were minstrel shows at the Bellaire High School Auditorium, which we attended. In 1956, the Elktown Follies brochure billed my Dad as singing "Carolina Moon". I remember Dad practicing this tune at home before the big night. Another year, he performed as the clown in Caruso's famous 'Vesti la Giubba.' In 1957, the Elk's Lodge performed Bogey's March in the Bellaire Christmas Parade, patterned after the theme shown in the 1957 hit 'The Bridge on the River Kwai.' I remember summer picnics for the Elk families, where all the other children of members could get together for a day of fun.

I think Dad's proudest Elk moment, however, occurred in September 1978 when he posed, as a Past Exalted Ruler of Bellaire Lodge No. 419, with his five sons who were being taken into membership of the Lodge. The photograph appeared in the Elks Magazine, and included Jeff Durant, Exalted Ruler of the Bellaire Lodge, and Clarence Schlarb, the District Deputy of the Benevolent and Protective Order of Elks. Dad was very happy that night when each of his sons was initiated as a new member into the Bellaire Lodge No. 419, where he had served as Exalted Ruler twenty years before.

Beginning School at West Bellaire

When school began at the end of summer, and the days grew shorter as fall approached, the adventures of summertime would come to an end. I began Kindergarten at West Bellaire School before I had reached my 5th birthday. My birthday was September 15, and I just squeezed into my class by a few days before class had started in 1957. Now this would make me always one of the youngest kids in my class. When my Dad was my age, he attended Rose Hill Grade School. He told how he walked along '*Back Washington Street*' to the schoolhouse about half a mile away from the store on West Washington. Rose Hill School was considered to be in town and took in most grade school students living in the second ward of the city. My mother, Nancy, however, grew up in West Bellaire, and she had attended West Bellaire Grade School. West Bellaire was the newest residential area of the town. My other set of Grandparents, George and Neva Robinson, lived in West Bellaire, and if I could go here for school, I would be able to walk home after school to their house. My Grandfather, Abe, also lived in West Bellaire, and for similar reasons, my parents were glad to know that I would be assigned to Kindergarten in Miss Kirkland's class at West Bellaire School.

Even more convenient was the fact that our grocery store was the bus stop for West Washington Street students enrolled at West Bellaire. I did not have to walk to the bus stop, except down the steps to the sidewalk. My Grandfather Abe opened the store early, usually being there by 6 o'clock each morning. So when the bus students began to arrive, he was there to greet them. Many times we needed something for our lunch boxes, like Hostess Twinkies or Cupcakes, or a box of cough drops if we had a sore throat. You could always get something that you needed at the store. There was a small section of school supplies, including paper tablets, pens, pencils, and erasers. So students could do a little shopping before the bus arrived. On particularly cold mornings during winter, my Grandfather would allow us to stand inside the store to keep warm until the bus arrived.

On my first day of riding the bus, I was the youngest bus rider. All of the other students were established bus riders from prior years, and so they knew who the bus driver was and what the drill would be. My bus driver was to be Zygmont Rataiczak. He was known by my parents as 'Zyg.' He was a no-nonsense bus driver. You did not act up, you did not shout out loud, you stayed in your seat so as not to arouse a response from 'Zyg.' Because West Bellaire was K through seven, there were many older students who would be riding the bus with me. Christy Pallisco was a year older than me, and she was a friend from across the street from our store. So Mom told me that I should "not be afraid to get on the bus because Christy would watch out for you." I am sure that Mom had talked to her mother, Ida, beforehand. Both dad and mom were there to watch me climb aboard the bus and walk to a seat by the window. When the bus pulled away, all of the most important people in my life were being left behind, standing on the sidewalk in front of our grocery store, or upstairs, still sleeping in bed. I waved to them, and the bus rolled away. The bus made another stop at 26th Street so that the Dudek twins and Sharon Hollingshead and her brothers could board the bus. This bus stop was in front of the duplex where my aunt Kathryn lived with cousins Steve, Kathi, and Gary. Next year, Steve would be riding the bus with me to West Bellaire, and the following year, Kathi would be joining us. The ride in all was less than 5 minutes before we pulled up to the schoolhouse. When my school day ended, I could either ride the bus back home to the store or walk to either of my Grandparents' homes.

Throughout my grade school years, this was repeated for each of my brothers by our parents. They did not need Christy by then to feel comfortable on their first day, since they had an older brother riding with them. As we grew older, that bus stop also increased in the number of students. Christy's younger brother Steve was a year behind me, and so he would join us the following year. Steve was always assigned as the lookout for the approaching bus. He would stand on the sidewalk where he could see the bus make the turn from Hamilton Street, and when he saw it, his memorable exclamation was always the same. He would yell loudly for all to hear the letters 'B-U-S' to alert us to get into line. I can remember one day, I was not going to school due to illness. I could hear the students at the bus stop, and Steve's patented 'B-U-S' even alerted me inside the house that the bus was soon to be there.

When I entered 1st grade, I was absent from school a lot due to sore throats and the flu. I was falling behind in reading and other work simply by not being there to learn with the other students. I remember my Mom working with me while I was in bed, going over the homework that came from Miss DeVendra. As a consequence, and despite my mother's efforts, I was behind when I finally became well enough to return to school. Miss DeVendra had already arranged students into reading groups. There were the *'Redbirds'* and the *'Bluebirds.'* The 'Redbirds' were the better reading students. I got placed into the *'Bluebirds'* because I was behind. Both colors are pretty, however, I longed to be a *'Redbird!'* As the year progressed, my reading ability considerably improved, and Miss DeVendra repeatedly told some *'Redbird'* students struggling with words that *"I am going to put Danny into your place as a 'Redbird' if you don't do a better job in reading from the book!"* Oh, how I longed for her to do it. As I would listen to some students reading, and Miss DeVendra admonishing them, I sat there saying to myself, "Do it! Do it, Miss DeVendra!" She never did, and I finished 1st grade as a *'Bluebird,'* but I had fully mastered reading those stories about *"Dick, Jane, and Sally!"*

In 2nd grade, my reading continued to get better, but my struggle was always with arithmetic and those darn time tests. So once again, it was my mother who helped me through the addition and subtraction, the borrowing and carrying, and all those other tools of the skilled mathematician. I really think that when I began working at the store, I finally got the hang of things. Adding the numbers of a customer's order was real. There on the counter were actual items, each costing something different, and adding the costs together had real meaning. Oh sure, I made mistakes. My Dad would catch them and show me where I made the mistake. By the time I graduated to 3rd grade with Mrs. Dick, I had a fairly good idea of keeping account of customers' purchases. I was never as good as the best students in my class, but I was never far behind them. It was finally time to step into the business world at Frizzi's AG Food Center on West Washington Street.

Our Cub Scout Troop

In the second grade, the boys in my class reached the age to join the Cub Scouts. My mother Nancy, and Donald Cetorelli's mother, Midge, agreed to become the Den mother's of the West Bellaire Pack 110. We were assigned as Den No. 4. We had to have a place to meet, and some of the meetings we held at the 'picnic grounds' which at that time was just recently acquired by the West Bellaire community from the Co-Masonic Lodge. This was a far bigger hall than we needed, so Mom talked to Grandfather Frizzi about using the basement of his house in West Bellaire for our den meetings. He agreed, and so our pack meetings of six and seven-year-olds met high on top of the 'Mystery Mound' in the new home. There, we studied to learn our Cub Scout pledge, which we had to recite in order to get our first badges. One by one, Mom and Midge took each of us into the next room and made us recite the Cub Scout Promise, which I still remember today. When it was my turn, I told Midge, *"I, Danny Frizzi, promise to do my best, to do my duty, to God and my Country, to be Square, and to obey the Law of the Pack."* Some things you can just never forget.

Not everyone in our den had their uniforms. Some had shirts, but no pants. Some only had hats. Only Johnny DeBlasis had an entire uniform. I got my Cub Scout shirt, hat, and neckerchief all because of a flag presentation made by our U.S. Congressman, Wayne L. Hays, to the West Bellaire School. The flag had been flown over the Capitol Building in Washington, D.C., and our congressman was to present it to our school for a photograph for the newspaper. The principal decided that representatives of the Brownie troop for the girls and the Cub Scout troop for the boys should be in the photograph with Representative Hays. The problem was that not all brownies and Cub Scouts could be in the photograph. So Mrs. Dick decided to use a lottery system to select who would get this honor. Now we all wanted to be in the photo, but only a few could be chosen. The lottery was held, and I was one of the Cub Scouts chosen. I did not yet have a uniform! How could I be in a photograph as a Cub Scout without a uniform? Well, as always, my mother, Nancy, came to my rescue. We went to Wheeling to Stone & Thomas, and picked out my shirt, cap, and neckerchief specifically for the photograph. Johnny DeBlasis was the other Cub Scout selected. We took the photograph in the basement of the West Bellaire Schoolhouse gymnasium, and a few days later, it appeared in the local paper. I had a huge smile on my face for that photo!

After that photograph was taken, I had no occasion to ever be in the presence of Congressman Hays again until after starting my first job as a lawyer back home in Bellaire. I received notification in the fall of 1977 that I had passed the bar examination. My future partner, John 'Jack' Malik, Jr., asked me to go to the Belmont Hills Country Club with him to celebrate this important day in my legal career. Jack told me, "We are going to have lunch with Wayne today." Wayne was no longer our congressman, having resigned from his powerful position as Chairman of the House Administration Committee and his Congressional seat a few years before, when it was discovered that he had hired a young secretary named Elizabeth Ray. She admitted publicly that "I can't type. I can't file," and that Wayne had hired her for other reasons. Well, this luncheon with Wayne was filled with so many fascinating stories about his time in Washington, D.C., representing our district. He talked about President Johnson and battles with other Congressmen. No one brought up the secretary who could not type. I found it ironic that I was now with Wayne once again, with a smile on my face just like 20 years before!

West Bellaire Methodist Church

My brothers and I were raised in the Methodist faith. We attended the old country church of my mother's family, located on Brooks Run, called the West Bellaire Methodist Church. In our early years, this was the same church that was attended by our cousins Steve, Kathi, and Gary. This little church sat along the State Route numbered 147, which followed Brooks Run high up into the hills of Pulteney Township. This was the church that was attended by my Great-Grandparents, John Howard and Daisy Robinson, and by my Grandparents, George and Neva Robinson. My mother, Nancy, and her sisters had all attended this church as little girls, and it was natural that we would attend this church as our place of worship.

My first experience at public speaking took place here during a Sunday School exercise when I was about 5 years old. Sunday School children had a part to memorize which we were to recite during the program in front of the church congregation. I had memorized my part well and rehearsed it for my family at home. I found that performing around the kitchen table was so much different than when standing in front of the congregation of this little church. I began to recite my part and then realized that there were so many people sitting there with their eyes fixed on just me. I went blank...completely. But when I stopped reciting, it was my mother's reassuring words that I heard as she began to assist me with speaking the words that had vanished from my mind. Focusing on her, I began to pick up where I had gone blank and finished my part. At this age, stage fright was always something that seemed to plague me. With time, however, I began to overcome this common childhood fear so that it did not follow me into adulthood.

The only pastor that I remember at West Bellaire was Reverend Ralph Hudson. He had three sons, two of whom were older than I was. The youngest was Jim, and he was just 1 year younger than me. We attended Sunday School in the basement of this church, and Daisy Jackson was the leader of our opening exercises each Sunday morning. We always began with the song "For God So Loved the World," which was a simple little song that even a child could understand about salvation and resurrection. My favorite Sunday School teacher was Helen Smith, who was always so kind and whose faith was evident, even to a youngster. After we finished Sunday School, we met Mom and Dad upstairs to attend church. When we were smaller children, we sat with Mom and Dad in a pew all together. But as we grew older, we wanted to sit with our friends. Mike Johnson and Dave Hudson always sat in the back pew against the front wall of the church, and so we drifted back to this last row as we got older.

Reverend Hudson was a good man who was staunch in his faith and belief that the salvation of souls was his personal responsibility. He preached not in fire and brimstone but assured us with great conviction that our salvation was essential to avoid it! Many of his sermons were made with the typical altar call offered up to the congregation in the

Methodist faith. He would make the point through biblical verses using the words of Jesus that "no man cometh to the father except by me." His sermons were stirring, and oftentimes, I felt he was talking to those of us young people sitting in the back row. I recall one Sunday, my youngest brother, who was just a baby, was being held by my mother, sitting with my Dad in a pew. My younger brothers were with them, but brother Dick and I were in the back row with our friends. My baby brother belted out during Reverend Hudson's sermon a loud cry, interrupting everyone's concentration. Reverend Hudson, after pausing, pointed at my baby brother and was quick to remind all there that Jesus said that "unless you turn and become like little children, you will never enter the kingdom of heaven." When I graduated from high school, I received the Holy Bible from this church with my name inscribed in gold on the black cover. That Bible sits on my desk today, as a reminder of the days of my youth in this little church.

One of the other important men of faith that I remember as a child was an Italian priest named Father Ralph Salciccia. My first encounter with Father Ralph was at the Bellaire City Hospital, where I was recuperating from a tonsillectomy. My mother had decided that all four brothers should have this procedure at the same time. After surgery, both Dick and I were really in pain. I recall that we tried to talk, but could not. Our younger brothers were up and running about, but Dick and I were suffering from the worst sore throat I ever had. Back in the 50's, this was not an outpatient procedure, so we stayed the night in the hospital. Dick and I both had ice collars around our necks and were unable to eat anything except Jello or ice cream. After the lights were out for visitors, the halls were darkened, as was our room. I was still awake when this man of the cloth entered our room. It was Father Ralph. He carried with him a sack which was clearly marked as coming from the Dairy Queen in town. He approached both Dick and I and asked us to take a Dilly Bar, which was chocolate-coated ice cream on a stick. He assured us that he had checked with nursing and that ice cream was an approved treat for us to eat. Father Ralph was making his rounds at the hospital and ministering to the needs of the sick.

Father Ralph was from Italy, and he was familiar with my Grandmother Minnie's sisters, who attended the St. John's Catholic Church. Often, he would walk to the little market of my Grandfather's nephew, Sam

Cicogna, at Crescent Street. Here, Father Ralph and Sam would speak to each other in their native tongue, allowing both men to retain the Italian language of their former homeland. When my father received letters from relatives in Italy, it would be Father Ralph that he would call on to interpret those letters into English. Always pleasant, always kind, always a servant of his parish for the Lord, the hospital visit was my first experience meeting him. As I grew older, I could see his strong faith and his service to humanity, regardless of one's religious faith. That night in the hospital, he saw only little boys, to whom he wanted to bring comfort. His reputation for service to others and his ministry to the Italian community continued to follow him wherever he passed.

Father Ralph ministered to all people, and this included my Grandfather Abe. He once approached my Grandfather and wanted him to return to the Catholic faith of his boyhood in Italy. They discussed the reasons why my Grandfather chose to reject the Catholic faith. I only learned of this conversational attempt at conversion long after both my Grandfather and Father Ralph had passed. Father Ralph, however, was not successful in his attempts at persuasion. He never gave up on my Grandpa Frizzi and came to offer his condolences on the passing of any relative in our family. He was a true and faithful servant of God to all.

Making Road Trips for the Store

One of my first memories of our store business was when my brothers and I, along with Mom and Dad, piled into our 1955 Chevrolet Bel Air and drove to South Wheeling. We did this once each week, after our grocery store closed. The purpose of the trip was to deliver to the Associated Grocers Warehouse on 23rd Street our weekly order for stock. Later that week, our order was delivered by an AG Truck to our storeroom on West Washington Street. We always traveled over the Bellaire Bridge to Benwood and then proceeded north to 23rd Street, which was a part of the warehouse district (among other things) in South Wheeling. After parking the car, Dad would get out with the order slips and walk up a short flight of steps to the doorway that entered the business office of the AG warehouse. A mail slot was used to deposit the order, which the office staff would find the next morning. The warehouse had loading docks to the west of the door where the delivery trucks would load our order for delivery.

My Dad and Aunt Kathryn would sometimes attend the grocer's meetings that were attended by my Grandfather Abe. Once Dad returned to work at the store, he and my Grandfather would attend together. These meetings were held upstairs in the meeting room. It was filled with school desks for the individual grocery store owners to sit in during the meeting. The older and more experienced grocer entitled you to a seat in the front of the room. The boardroom had a large head table, where the warehouse superintendent, Ray Young, sat, along with the other board members and officers who were elected by the members of the Association. I remember going to one of these meetings as a boy when my father had been elected as President of the Association. There were many deliveries made from this warehouse to other AG Members who also had small neighborhood grocery stores in Bellaire. Stadium AG, operated by the Elga DeBlasis family at 2653 Belmont Street, would be one delivery stop located near Nelson Field. Then another delivery at Diamond AG Food Center at 423-37th Street, operated by Anthony 'Tony' Berher. The delivery truck would then make its way to Frizzi's AG Food Center on West Washington to make the delivery of those items listed on the order slips that my Dad had deposited in the mail slot earlier in the week. We always looked forward to these weekly trips to South Wheeling.

One particularly memorable trip occurred when I was probably five or six years old. We arrived just as we always did, and Dad parked the car and then walked up the steps to the office door. He deposited his order into the mail slot of the door as always. This night was different, however, since as dad was walking back to the car, we saw him bend down and pick something up from the brick street. He walked a few steps further toward the car, and then we saw him bend down again, and this time he picked up what looked like a piece of paper. When he got back to the car, he turned the overhead light on and said, "Look what somebody dropped on the ground!" To our amazement, he held a $10 bill and a $20 bill, which some poor soul had let escape from their pockets. We were excited by this discovery and my Dad's good fortune. Dad addressed my Mom, telling her, *"Someone going around the corner for a good time probably dropped this on the ground!"* A good time? What kind of good time was he talking about? He would not elaborate, but my Mom seemed to understand. Some years later, I reminded Dad about finding that money, and he remembered that night very well. Being older now, he expounded on the subject that he had intentionally left vague at the time. He said, "Someone who was heading to the 'cathouse' back by the railroad tracks probably dropped it when they were checking their cash." As I grew older, I knew that the term "South Wheeling" often referred to houses of prostitution in the *'Friendly City.'* At the end of 23rd Street, beyond the warehouse, and back by the sandstone block wall supporting the railroad tracks, there was in fact a walkway to a well-known house of prostitution. In those days, $10 to $20 dollars would have provided a really 'good time' to whoever lost those bills. We had a different kind of good time, too, with that money. The night my Dad found those bills, we celebrated all the way home, thinking of how we might use that extra cash!

Trips to Naylor's Wholesale House in Wheeling were also fun. Naylor's was a place you could buy all kinds of bulk items at discount prices. Because the grocery store was a retail business, Dad never had difficulty getting access here to make purchases. The building was several stories tall, and on each floor there were boxes and boxes of all kinds of things, from clothing to tools. Once we were there, I remember boxes full of socks in all different colors, and other garment goods like t-shirts and underwear. I remember Dad getting several of those boxes of socks and bringing them home. On many of these trips, my brothers and I had to sit in the car as shopping was better without us. But when I got to go in, I recall how many different piles of boxes and products were for sale. Naylor's was not our favorite place to go, however, which was always back in Bellaire on Franklin Street.

Dad and Mom would often go to Cifaldi Distributing Company, operated by Lou Cifaldi. This was a small building that sat below the grade of the road, and Cifaldi sold all kinds of trinkets, toys, candy, and other products at wholesale to our grocery store. Once again, we were usually kept in the car while Mom and Dad looked over the merchandise. This building along Franklin Street was crammed full of different kinds of 'stuff.' Sometimes my brothers and I got something from inside this little distribution company before my parents finished their shopping for the night. One toy I remember was a balsa wood airplane that was assembled from a kit. We usually get at least twelve hours of flying time before it suffers disabling damage from a crash into the ground. We might try to repair it with scotch tape or glue, but we never could get it back to that first flight of the day.

I also remember going with my Father to the B & O Freight Station along Crescent Street to pick up fresh produce delivered from California. We took the old Chevrolet Panel Truck down to the station and backed up to the long row of docks facing Crescent Street. Behind the freight station was the B & O railroad siding, where product shipped by rail would be offloaded to the station warehouse. The siding also doubled for the railroad siding used by the Imperial Glass Factory. From this railroad siding, boxcars were placed for moving the produce to the docks for pickup by local vendors who were awaiting its arrival.

Another trip I recall was to pick up poultry from a farm on State Route 9 outside of St. Clairsville. My brothers and I, along with my mom, piled into the back of the 1961 Corvair Van, which had no windows. My Dad drove, and my Grandfather Abe sat in the passenger seat. The long twisting road of State Route 147 to Centerville caused us to roll around all over the cargo bay as the truck negotiated the turns. This was fun for us, but for my mom, it was a nauseating experience with no windows to look out of. We finally found the farm and loaded the boxes of chickens on ice. The return trip, however, was not as much fun since the chicken boxes prevented us from tumbling around. My poor Mom was never so glad to have this trip come to an end!

A 1950's view of West Washington Street and Frizzi & Son AG Food Center. The Chevrolet Corvair delivery truck sits at the prized first public parking space beyond the reserved parking for customers. Abe Frizzi stands in the doorway to the store. As a customer stands on the sidewalk. (Wallace Collection circa 1959)

Three generations of grocer's and sons. Abe at left and his son Danny standing, with his son Danny Jr. in the truck and son Dick in the stroller. Photo taken at Abe's home on the Frizzi Knob. (Frizzi Collection 1954)

The back yard above the store on Washington Street was a hillside that had to be terraced to make flat usable yard space. These steps gave access to the duck pen. (Frizzi Collection circa 1954)

Anthony and Rose Andriano stand beside their terraced garden fence with some freshly harvested onions. (Frizzi Collection 1957)

Customer, Clyde Schaffer, and son Junior, who visited Dan Jr. and Dick while his parents shopped at the store. (Schaffer Collection circa 1957)

Danny Jr. with his mother Nancy at the Washington Street upstairs apartment over the store. They are stepping out for some event. (Frizzi Collection 1957)

Josephine Andriano receives Holy Communion on Christmas Eve from Father Malara of the St. John's Catholic Church, with Richard Massa assisting at left. (Massa Collection circa 1954)

Nora Andriano joins with my mother, Nancy Frizzi, as a birthday celebration takes place. Nora was always so helpful with the Frizzi boys (Frizzi Collection 1956)

Cyril Scott stands in front of Frizzi's AG Food Center on Washington Street with his distinctive mischievous look. He was always finding ways to get into mischief and sought out the young Frizzi boys when he went looking for it. (Frizzi Collection 1959)

Chapter Six

Retailing From Behind a Counter

Learning the Ropes

When I was in the third grade and 8 years old, my brother Dick and I were introduced to working at the store on Friday and Saturday evenings. During the summer, we would have to come in from play early so that we could be at the store by 5 o'clock in the afternoon. We would closed at 10 o'clock on Fridays and Saturdays. Our Grandfather Abe would leave the store at 5 o'clock and entrust it to our Father. To learn the business, and also probably to give my Mother a break from caring for all four brothers, we were assigned days. My day was Friday, and my brother Dick was assigned Saturday. We would work with Dad until closing time, although sometimes, we might get to go upstairs at 9 if we were not busy. Customer traffic usually got quieter after everyone had returned home from town later that evening. Because we would be working at the store, we would both be unable to watch television shows on the nights each of us worked. We had always enjoyed watching TV together, but would now be on our own with our little brothers.

I would miss 77 Sunset Strip, Route 66, and Rawhide on Friday, while Dick would miss Have Gun Will Travel and Gunsmoke on Saturday. We decided that the only way to keep up with what was happening on these shows would be to remember the storyline and repeat it, so that one of us wouldn't miss the show. Later, we got a tape recorder and decided to infringe copyright by tape recording the programs so that they could be replayed after work was over. Mom often had a difficult time with Dick not wanting to work his Saturday night shift. He did not want to come in from the backyard to get a bath and groomed for work at the store. Often, she would have to go up to get him when he would not heed her call to him from the back porch. When he persisted in his refusal to go, I was usually asked if I would go and take his turn. I usually did as my mother requested, and Dick got a reprieve. I did get his pay for that evening, which was 50 cents and an ice cream cone or candy bar.

Now, as kids working in the store, we would sometimes sneak a piece of candy. This was called 'eating the profits!' In order to do this without getting caught, we would wait until Dad left us alone in the store as he headed across the street to the storeroom. I had a particular taste for maple creme candy. These unwrapped candy pieces were in the shape of a rounded dome, covered in chocolate and filled with maple creme. We sold them individually for two cents each. They sat on the counter in front of the cash register in a large wooden tub with a wire handle. The lid on the tub could be lifted off so that the maple crèmes' could be snatched. After Dad was safely inside the storeroom, I would lift the lid on the tub, pull out a single piece of candy, and pop it into my mouth. This was my 'modus operandi' for the proverbial eating of the profits! Now, brother Dick did not like the Maple Creme candy. He liked candy bars. One day, Dad was cleaning out below the meat slicer, where supplies were kept, and he found a pile of candy bar wrappers that Dick was disposing of after he had eaten a candy bar. Dick obviously had to hide them somewhere other than the trash can where Dad was sure to find them. I know that Dad questioned us, and I think Dick confessed. Whew! If Dad had questioned me, what would I have said? Probably something like "It wasn't me, Dad, I only eat candy that does not come in a wrapper!"

"Presentation is the Key"

What would a Friday night look like at our store? My first jobs were menial, but essential. Dad taught me that when you are trying to sell something, anything at all, Presentation' was the key. I would watch my father cutting pork chops from a long pork loin. Each cut was carefully severed from the loin so that its thickness was uniform throughout. He would cut six or seven in a row, and then take the meat cleaver and sever them from the bone at the base of the loin. He would then arrange them neatly on a cardboard plate after dressing them with a knife and scraper, trimming each chop. He would arrange them so that they looked as though they had been woven together. I watched him cut T-Bones, Porterhouse, and Filets as he worked his magic on the cutting block. The cutting block was just a large tree trunk that had been cut to a thickness of about 30 inches. It was supported on four sturdy legs, which placed it at waist height. I remember that on one side, the block was starting to split open, but because it was so large, there was plenty of cutting space left. Above the cutting block, on the wall, was a diagram of a side of beef, showing how it could be cut into various parts. Dad would show me on the diagram where each cut of meat was coming from as he made his cuts on the large piece he was working with.

Our meat cooler was not located inside our grocery store since there was not enough room. It was located across the street in the storeroom where the stock and inventory were kept until needed. All meat products would come from the Sugardale Company in Canton, Ohio, in a refrigerated truck once each week. The man in charge of the route that delivered to our store was a little Italian man who was probably no more than five feet tall. He was extremely agile, however, and knew exactly how to handle the large sides of beef as he carried them from the Sugardale truck to the meat cooler across the street. The beef came in either whole sides, front quarters, or hind quarters. It was cheaper by the side, and Dad would get the whole side of beef and then break it down himself. These quarters were then manageable for carrying over to our store and the butcher block for making individual cuts of meat for display. Attached to the butcher block was a metal contraption that held an array of cutting utensils. There were all sizes and shapes of knives for cutting large steaks and for deboning meat from a bone. There were knives for trimming the fat from the steaks or chops. Meat saws hung from a shelf, along with the powerful meat cleaver, and other tools used by an experienced butcher.

I enjoyed watching my father as he prepared to take on the role of butcher. He would always pull out the sharpening tool that was on a wooden handle with a long rod, similar to a rat-tail file but with much finer cutting edges. Dad would take his knife in his right hand, and the tool for sharpening in the other, and in rapid motion run the edge of the knife from side to side along the sharpening tool. With each stroke, he rotated the blade of the knife to the other side. He could do this about as fast as a boxer might strike a speed ball before entering the ring. There were also scrapers for removing meat and bone scraps from the individual steaks or chops. There was also a large metal brush that was used to clean the meat block by scraping off the scraps and fat that adhered to it. Dad always said, 'Presentation' was everything. When the meat case was fully stocked with fine cuts of meat, leftover scraps were placed into a large stainless-steel pan for making ground beef.

Aside from watching my father at work, cutting meat was not something that a small boy was able to do. Sometimes Dad would give me a bone with meat scraps, and ask me to take a smaller and narrow boning knife and get all the meat off the bone. He instructed me on how to handle the knife and watched me, making sure that I could accomplish the task safely. I used to watch my Grandfather handle the boning knife. He could take that knife and absolutely clean a bone so that you could not find a scrap of meat left on it. When Grandpa Frizzi finished with it, a hungry mutt would be disappointed that the red meat was all gone. The bones were then cut up and packaged as soup bones.

The most important duty assigned to me, however, was just stocking shelves or dusting them with a feather duster. This had two important purposes: First, by stocking shelves, I learned where different products in the store were located; and Second, I learned that 'Presentation' was important. When my mother prepared a meal, I saw that it came in a can or package, but I had no idea where it might be on the shelf. By stocking shelves, I was able to become familiar with where things were shelved in the store. Soon, I knew that the soups were behind the gas stove on a shelf. I learned where I could find the cereal on the shelf above the produce table, and that cans of Pet Milk were to the left of the cash register. I could find all those things my mother used to cook a meal, including the 'Ceci' that we ate at every meal. I knew where the pickled pigs' feet were, so that when a prankster called and asked, "Do you have pickled pigs' feet?"

I could answer, "Yes," and then await their line, "How do you get your shoes on?"

In the 1950's and 60's, the product line was limited, and in our small store, it was even more limited because of space. By knowing where everything was located, I could always be a help by 'fetching' whatever grocery item was being asked for. When orders for delivery were being filled, dad would call out what item he wanted, and I would return with it to the counter to be boxed with the order.

Sometimes dad would go to the storeroom across the street after deliveries had been received to bring back on the two-wheeled dolly cases of products to be stocked. We did not always have shelf space for a whole case, so usually we returned whatever would not fit on the shelf. You could not just stack the cans or products, you had to stock the shelf imagining how it was going to look when you finished. Each can had to be turned to make sure the label was directly facing you, as though you might be the customer searching for that product. Also important was the concept of rotation of product on the shelf by placing the older cans on the floor first, stocking from the box to the back of the shelf and then placing the old cans in front. This was less important for canned goods but was essential for other perishables with a shorter shelf life. Dad always said that no matter what you are stocking, remember to rotate the stock. This is a practice that has followed me to this day regardless of what I am doing. I learned the accounting principle of FIFO before I ever had an accounting class in college. Once the stocking was done, the half full boxes could be returned to the storeroom across the street.

Pricing of the product being stocked was accomplished using a metal hand stamper with an ink pad. The price was entered by rotating a small rubber belt for each digit in the price. Most items were less than $1.00, so this required rotating four of the rubber belts to the digits giving the correct price, a decimal point, and a dollar sign. Each time the stamper was depressed upon an item, the numbers were recoiled back to the ink pad, making it ready for pricing the next item. Prices were based on the price list that came from the warehouse, which listed the suggested retail price. Sometimes the stock still on the shelf had a different price. With cans, steel wool was used to remove the old price from the top of the can before it was stamped with the updated price. For products in paper or cardboard containers, a small blank adhesive price tag was placed over the old price, so that the new price could be stamped on the tag.

Feather dusting was also a task given to me as a stockboy. Our store did not have air conditioning, and our front door had a screen door to allow air to circulate. We did have ceiling fans that had been installed when the store was built in the 1920's by my Grandfather Abe, but Dad always said he did not like to run the fans because they would stir up dust. Feather dusting was a way to occupy my time and to keep the tops of the cans and boxes on the shelf nice and shiny. When I was feather dusting, I could also reface the cans that had been shuffled about by customers and pull the cans to the forward position on the shelf. Once again, as my Dad stressed, 'Presentation' is important. One thing you never wanted to do was drop a metal can so that you placed a dent in the side. Sometimes, you find dented cans in the box from which you were stocking, caused by rough handling at the warehouse or during delivery. The product of a dented can is most often safe to eat unless the can is a 'leaker,' where staining appears on the labeling. If a can is dented on the seam or dented at the circular edge on the top or bottom of the can, you might consider it unsafe. Dents in the side, while not really appealing, are of little consequence. The problem, however, is 'Presentation.' No one ever wants to purchase a dented can, even if it just happened in front of them. A one-dollar bill that has writing on it, or a slight tear, gives a similar reaction. Even though it is still good, there is some innate fear of anything that has been marked, dented, or defaced in some way. For this reason, handling the merchandise carefully while stocking shelves was extremely important.

Once I had learned these rather simple tasks of a stockboy, I was able to start going to the storeroom by myself, finding the product needed at the store, and bringing it back for stocking. Sometimes I would get carried away, and I would place too many cans or boxes on the shelf that exceeded the allotted space for that product. Dad would tell me to put some back in the box to return across the street to the storeroom. The storeroom was the place where we received our deliveries from the Associated Grocers' Warehouse in Wheeling. The truck would pull up to the door of the storeroom, and tracks with rollers were set up to send the boxes from the truck into a waiting stockboy in the storeroom to unload and stack the boxes. I was too small to handle most of the heavy boxes at seven and eight, and was just able to watch. Watching, however, was a way of learning.

Another task assigned to me was performed in the back room of the store. We kept cases of soda pop, empty pop bottles, and a refrigerated cooler there. Pop bottles were returnable to the grocer at two cents a bottle, unlike today, where containers are thrown away or recycled to make a new container. In the 1950's, a carton of soda pop usually consisted of 6 glass bottles, although some came in an 8-pack carton. If you returned empty bottles in your used carton, you had paid your deposit on the purchase of another carton. Most people purchasing a carton of soda pop did so on a regular basis, and they most often were able to bring the previously purchased empty bottles with them. If a customer purchased a carton of soda pop, without empty bottles being returned, they would be charged a deposit on the bottles in the carton. One of the things that kids my age used to do was collect pop bottles along the highways and anyplace where someone may have discarded them. They could turn them in for cash at our store and then spend the cash on candy. The bottles they found were generally very dirty and usually not of the same kind of bottle. Most often, they did not have cartons to place them in. My job was to arrange all the bottles according to distributor into pop cases that could be tallied and returned for credit with the truck driver who delivered a fresh case to our store. Drivers would check to make sure that they were only accepting those bottles that they could return to their own bottling company for credit. Because we had several distributors, my job was to make sure that I was separating all bottles before each new delivery.

The access to the pop room was provided by an exterior door from the sidewalk. This was a delivery entrance that was separate from the customer entrance. It was used by drivers of beer and soda pop delivery trucks using their own two-wheel dollies. Several of the drivers were large and muscular and would carry full cases under their arms. One I remember in particular was 'Jumbo Joe' Pabian. He played football for the local Wheeling Ironmen professional football team. He was a huge man with huge, muscular arms. On one of his visits to the store, he was carrying cases of pop when he accidentally ran into one of my little brothers. The pop case struck my brother's head. 'Jumbo Joe' was very upset about the incident and offered some treats to my little brother, who, other than sporting a small goose egg, was not seriously injured.

We also had beer deliveries with returnable bottles as well. Frank Ragni was a boyhood friend of my Dad who grew up just across the street from our store on Washington Street, and his father, Innocenzo, was a good friend of my Grandfather Abe. You could not help but like Frank, who always seemed happy and friendly. Frank was our delivery driver for Duquesne beer, which came in heavy cardboard cases of twenty-four bottles. Whenever Frank delivered to our store, our greeting was always the same. I would say "Hey Chen-Cho," which was short for his father's name, Innocenzo. He would always reply, "Hey Fritzo!"

My father once told me that when they were young boys, he and Frank were playing on the sidewalk, running back and forth, and they tripped.

Dad said, "My nose is a little bit crooked because Frank Ragni fell down on my head and broke my nose!" I remember Innocenzo, Frank's father, who died while I was a small boy. I will always remember his wife, Gina, who continued to live just across from our store. She was kind and always friendly with my mother, and with me and my brothers during our childhood.

Learning the Tools of the Trade

The next task that my father taught me was collecting money from customers, counting change, and using the cash register. This was obviously a critical part of the operation of a retail store, since mistakes could cost the business losses, or worse yet, anger a patron. We had an old National Cash Register from the 1920s that was purchased by my Grandfather Abe. When I started to work at the store, I had to learn how to use this contraption. The register had several rows of keys, each with a monetary amount listed on each key. By using the combination of keys, a clerk could always tally the total purchase. A total sale price could be punched on the keys in sequence to show the amount of the purchase. For example, if the total sale was $15.85, you could depress the $10.00 key and the $5.00 key to get the $15.00, and then the 50-cent and 35 cent key to total the sale. The buttons were depressed halfway until all buttons were pressed to record the sale. Then, by pressing the purchase button or by pulling the crank handle along the side, a bell would ring, letting all know the cash drawer was being opened. A glass display at the top of the register would show the amount of the sale through numbers that popped up, visible to both the customer and the clerk. The sale would be recorded on an internal inked paper tape showing that sale, along with a mechanical counter showing that the cash drawer was open for the sale. At the close of business, the tape could be removed, showing all sales for that day, the total times the register had been opened, and how many times the cash drawer had been opened other than for making a sale. The button marked 'No Sale' was to open the register without a sale, and usually just to get access to the drawer for some other reason.

Before going to the register, however, the clerk would have to total the price of the goods being purchased by using an adding machine, or manually on paper, or in their head. We had only one good adding machine on our counter, and often it was in use when there were multiple customers in the store at the same time. When this occurred from time to time, we needed to use a pad and pencil to total the sale using only our arithmetic skills. The adding machine also had a tape which we could use to double-check the order before giving the customer the total sale price. My Father was patient with me while learning these skills and gave me the easy ones at first until I mastered the basic skills. In time, I could then begin handling more complicated orders and purchases.

Arithmetic was never my best subject in school. I especially hated time tests for doing math problems. Those are the tests where you had a full page of math problems on which you used a folded paper placed under each line to record the answer to each row of problems. Once each row was completed, you were to open the fold to a blank fold and go to the second line of problems. I hated these tests because I did not like working fast, and of course, we were being timed. I especially disliked these tests just before lunchtime. Some teachers allowed those students who finished the timed test early to get up and go get their hat and coat for lunch and recess, while I, and the other slower students, were trying to concentrate on solving our remaining problems. Working fast often caused errors, but in the workplace, speed with accuracy was a must. Dad would always check my addition and subtraction before we would go to the register to ring up the sale.

The next task for money handling was just learning how to handle the money. The cash drawer was arranged for the bills and coins, no different than a cash drawer of today. Placing the money in the drawer, however, was never to be done in any way except neatly and uniformly. My Dad explained to always turn each bill face up, with the bottom of the bill to the left side of the drawer. Each succeeding bill was to be placed upon it in the same way. Placing the bills with the wrong side showing, or backwards in the drawer, was just not acceptable practice! This rule made counting back the change to a customer easier, and with excellent 'Presentation!' Even today, when someone gives me change, and the bills are upside down and backwards, I recall how unacceptable that practice would have been to my Grandpa Abe and my Dad. Even if the change returned to me is correct, it just is not the professional way of doing things as Dad taught me at Frizzi's AG Food Center. All of this was reinforced by my Mother Nancy, who had worked at her first job at Union

Savings Bank in Bellaire. She, too, was supportive of my early money-changing habits that were developed by my Dad.

Now, the task of counting the change back to the customer also had a ritual that had to be followed. Coins were counted first, then bills, to arrive at the amount that had been tendered. A kid operating a cash register was always going to be susceptible to advantage taken by an unscrupulous adult. Dad always said to remember, "When the cash drawer opens, always place the bill you were handed on the marble top shelf just above the drawer. Don't place it into the register until you have counted back the change to the customer." The obvious reason was to make sure that the customer was satisfied that you returned the correct amount of change, instead of saying something like, "I gave you a ten, not a five." As long as there was a five-dollar bill on that shelf above the cash drawer, you could not be tricked.

Counting the change was also a more professional way of returning funds to the customer than just slapping the bills and coins into their hand. So starting with the smallest coins and working your way up to the largest bill, it was a way of checking yourself. So the process on a $3.77 sale where a $10 bill was tendered would follow: first, the tendered $10 bill was placed on the marble shelf above the drawer; Second, three pennies were taken from the drawer; then two dimes; a one dollar bill; and one five dollar bill; Third, counting to the customer was always "78, 79, 80; 90 and four dollars; one-dollar makes 5, and 5 dollars make ten, and thank you Sir!" Yes, it did take a little bit longer, but you were checking yourself as you did the counting, and the customer was able to check the amount being returned as it was being counted, rather than counting it once it had been handed to them. Just the other day, I was getting change for two ice cream cones that tallied $10.20. I tendered the clerk a $50 bill and a quarter. My change was $40.05. When the clerk counted back my change, he counted it out as he should, and when he reached $50.00, he realized he was still holding an extra $20.00 bill in his hand. If he had just placed my change into my hands without counting, his employer would have suffered a $20 loss. This process of handling money and making change was not only about accuracy, but it was also about establishing trust with the customer. Each transaction became an opportunity to demonstrate care and professionalism, reinforcing the reputation of our family business in the community. This small routine instilled confidence in both the clerk and the patron, ensuring smooth and pleasant interactions at the checkout counter. Fortunately, this young man's training prevented his employer from sustaining an unintended loss.

Some might call this process unimportant, but my Dad called it professional retailing. Think about this the next time you get change at a register, and you will see how little professional retailing is left. I got coffee not long ago at a small diner in St. Clairsville before heading into the courthouse. The young lady who took my order, much to my surprise, handed me my change by counting it out, and I commented that she 'had been trained well as a clerk.' She said, "Thank you sir. That is the only way I know to do it!" Someone like my Dad must have trained her!

Now, remember that these early cash registers only recorded the amount of the sale. The register window only displayed the total amount of the purchase, and not the change to be returned. So as I was learning this process, I had to tabulate the correct change to return since the register was not going to tell me. Even when you were able to master the amount to be returned, some customers would unintentionally complicate the task of the clerk. Now, on today's registers, this is not problematic at all because the register does your thinking for you. In my day, however, returning the correct amount of change depended upon your ability to think through what the customer was doing.

If someone purchased a gallon of milk at eight-nine cents, five loaves of bread at a dollar, and five candy bars for the kids waiting in the car, the total sale would be $2.14 in 1962 prices. Can you believe that? Customers often would tender coins to reduce the amount of loose change in their pockets. If a customer tendered a five-dollar bill and four pennies, they were actually tendering $5.04. The four pennies made the amount from which to begin counting change $2.10, since the 4 pennies had already been paid. So you would count back one dime, one nickel, three quarters to make $3.00, and two $1 dollar bills to make change for the $5.00 tendered. The customer eliminates 5 pennies in their pocket that would have been there had they not tendered the four cents. If you want to see a deer in headlights today, go to a high school vendor at a ball game where there is only a money box to make change from. Without the register to tell how much to return, many clerks are at a loss as to what to do when you hand them a bill with some pocket change.

If you have ever worked in retail, everything I have described is a very basic retailing tool for handling money. I certainly was not a genius at 7 and 8 years old, but I learned basic retailing because I was taught the right way to do it. I have never forgotten those early lessons, and many of them I still apply today for a variety of daily tasks. My wallet always has the bills ordered just like a register drawer. I routinely tender change from my pocket with bills when paying for merchandise to reduce unwanted coins. More than anything, these tools taught by my Dad and Mom amounted to training that I will carry with me throughout life. They helped to make a young person realize that there is a right way to do things, even with what some would consider to be menial tasks. Believe it or not, there is a right way and a wrong way to do something as simple as driving a nail into a piece of wood. How to hold the nail, how to hold the hammer, and how to strike the nail. An old carpenter by trade taught this to me. Learning the right way helps to prevent bent nails, dented wood, and bloody fingers. Counting back change the right way is no different.

I also had to learn how to operate other important pieces of equipment when working at the store. Our store had two sets of scales. One was for weighing meat on a flat porcelain surface, and it sat on top of the meat case. The meat scale gave you the weight of the item after adjusting the scale for any tare. Tare was the weight of the container that would hold the food product. Meat items were in a cardboard pan, and the scale had to be adjusted so as not to include the weight of the pan in the price charged per pound for the meat product. The scale display was a rolling cylinder behind glass, which moved when the product was placed on the weighing surface. It was scaled so that a particular price could be viewed along a red line across the window, with the rolling cylinder moving to the exact weight of the product. By finding that weight, the price per pound would stop the cylinder at the exact price to be charged for the meat by the weight shown, less tare. There was a magnifying glass that you could slide across the window to view the small numbers on the cylinder behind the red horizontal price line.

The other scale was for weighing produce, candy, and other bulk items. This scale had a large stainless steel bowl into which the bulk items could be placed. This scale sat on a small shelf my father had built in front of the produce display. The tare weight of the stainless steel bowl was built into the scales so that no adjustment was needed. Our produce scale could weigh up to 10 pounds by moving a weighted lever from one side to the other end of the scale. Produce would be placed into a stainless steel bowl for weighing. Unlike the meat scale, this scale had a moving arm inside a glass display that would swing right when weight was placed into the basket. It also had a display readout behind the moving arm where the price could be calculated based on the per-pound price of the item being weighed. A thin black line on the moving arm against the background of the scale chart could be viewed to get the exact price to charge. The scale was very heavy and was coated with porcelain for easy cleaning. These scales would be antiquated today, but using them correctly would still give you the same price as the more expensive and modern models.

We also had an electric coffee grinder that I always enjoyed operating. We sold Viking coffee that came in bags of bulk coffee beans. We also sold ground coffee in cans, but some people liked to have their beans ground fresh. Some were one lb. bags, and we also sold larger 3 lb. bags. The bag was opened at the top, and the beans were poured into the top of the grinder by raising the lid. The grinding bin was sloped inside so the beans would automatically fall into the grinder as it operated. Before grinding, the customer would be asked how they preferred the coffee to be ground. There was a dial on the front of the grinder ranging from 'coarse' to 'extra fine.' The dial was turned to the setting preferred by the customer, and then the toggle switch was flipped on. The sound of that grinder for me was unforgettable. It hummed along, grinding the beans as the smell of freshly ground coffee filled the air. The ground coffee would fall into the spout of a tin pot below the grinder. Once all the beans had been ground, the same bag the beans had come in was placed on the spout of the pot, and both were turned quickly upside down. The freshly ground coffee was then filled into the coffee bag that had held the beans, which was now sealed for the customer.

The one piece of equipment that could easily cause injury, however, was the meat slicer. We gave that slicer a workout every day, because we sold a lot of deli meats. Bologna, which came in a round cylinder, seemed to be our best seller since it was the cheapest deli meat in the refrigerated case. At the time, I remember it being only $.69 lb. We also sold chipped ham, either sliced or chipped, depending on the customer's preference. But in addition to these standard luncheon meats, we also had three types of salami. The cheaper cooked salami, and then either hard salami or Genoa salami. We also had prosciutto that was expensive but very popular. We had baked ham, which came in a long rectangular block, and meat loaf, also called Dutch loaf, that came flat on the bottom and heaped up at the top. We also sold a couple of other meats that not everyone had acquired a taste forgoose liver and headcheese. In addition to these meats for slicing, we also sold all kinds of cheeses for slicing. There was casino brick cheese and a Swiss cheese that were popular. We also had beautifully colored longhorn cheese. And of course, there was Romano cheese, which we did not slice, but cut into blocks. The meat case was a colorful place to view from the window on the customer side of the meat counter.

Slicing meat required that you peel back the rind that came wrapped around the loaf that you were going to slice. A protective rind came around each foot-long meat block for freshness. You had to make sure not to peel back more rind than what you were going to slice from the block of meat. You had to gauge this by how much the customer told you to slice. If they wanted a pound, you would take back about two to three inches of rind, depending on the type of meat requested. Each type of meat came in differing shapes, so you had to gauge how much rind to remove. Most customers did not want to get meat sliced and have the rind still on the meat. Bologna, however, seemed to be the exception, and customers seemed not really mind. Once you had sliced the meat into the weight that was desired, you used the scale to see how close you were to the desired weight. Because each block of meat was a little different in shape and size, you really could not judge by just counting slices. After getting some experience, I could usually come very close to what was ordered. If you sliced more meat than what the customer wanted, customers were not obligated to take the excess. Most did agree, provided it was just an ounce or so over. If they did not agree, these extra few slices would usually become a sandwich to be eaten later. Under the slicer was a large roll of wrapping paper that was waxed on one side. We would tear off enough to wrap the meat neatly, and then we used string to tie the package together with a bow. Periodically during the day, depending upon what we were slicing, we might need to clean the slicer. When you sliced goose liver, for instance, it left a fatty residue on the blade that would come off in the next meat or cheese to be sliced. We had to be careful so that this did not happen to make sure that when the customer opened their package at home, it was properly presented to them, remembering that 'presentation' was everything!

We also had a meat grinder that we used to make hamburgers and sausage. We sold a lot of ground beef since hamburgers were a popular mealtime sandwich, especially during the summer months and outdoor grilling. We tried not to make it in bulk to last beyond the day, since it was always better to make it closer to the point of sale. The meat was cut into small chunks that could be placed into the throat of the grinder. These were mixed in a large aluminum or porcelain pan. The chunks of meat were then fed into the grinder, and a wooden plunger was used to push the chunks through the throat and into the grinder. As the ground meat exited the grinder in fine threads of meat, they were placed into individual flat cardboard pans. Once again, proper presentment was important. We allowed the ground meat to fall into the pan, making sure that it held the same shape as when it came out of the grinder. We never wanted to smash down the individual threads of meat as they had come out of the grinder. If we were making sausage, after it was ground into a large aluminum pan, seasoning was mixed with all the ground pork before we encased it for sale. A funnel fitting was attached to the grinder to squirt the ground pork out in a stream. The funnel was about eight inches long, and we placed pig intestines on the funnel, which was used as a casing to hold the pork. As we fed the seasoned ground pork through the grinder a second time, it filled the casing, and beautiful sausage was made. We made two kinds, regular sausage and a special hot sausage for those who liked it tangy.

Both the meat slicer and the meat grinder could be dangerous to fingers, so the utmost care was used when slicing and grinding. You had to remain conscious of where your hands and fingers were when using either piece of equipment. Fortunately, I had no mishaps during my time using either. Cleaning the equipment was essential to maintain them in a sanitary condition, so each night, both the slicer and grinder were broken down and washed in hot and soapy water, then rinsed until all traces of soap were gone. Only then were they reassembled for use the next day. Cleaning would, of course, require the utmost care to prevent a mishap caused by a slip of the hand.

Until each of these skills was mastered, I was not going to be much assistance my Grandfather and my Dad. Over time, the skill came, and I could better contribute to managing the store. When I was in the 4th grade, my father was scheduled for some surgery that would take him out of the store for a few days. My Grandfather Abe, would have to be there by himself during the daytime hours when he would be going back and forth between the grocery store and the storeroom across the street. My parents talked with Mrs. Dick, the Principal at the West Bellaire School, and explained to her the dilemma. They requested that I be allowed to miss classes during the day so that I could work at the store with my Grandfather Abe. Permission was given by the principal, and Mom and Dad also talked to Mrs. Penn, my 4th-grade teacher, to explain why I would be missing class.

On the day of the surgery, instead of catching the bus in front of the store with my classmates, I stayed behind at the grocery store to work with my Grandpa Frizzi. While he ran between the store and the storeroom across the street, I was left in the store to wait on customers as they would come in. At 9 years old, I got my first taste of what each of us would face when our schooldays were over, and I began going to work in the morning! Luckily, I had several years of school remaining before starting my career. I don't recall much about those few days when I was filling in for my father, but I do remember my classmates' inquiries about why I was not in my 4th-grade class. My standard comment was that "My Dad was at the hospital, and I had to work at the store with my Grandfather." Some seemed puzzled at the thought of a 9-year-old having to work instead of going to school, but most seemed satisfied with my response. The surgery for my Dad was not serious, and so he was back at work in a few days. My absence from school ended, and I returned to Mrs. Penn's 4th grade class.

One of those memorable duties that I recall was making milk runs with my father in the early morning hours before school. We could get a better price by picking up our own milk from the Farm Dairy Company plant in Tridelphia, West Virginia, instead of taking delivery from their dairy trucks. To get a better price, however, the milk had to be loaded in our truck at the plant before loading their own large delivery trucks. This required us to be loaded early at the dock by 5:30 a.m. in the morning.

Frizzi & Son AG Food Center now had a newer Chevrolet Truck that we used to make these milk runs. It was a 1961 Corvair model panel truck that Dad had purchased new at Kuchinka Chevrolet in Bellaire. The motor compartment was in the rear of the truck bed between the rear wheels of the vehicle. The standard transmission and engine were connected directly to the drive shaft for each rear wheel. To accommodate the rear engine, the cargo floor was slightly higher in the rear of the truck than in the middle. It had a six-cylinder engine and could handle the milk run with no problems.

Dad would get my brother Dick or me up about 4:30 in the morning to accompany him to the Farm Dairy Company plant for pickup. The plant was in West Virginia on National Road. Before we would leave the store, we had to first load into our panel truck the empty glass gallon jugs that were returned to us by our customers. Just like the pop bottles, the gallon jugs carried a deposit. They were housed in metal milk crates that could handle four gallon jugs in each. These crates were made to be stacked. Once the empties were all loaded, we were ready to roll.

We would travel across the Interstate toll bridge from Bellaire to Benwood, West Virginia. The sun was not up yet, so all the street lights were lit up in downtown Bellaire as we proceeded to the bridge ramp on 32nd Street. The only person we would see this early in the morning was the toll taker on the bridge to whom I would hand a ticket from the book of tickets that Dad kept over the sun visor of the truck. My schoolmate Rodney Crosby's dad was a toll taker, and sometimes he would be the person taking our ticket. Over the river to Benwood, we would drive north to 29th Street Boulevard in South Wheeling, where we would begin the long nine percent grade up to the top of Bethlehem Hill. The little Corvair Van had no trouble pulling this grade with empty crates. Once we crested the hilltop, we traveled down to Elm Grove. We would follow Route 40 past Monument Place and proceed east on the old National Road. After a few miles, we would arrive at the Farm Dairy Company plant. This dairy had a little lunch counter in front of the building where early risers would go for breakfast. The loading docks were on the side of the building.

When we arrived, the plant would soon be ready to begin loading milk onto company delivery trucks for distribution to the surrounding communities.

We had to pull up to the loading dock first, and my Dad would give our milk order to the dock worker. He would bring out our order, stacked on a dolly with four wheels, to the edge of the dock, and he would help load by handing each milk crate to my father in the cargo bay of the truck. Each crate would be stacked inside the cargo bay of the Corvair Van. Because the rear of the cargo bay was somewhat elevated due to the engine and transmission, the crates fit neatly into the center, where they would not shift once the truck started moving. These were stacked about three crates high. We used to get about 140 gallons of milk, or 35 crates, plus crates with other dairy products like cottage cheese. Once we were loaded, we started back to the store. The crates of milk were interlocked; however, sudden stopping or starting could sometimes dislodge them. My job was to climb into the back of the bay and make sure that the crates were reset.

Once we got to 29th Street hill in Elm Grove, the drag up the hill to Bethlehem would begin. The six-cylinder engine of the Corvair Van would begin to whine as Dad shifted into lower gears as we climbed toward the hilltop. The pace was slower than it had been with the empty jugs, which were now full gallons. The weight of each gallon of milk, not counting the glass jugs and crates, was about 8.5 lbs, so we were carrying more than 1,200 lbs of weight just from the milk itself. Once we got to the top of the hill, we cruised down the other side to South Wheeling, and then proceeded south to the Interstate Bridge, which would take us back over the Ohio River to Bellaire. This time, there would be a different toll taker than before, since our round trip would place us at the toll booth on the westbound side of the bridge. Once the toll was paid, we were on our way to West Washington Street for unloading.

When we arrived, it was still before 6 a.m. Dad would drive the Van up on the sidewalk at the store room with the side bay doors opened. He would get as close to the storeroom door as he could. One by one, the milk crates were taken from the truck and stacked by us 4 crates high on the floor. Once we had all the crates stacked, the process of dragging them to the back of the storeroom would begin. If I had made the trip that morning, brother Dick would have joined us at the storeroom to help with this process. We used a long hammer with a hook on the end of the handle to latch onto the bottom milk crate and slowly drag the entire stack back to the walk-in cooler. Each crate would be taken off the stack, and the re-stacking would take place inside the cooler. Each crate was over 50 lbs, so we got an early morning workout before school was to begin. Sometimes Dad helped in this process, but usually he would go into the store while Dick and I completed the work of placing the milk inside the cooler.

Now this cooler was not just for the milk order. This is where the sides of beef and luncheon meats were also kept. One morning, I remember working with Dick, who was stacking milk crates inside the cooler. He was stacking a crate on the floor, and bent over to place it, when the weight of the crate pulled him closer to the cooler wall than he wanted. The top of his head hit a meat hook fastened to the wall of the cooler, and momentarily, his scalp was impaled by the hook! He slowly jerked his head back to free himself, and except for a little blood, he was fine. Once the door of the walk-in cooler was closed, our milk run was over for the day. We would head back to the house above the store to wash up, eat breakfast, and get ready for the school day. We usually did this twice each week as we sold a lot of milk at $.69 cents a gallon.

The gallon jugs of milk were glass and subject to being broken. Each jug had a hard plastic handle molded around the opening of the neck of the bottle. It was flexible in that you could put your fingers through the handle and pick up the jug to carry it. The plastic handle would flex with the weight of the jug. One of my truly embarrassing moments working in the store was on a busy Friday night. Dad was helping other customers, and a man came in and wanted three gallons of milk. I went to the meat cooler where we kept our milk in the lower cooler compartment. I took out 3 gallon jugs. Now, to carry them to the store counter, I used the handle on two of the jugs to pick up two gallons in one hand, and used the other for the single jug. I had seen my Father do this numerous times and decided that it would work for me as well. When I reached the counter, I put the single gallon on the counter. Now, the other two gallons still in my other hand posed the problem. I was going to separate the two jugs now since I had a free hand. What I did not realize was that when I picked up two jugs in one hand, the bottoms of the jugs separated by about three inches. When I allowed my free hand to pick up one of those jugs, the bottoms of both wanted to come back together. They did it with a 'clinking' sound of glass bottom touching glass bottom. Both glass bottoms immediately broke, and two full gallons of milk in a tidal wave exploded all over my pants, shoes, and the floor! Dad did not say too much as I headed to the sink in the back room to get the mop and bucket. My mistake had been that the two should have been set down on the counter or floor first, and then separated. An embarrassing lesson was learned that night for sure! I never forgot the trick to separating two-gallon jugs in the future!

Another embarrassment that I was forced to endure was the afternoon I caught the hillside on fire above the store. We had a small burn pile up in the yard behind the store. When we got too many boxes or paper, we would often dispose of them by burning them on this pile. Everyone along the street did this, and all considered it acceptable practice. I did this in the past. But one day, I recall boxing up some scrap cardboard and papers with the intention of going to the burn pile. Dad's last words to me as I went out the door were, "It's a little windy, so be careful."
I replied as most kids would have replied, "I know Dad, I know!"

Many years later, in an insurance law class, I learned the legal definitions of fire as a potential hazard. A 'friendly fire' is one that is controlled and serves a useful purpose. An example would be a pilot light on a hot water tank or furnace. A 'hostile fire,' on the other hand, is defined as one that is not controlled and serves only one purpose. It burns things up that you don't want burned up! The wind on this day soon turned my 'friendly fire' into a 'hostile fire,' moving to the brush surrounding the burn pile. I tried frantically to control it, but the wind was my enemy this day. As it burned further up the hillside, other neighbors came out to help me stamp out the burning grass and brush, but to no avail. I ran back to the store to inform my Dad that I needed some help, and he reminded me of his last words when I left just 15 minutes earlier.

Someone called the fire department, and soon the firemen were racing up our steps and the neighbor's steps to the hillside above the houses. They pulled up their fire hoses, connected to the fireplug across the street from the store, and soon had the 'hostile' brush fire under control. I was relieved to see that nothing except the brush was burnt, but I was wondering whether I would be arrested for starting the whole affair. Everyone was telling me as we walked back down to the street that 'it was too windy today to be burning!' I felt so embarrassed in front of all the customers and neighbors who had come out to witness for themselves my carelessness. Dad told me later that the same thing happened to him once, and he said not to worry. He never forgot my response to his warning, however, and if we disagreed on something he was trying to tell me, he would always respond by saying, "I know Dad, I know." This was his way of saying "listen to what I am saying!" He would often repeat those words to me whenever I shrugged off his advice as a way of reminding me of my 'friendly fire' turned 'hostile!' Sometimes, warnings from a parent are based on knowledge they have acquired from their own experiences. Well, I did not get arrested for burning up the hillside, but I did have to endure the embarrassment of that day, and years of being reminded of my words, "I know Dad, I know!"

Our Customers

Friday nights at the store with my Dad often became busy in the early evening as people passed by on their way to town. Some were heading to movie theaters, while others were heading to a local bar or tavern for a drink. Some were heading there to do some shopping. Many were heading to town for a meal at a local restaurant. The sidewalks in Bellaire would be filled with people as many retail merchants remained open on Friday evening. The roller skating rink on Belmont Street attracted many kids my age, some walking and others being transported by their parents in the family auto. The traffic into town began about 5 o'clock, and our store would get busy. Friday was also a scheduled payday for many workers, and after the banks closed, they would need to find a place to cash their paychecks. My Grandfather Abe had long stocked up cash so that he could cash those paychecks, a service that had the effect of attracting customers to the store. I remember many times when our store would be filled with three or four customers waiting to make purchases and cash checks.

Along with all the customers driving by, there were many customers who walked to our little grocery store along the sidewalks and from across the street. I remember Yogi Wallace and his wife Lois, a young couple that lived in a duplex across the street. They lived next door to Paul and Yolanda Nattichione. The Clutter family lived in the duplex that was directly across from our store. Then the Pallisco family and Gina Ragni lived in the second half of the duplex. Down the street was Mamie Curran, and her husband and sons. The Byles family came next, with sons John and Greg, followed by the Hepburn family and all their children. Mr. Presutti and his wife, Teresa, who owned the fireworks plant, were next. A large three-story home of the DeBlasis family with Rose and daughter Mary, and the Clark family above them on the third floor. The Andriano family was on the other side of the store, followed by the Tellitocci family and the Kent family. At the junction of Hamilton and Washington was Albert DiGiandomenico, his wife, and his children. The Eden family lived near them in a tiny house. The Velegolla family lived above our store room after my Aunt Adeline and her husband Marion had relocated to Shadyside. Each and every one of these families patronized our little grocery store, and on Friday nights, I got to meet many of them when I was being introduced to the store business.

Many times, customers would come in with their children. Others would drive to our store and leave their children in their automobile while they shopped. Minnie Taffe was one of those customers who would always bring her nieces with her when they walked to our store to shop. They were little girls about my same age, and they would watch as I worked with my Dad and Grandfather. Their aunt Minnie was always friendly, and you could tell just by watching her interaction with them that she was truly a favorite aunt. Minnie made shopping fun for them, and I think they enjoyed their shopping trips to our store as much as I enjoyed accompanying their aunt Minnie. After they had bought the groceries they needed, they would exit our door and begin the walk down the sidewalk to return to Minnie's home.

There were two different Wallace families that frequented our store. The first was Philip and Nancy Wallace, who had a large family living outside of Bellaire at Rock Hollow. They had many children ranging in age from teenager to toddler. Often, the children would sit inside the automobile while their parents shopped inside our grocery store. From time to time, one of the children would meander into the store, asking their parents about something going on in the car, or how much longer it would be before they were done shopping. Philip and Nancy would 'shoosh' them back outside to wait for them to finish shopping. Waiting patiently sometimes rewarded them with penny candy. Daughter Kathy was the same age as me, and we became classmates in Mr. Griffin's eighth-grade class. I had known her even before through her family's trips to our store for groceries. I remember that when the family's shopping was finished, our grocery counter was completely full and overflowing! We brought bags of groceries and boxes to the waiting vehicle, and somehow the kids and the groceries all seemed to fit. The family had many mouths to feed, and their grocery bill was always a big one. Another good customer from Rock Hollow was Joe Albaugh, who worked as a carpenter, and his wife, Polly. Sometimes they would bring along their daughter, Diane, who was just a year or so older than me. Rock Hollow was just a narrow hollow on the road to Neffs, but it yielded some of the finest people you could want to meet.

The other Wallace family was Lawrence and Lois, who lived across the street from our store. Their children were very small, and I did not have much contact with them. Lawrence was nicknamed 'Yogi,' and that is the only name that I ever knew to call him. 'Yogi' was in many respects a grown man who still had the heart and mind of a little boy. He loved to build models, which was a hobby in which I also found great pleasure. One day, I saw 'Yogi' placing outside on an upstairs window ledge what looked like model army tanks. I asked my Dad why he was putting them outside on the ledge and not on a shelf in the house. When Dad inquired of 'Yogi,' he responded that he had "painted each of the models with a different kind of paint," and he wanted to see how each model would weather outdoors. Lawrence, although an adult, became a child relating to such things as locomotion, trains, and model building. His early work on Washington Street as a modeler became the foundation for a lifetime of master craftsmanship, with skills of creating all kinds of model structures to complement his huge model train layout. He was always building something that would complement his train layouts.

And then there was Clyde Shaffer and his wife, Minnie, who drove a 1949 or 1950 Studebaker. This car was different than most of that day because of the distinctive chrome 'bullet nose' on the front end of the vehicle. It had big chrome bumpers and a rear window glass that was rounded at the sides. Over the windshield were exterior sun visors matching the color of the car. Clyde was a scruffy man with a gray beard, an old cap, and thick, round glass spectacles. He always wore bib-overalls and a T-shirt when it was hot, or a long-sleeved shirt when it was cold. Clyde always seemed to be a bit gruff and rough around the edges, but he was always kind to our family and me. Clyde had a son named Clyde Jr., whom everyone called 'Junior.' He was a little older than I was, and if I was not at the store when they came shopping, Junior would come upstairs to our residence and play while his dad and mom were purchasing groceries. Living at what was called 'Red Town,' near the brick factory at McClainsville, Clyde and his family lived on the fringes of poverty in an old company house. I remember when I was five years old, my Dad told me that Clyde's son, Junior, would not be coming to the store with his mother and father anymore. Junior had taken ill and died from some sort of kidney disease. My father told me that, "Junior drank a lot of Coke, and it affected his kidneys." His death at such a young age, someone that I knew as only a boy my own age, was very upsetting to me as a child. I could not understand how death could take someone my own age. My brother Dick and I were saddened at the loss of Junior as a playmate.

Max Wallner from west of town at Moss Run would always stop on his way home from Steubenville, where he worked as a mechanic. Every day, he would make the round trip from Bellaire and back, and he was always returning about the same time each evening. He drove a Volkswagen Beetle and got great gas mileage with the VW on the 80-mile round trip each day. When he came in, his purchases were the usual gallon jug of milk, bread, and anything that Mrs. had asked him to pick up on the way home. With a growing family, milk and bread did not last very long. Max's arrival time at our store each night was always within minutes of being the same. When he had gathered his purchased groceries, Max would get in his little VW Beetle and speed off, shifting those gears like he was an Indy driver, heading home to his family and the finish line!

Many years later, when I got my first car, it was Max who made the repairs for me. The car was a 1965 VW Beetle, just like he always drove. I had paid $175.00 to the seller. It had a blown piston, the clutch and throw-out bearing needed to be replaced, and the king-pins were also shot. The hood was dented, as were several fenders. When I showed the car to Max, he asked me how much I had paid for it. When I told him, he responded saying, "Did you wear a mask when you robbed that lady?" After repairs were made by Max, and I had replaced fenders and the hood, it was ready to repaint. I had Labe Smith paint the car for me in a beautiful Chevrolet Blue color. I was able to sell the car for $975.00 a year later, covering all my repair costs and leaving about $100.00 to spare! Max knew his VW's!

Another customer from 'out the road' was Tommy Steele, and his wife, Hazel. Tommy would always accompany his wife when shopping, and we would find time for small talk as she looked around. I remember on one occasion, while they were in the store, a little toe-headed boy in bare feet came into the store looking for candy. He picked out what he wanted and then raced out the front door to the sidewalk. He had come down the sidewalk this day without an adult, as he would usually do. In haste to get back across the street, he ran out from between two cars parked along the curb and was struck by a truck driven by Mr. Rataiczak, who was heading home after work. The screech of the tires on the pavement and the thud left no doubt about what had happened. The little boy was lying there unconscious, with a crowd of onlookers. Hazel was so visibly upset inside the store and began to cry. Tommy came to her side and attempted to calm her and give her assurance that the boy would be alright. She had just seen him leave and had mentioned that he should not be running around without someone being with him. I ran outside to see how the boy was and found him lying on the pavement of the street unconscious. As someone talked to him, he began to cry, which we thought was a good sign. Mr. Rataiczak, who struck the boy, was naturally shaken up by the incident. The police arrived, and an ambulance took the boy to the hospital. What could have been a tragic ending was not. I remember this little guy returning to the store with an adult about a month later. He had a scar on his forehead that was healing well, and he did not appear to have any broken bones. He wanted to buy more penny candy. We told Mrs. Steele the next time she came into the store that he was recovering well, and she smiled with relief at the news.

We had many Italian customers. I remember the Beltrondo family. Johnny and Marie, who would always shop in our store together on Friday. They lived south of Bellaire on New Cut Road. Sometimes their son David would accompany them as they did their shopping. Their children, like David, attended St. John's Catholic school in Bellaire. Johnny was always a talkative guy while Marie did the shopping, and he would engage me about school, sports, and just about anything that came to mind. Johnny, however, sometimes came to the store without his wife. When he did, he always waited until the store was empty of customers, or when we were not busy, and could be waited on right away. He would then tell my Dad or Grandfather, "Give me one of those in a sack." One of what, I would say to myself? What was 'them' that he wanted in a sack? I didn't learn until one day when I asked my Dad, "Why does Johnny always say give me one of those in a sack?" Dad told me that Johnny never wanted anyone to know about the dark Port wine that he enjoyed. Dad explained to me that 'them' was a 5th bottle of Dark Port wine. When I grew a little older and could reach the top shelf behind the meat case where the Port was kept, I too, began to deliver to Johnny 'one of them in a sack!' He always called me 'Young Frizzi,' and then would say, "Give me one of them in a sack!" That was Johnny's cue to me, to get a sack, go to the back and place a fifth-size bottle of Port into it, and only then return to the counter to deliver it to him. I always honored Johnny's wishes, and with that purchase, he would be off until the next time.

Of all the Italian customers, however, I remember Italia DiMattia. She was a short, stocky lady who walked very slowly. Her voice was soft spoken, as I recall. Italia came to our store often when my Grandfather Abe was working. They would converse fluently in their native Italian tongue, which both seemed to enjoy. Often, my father would also join in the conversation. Italia would sometimes correct my father on the pronunciation of Italian words that he may have been unfamiliar with. Sometimes, I would ask her how certain items she was purchasing were pronounced. She was polite and responded by saying the Italian word for each item on the counter. Some were already familiar to me, but I learned many words by listening to her. Sometimes, Italia would walk to the store with her daughter, Mamie, who lived just down the street from our store. Other times, it would be with her daughter, Yolanda Nattichione. These encounters with Italia, just an older Italian lady, were educational and memorable.

Yolanda and her husband, Paul Nattichione, lived across the street from our store in a duplex next to 'Yogi.' I remember that they had a very pretty daughter named Carol. She was older than me by at least ten years, but as a youngster, I always saw her as so beautiful. Paul would often be in the store during the day while Yolanda worked in the decorating department of the Imperial Glass Factory. I remember that she was always called 'Yulie,' and it was not until many years later that I even knew that her real name was Yolanda. Her husband, Paul, was always a sociable and friendly guy with me as a kid. He is the one who told me that the correct pronunciation of my surname was "Fritza" as it was pronounced when my Grandfather Abe, moved to America.

The Hepburn family of Clarence and Lillian were also customers who came to our store. They had a number of children who were older than I was, but Karen, Danny, and Michael were closest in age to my brothers and me. Sometimes we played together in our backyard and on the sidewalk between the store and their house. They rode the bus with us to West Bellaire each morning. Their family was larger than ours, with many mouths to feed. When my Grandfather Robinson died in December 1964, my Grandma Neva was left all alone in the big house on 4th Avenue in West Bellaire. She needed to sell it. This home was spacious with a big yard, four large bedrooms upstairs, a parlor and large living room, and a big kitchen. This house was so familiar to me because my brothers and I spent many days as young boys during my grade school years. Those would now be memories as my Grandma Neva sold this home to the Hepburn family, and they moved to West Bellaire from Washington Street. My Grandmother Robinson was so pleased that the home would be once again filled with a family and the laughter of children!

The Unforgettable Sounds of the Radio

The entertainment on Friday and Saturday nights during the 1950s and 1960s while working at the store was provided by a radio. The radio sat on a shelf above the freezer behind the counter. It was a brown Zenith Bakelite AM/FM radio through which came the voices and sounds of the times. My Grandpa Frizzi always liked to listen to the Polka Party on Sunday mornings when he opened the store for half the day. Mom sometimes asked me to run down to the store to get change for two dollars. She wanted four fifty-cent pieces for my brothers and me to drop in the collection plate at church during Sunday School. Polka music was always on the radio. The Polka Party played many of the same songs that my dad played for us on his accordion, but somehow, Polka music on Sunday morning always seemed a little bit out of place on the Lord's Day.

On those Saturday nights when I would sometimes work for brother Dick, the radio was always tuned to WWVA in Wheeling, West Virginia. This live show of country music brought into Wheeling singers from all over the United States. Some of the biggest names in country music were at the Jamboree. In addition to big names, there was an abundance of local talent that would be previewed before the big names came on stage. The show originated at the Capitol Music Hall in downtown Wheeling, which was, and continues to be, a magnificent theater for the performing arts. But the Jamboree in the 1960's was all Country with a capital AC.' You had to like Merle [Haggard], Charlie [Pride], or Marty [Robbins], or duets by George [Jones] and Tammy [Wynnette] if you were going to listen to WWVA. I was beginning to listen to rock-n-roll music during this period, and preferred to listen to other channels. 1170 AM on the dial always had a strong signal, and so that is where we normally kept the dial. The Jamboree and country music back then were not as popular with the younger crowd. Nonetheless, the sound of country music coming through that old radio on the shelf by the frozen food freezer will always be an unforgettable sound of my childhood at the store.

Some evenings we would listen to high school football games on the radio during the fall. During the winter, we would listen to high school basketball games broadcast for local fans. I usually attended these games with schoolmates when Bellaire played at home, but the away games could only be attended with a seat beside the radio. In the spring and summer, Major League Baseball provided entertainment for the evening. Our radio stations gave us a choice between the Cleveland Indians in the American League and the Pittsburgh Pirates in the National League. We got the Pittsburgh channel on television, which broadcast the Pirate ball games, so naturally, I became a Pirate fan early on as a boy. In 1960, the Pirates defeated the New York Yankees in the World Series in the 7th game. Local Jefferson County native Bill Mazeroski was the hero for the Pirates, and I can remember when he hit the winning home run over the left field scoreboard at old Forbes Field to win the game and the series. Walking to my Grandparents' home that day after school, we learned of the 'shot heard round the world,' and any doubt about who I rooted for as a kid was settled. Dad listened to that 7th game at the store. I continued to follow the Pirates throughout my childhood, but the 60s could not repeat the season that opened the decade.

Although Bellaire was in Ohio, we were closer to Pittsburgh in Pennsylvania than to Cleveland in Ohio. Not everyone was a Pirate fan, and old Bill Clutter, who lived across the street from our store, was one of those who disliked the Pirates. Bill would sit on his porch listening to the games with two radios. One was so that he could root for the Cleveland Indians, and the other so that he could root against the Pirates. He knew that I was a Pirate fan, and he liked to give me the razz whenever they lost. When I would cross the street to the storeroom, Bill would always have something to say about the Pirates. Bill particularly could not stand the Pirate announcer, Bob Prince, who was the legendary voice of the Pirates baseball team. The phrase that he used whenever the Pirates hit a home run was 'Kiss it Goodbye,' and Bill truly hated those three words.

During the 1966 season, Danny Whelan, the Pirate trainer, held in his hand a green rubber hot dog which he shook at an opposing pitcher during a game. Whelan shouted out to the opposing pitcher, pleading for a walk. The act of shaking the rubber hot dog was viewed as putting a 'jinx' on the pitcher, Dave Guisti, of the Houston Astros. Sure enough, Guisti walked the batter just as Whelan had shouted at him to do while waiving the green rubber hot dog. That walk created the idea that a 'Green Weenie' was good luck to the Pirates, and a jinx to their opponents. Thus, the 'Green Weenie,' a green rubber hot dog that could also rattle to make noise, became a part of Pirate history. These 'Green Weenies' immediately went on sale at Forbes Field at all games, and could be ordered by sending a few dollars to the Pirate organization. The marketing was promoted by Bob Prince during each game. So naturally, hearing this promotion on the radio, I had to order one. I kept checking the mail each day to see if it had arrived, and after about three weeks, my own 'Green Weenie' came in the mail.

The day it arrived, the Pirates were playing at home, and Forbes Field would be a sea of 'Green Weenies.' I brought the 'Green Weenie' with me to work that afternoon and hid it behind the counter. The ball game would soon begin. I did not want to display it unless it was for something to cheer about. I remember that when I heard those words 'Kiss it

Goodbye' spoken by Bob Prince, I made a beeline to the front door of the store with my 'Green Weenie' in hand. As Bill saw me approach, I held it high in the air and shook it long and hard! He looked aggravated, to be sure. But after a few more innings, and another home run, I ran back to the front door of the store and again shook it even longer and harder! Bill was now livid with the 'Green Weenie,' and my razzing of him that he put his radios away, folded up his chair, and left the porch for the tranquility of his own living room. There in solitude, he would not have to endure more of my jubilation! In the 70s, the Pittsburgh Steelers would have a similar fan item called the 'Terrible Towel.' The Steelers had much more success with the towel than the Pirates ever had with the 'Green Weenie!'

If we were not listening to a ball game, we knew it was getting toward closing time when the 30-minute radio broadcast of the famed evangelist Katherine Kuhlman began. This lady preacher would proclaim to her radio listeners the words, "I Believe in Miracles!" I often wondered what she looked like, but since her voice was the only clue, I had to use my own imagination. She spoke in a slow and deliberate way, and her words were drawn out until you thought she might never end them. She used an inflection with her words that placed emphasis on those words that were most important to her. When she opened with the words, "I believe in miracles," she emphasized the word 'Believe' by drawing it out to 'Beeee-Lieeeeeeve!' Sometimes she would have someone who needed physical healing with her, and during her radio broadcast, they were miraculously healed to the cheers and shouts of persons present at her rallies. I had never put much stock in these preachers like Katherine, or the other guy I used to see on TV, who was named Oral Roberts. But somehow, just listening to Katherine Kuhlmann's voice on the radio gave me assurance that she truly did 'believe' in what she preached, regardless of what others thought. Once she completed her sermon, the program would end, and closing time was nearer.

She was not the only radio evangelist whose voice came across the radio waves. I can remember listening to Herbert W. Armstrong of the Worldwide Church of God, and his program 'The World Tomorrow.' This was a mixture of current events with biblical teachings, much of it based upon issues of the day. Later, his son, Garner Ted Armstrong, took over the radio broadcasts. Both were powerful and easily listened to preachers. They spoke in plain language that was easily understood even by a young boy. Discussions on the World Tomorrow related biblical teaching to science and modern thinking. Garner Ted Armstrong often spoke of scientific thought as he addressed the bible and traditional religious doctrine. At times, we heard the unmistakable voice of Billy Graham at one of his outdoor crusades. He seemed so different from the others. His words were filled with simple explanations of salvation and why it was the most important decision we would ever make.

The protestant faiths of Christianity were not alone, however, as occasionally, Catholic Archbishop Fulton J. Sheen would also be heard on the radio. He also had a popular television ministry in 1952. Sheen was like a professor or teacher who explained biblical teachings as though you were his student in a classroom. He often would use a blackboard on his television show. He had a unique style that, regardless of your religious faith or persuasion, gave you an interest in wanting to hear what this man had to say.

Music at work was soothing, and helped the time to pass. Even if it was only AM radio, work would not have been the same without that old Zenith radio. The sound of the radio, however, was not the only music that I heard at work. My Grandfather and Father were both whistlers. That childhood song that you 'whistle while you work' was certainly true for both of them. Their styles, however, were different. My Grandpa Frizzi whistled, but it was always in a tune that was difficult to recognize. His whistle seemed like it began and went on for a few stanzas, and then suddenly would change into something that seemed to be totally unconnected. I am sure that he knew what it was, but often we did not. Now, when he arrived to open the store in the early morning, we upstairs in the residence above the store knew he was there, because we often awoke to the sound of his whistle.

Dad's whistle was different than his 'Pabby.' His whistle was strong and loud. You could generally listen to it and know what tune he was whistling. Dad had the ability to 'warble' his tune like a bird, and this made it easy listening for all within earshot. They both whistled tunes when they walked across the street to the storeroom, or whenever the mood struck them. One particular whistling memory that I recall was during the Christmas season in 1957, when Dad and the members of the Bellaire

Elks Lodge were to march in the Bellaire Christmas Parade. This was the same year when all moviegoers were enchanted with the movie 'The Bridge on the River Kwai,' a story about the building of a railroad bridge by American and English soldiers held in a Japanese concentration camp. That year was not just a super year for the Classic 1957 Chevrolet. This movie, starring Alec Guinness and William Holden, won 7 Academy Awards. Each day, to keep the imprisoned soldiers focused on survival, their Commander, played by Guinness, made the captured prisoners march as soldiers to work on the bridge. They whistled a British tune known as 'Colonel Bogey's March,' and the musical score that accompanied it became an inspirational part of the movie. The sound of those soldiers marching in unison and whistling this unforgettable tune was the Elks Lodge's re-creation of that scene in the movie for the Christmas Parade. I was five years old, and I remember them marching past the City Park at Belmont Street, perfectly in step and whistling this famous tune. We stood with Mom to watch all Elk's members, and Dad pass by, whistling 'Bogey's March' just like in the movie!

Activities and Co-Workers

When it was slow, Dad and I would sometimes do calisthenics to pass the time until closing. We would do deep knee bends, or toe touches, or some other exercise that limited space would allow. One night, I recall we performed a maneuver, something akin to a gymnast on the rings. Directly behind the cash register was a freezer whose top was about the same height as the counter holding the register. Dad suggested that we take turns supporting our body weight by placing one hand on the counter and the other on the freezer. We would bend and lift our knees from the floor so that our arms were supporting our entire body weight. Using our upper arms only, we would drop our body down until our upper arms were level with our shoulders. We then would have to extend both arms back to the position from which we started. Dad went first and did about five repetitions. Then it was my turn. This was harder for me since my shoulders were not as wide as the space between the counters, but I managed to do a couple. We repeated this a few more times and then rested before starting again. I remember how my arms felt like they were floating at my side after each repetition.

This slow night brought us to another exercise for our legs. Deep knee bends we did in school for exercise. Dad started off doing fifty reps, and I followed. Then I did another fifty, and then Dad followed. We decided to do as many as we could, each of us hoping to be able to do the most. I don't recall how many we did or who won, but I do remember the next morning. My legs and arms were feeling the pain from the night before. Later that day, my Mother asked me, "What did you and your dad do last night? He could hardly get out of bed this morning!" These friendly competitions would go on until a customer came into the store and interrupted our workout! My Dad was always very physically fit, so in most of our competitions, he was able to win the gold medal every time.

My Grandfather usually went home at 5 o'clock p.m. since he opened the store early each morning. Eventually, Dad hired some additional help to work at the store with me so that he could take off as well. The store always had delivery boys who lived on Washington Street. The first one that I remember as a child was Alfred Tellitocci, who grew up just a few doors away from the store. By the time that I was working, however, Dad had hired Greg Byles, who lived just a few houses west of the store. Greg was a good employee who was on the quiet side, but a good, dependable worker. We worked together some evenings when Dad had gone home. Greg was in high school and was at least three or four years older than me. He had a great knowledge of automobiles and how they operated, and Greg spent many evenings explaining to me about 'headers' and 'carburetors.' Both he and his older brother John worked on their automobiles in a garage below their house, and these vehicles were the pride and joy of the Byles brothers. Greg had a beautiful blue 1969 Chevrolet Nova, and John, his older brother, had a black Nova of the same year. They were built as drag vehicles.

When Greg or John started up their Nova down the street, it was loud enough to let anyone up the street know that they were heading somewhere. Greg used to pass the store going very slowly since his engine was rumbling as he went by. He did not accelerate to prevent emitting the loud roar of his engine from his headers and exhaust. Had he put the pedal to the metal, Washington Street would have sounded like a drag strip disturbing the neighbors. For this reason, Greg always proceeded so slowly past our store on his way to town. His car was always very clean! Greg became a machinist after high school, from the training he received from Marion Blind, shop teacher at Bellaire High School. Greg and those chats introduced me to the world of automobiles.

After Greg graduated from high school, he retired from the store, and my dad next hired Tom Breyer. He was only 2 years older than I was. Tom and I spent a lot of time talking about cars and girls. Tom also had some friends who had rented a garage on Harrison Street where they worked on cars and drank beer. Tom, however, did not have a car that was souped up like Greg's Nova. It was, however, a real classic that Tom called 'The Merc.' The 'Merc' was a 1949 Mercury Coupe with big front seats and spacious rear. The stick was on the column, and to Tom, this was his baby. Tom and I talked about school, teachers, and girls. I recall that Tom had one particular girlfriend who I believe always gave him a hard time, despite the fact that I think she really liked him. I learned a lot about girls from Tom and dating, and things that go along with it. Tom used to tell me about riding the loop in Shadyside with the 'Merc.' Tom seemed to know all the other guys his age with fast cars.

I learned many of the store delivery routes from Tom, so that one day I would be taking over when he graduated and moved on. Tom was a great guy, and in a way, I looked up to him as an older brother that I did not have. He would tell me about the 'Knotty Pines' bar in Elm Grove, which was a hopping place for high school students looking for a beer. I think his favorite beer was Past Blue Ribbon. When things got slow, we would stand in the doorway of the store and watch the traffic pass by and just talk. His friends, my friends, and girls from school would see us and honk as they passed by. I was sad when Tom finally moved on. So many things that you could discuss with an older brother, I lost when he graduated and said goodbye.

Abe Frizzi in the produce section with the scales and weighing bananas. Cereal shelved above the produce rack. (Frizzi Collection circa 1961)

The bus stop lineup waiting for the school bus to West Bellaire School. From front of the line, Dick Frizzi, Steve Pallisco, Terry Hollingshead, Danny Frizzi, Jr., Christine Pallisco, Sharon Hollingshead, Cyril Scott, Rossie Velegolla, in rear possibly J. Hepburn and sister Linda. Note the U.S. Postal Box on the cement pole. (Frizzi Collection circa 1961)

Behind the counter where orders were filled stand Abe Frizzi and son, Danny, who cease work to pose for this photograph.   (Frizzi Collection circa 1961)

Abe Frizzi waits on a customer standing at the counter. Beyond the counter are the produce racks. The white signs above the customer hang from a wire facing the doorway behind Abe so that one could see the specials as they entered the store. (Frizzi Collection circa 1961)

Daniel Frizzi takes the Presidency of the Associated Grocers while the board of directors of the Wheeling warehouse poses for a photograph. left front, Ray Young, Warehouse Manager, Frizzi with gavel, Phil McMillen; left back Gordon Cooke, two unknowns, Bill Kirchgessner, Charles Shutler, and Clem Estep. (Frizzi Collection circa 1960)

Chapter Seven

A New Home in West Bellaire

Eighth Grade, High School and College

As our family grew during the 1950s, we had finally outgrown the little house above the family grocery store on Washington Street. The home which my father had known as a boy, and which I had known for the past 11 years, was just too small. With everyone getting older, my parents began to find homes in the area with enough rooms for four sons. They looked at homes at Overlook Court, high above West Bellaire, and Belview Heights overlooking Gravel Hill. They settled upon West Bellaire. The home they chose was a new home that was built by a man named William Makofsky for his wife and sons. His unfortunate and untimely death left his wife without the means to keep it, and she offered it for sale to my parents. The house was made of brick, had three bedrooms, a couple of bathrooms, dining room, large living room, and kitchen. The living room had a fireplace which was not just an imitation. It really worked! There was a big yard, and garage under the house. The most appealing part of this home, however, was the basement which we never had on Washington Street. I remember how excited Mom and Dad were when we all drove to West Bellaire to look at it. Soon after we moved, another brother was born, and this was the home where our family lived during the remaining grade school and high school years.

Another important feature of this location was that it was close to West Bellaire School, so my brothers and I could walk to school each day. No more bus riding until eighth grade and high school. There were many of our schoolmates that lived in West Bellaire, so we would still see the same faces after school as we saw during school. The home overlooked Riley's field, the railroad tracks of the B & O Railroad, and my maternal Grandparents home. George and Neva Robinson, my mother's parents, lived along the Bellaire Neffs Road, and along the railroad tracks leading west out of Bellaire. As kids, we spent a lot of time at their home growing up, and this move placed them within walking distance. We were all very excited to make the move to this new home. In May of 1963, we packed up and said goodbye to the house that I had known for the past 11 years. Although we would not be living above the store any longer, I knew that I would still be working at the grocery store with my Dad and Grandfather. In a way, I was getting a new house, but I would still have a close connection to the old one. If I needed to work, I could ride the bus from school with all the kids from Washington Street. I could hop off the bus with them at the same bus stop by the store.

At age 11, I was working more than just on Friday nights. The extra time gave me spending money for hobbies that I enjoyed. During this period in my life, my passion was building models. I especially liked model airplanes of the WWII vintage, many of which my Dad remembered from his days in the Navy. I kept quite a collection of airplanes on the chest of drawers in my bedroom. Collecting rocks was another hobby. I got enjoyment trying to identify them using the popular Field Guide to Rock Collecting. I started looking for fossils as a part of that hobby. There was a whole series of field guide handbooks for rock collecting, star gazing, and stamp collecting, and I spent a lot of time reading these books. No longer the 'Blue Bird' that I had been in the first grade, these books appealed to me. Having a job and earning some cash allowed me to grow in these hobbies and interests.

Rock collecting was also a hobby of my Father. His collecting, however, was not for the purpose of identifying them, or testing them for hardness, or distinguishing them as sedimentary, metamorphic, or igneous. His were big rocks, not little ones like I collected. My Dad's enjoyment came from using rocks with his hands to build something. Our new home was situated above Birch Street with a sloping yard, and my father saw this as an opportunity to terrace the ground with stone walls. Brother Dick and I, being the oldest of the brothers, would be summoned by Dad to go with him on his rock collecting trips. In an old truck that my Grandfather Robinson owned equipped with a cable winch, the first few years at the new home were spent loading heavy sandstones suitable for building walls. Dad was always on the lookout for buildings that were being torn down where he might scavenge a few foundation stones. Some of these stones were small enough for Dick and I to pick up together and throw into the bed of the pickup truck. Others were so large that only Dad was able to handle them, and then, sometimes only with our help. Once the truck was loaded, Dad would drive us home and we would unload the truck. We always unloaded at the place where Dad had some construction project ongoing.

There was an old spring house located on the property that had been in my mother's family for more than a century. This spring house was made entirely out of sandstone and had been built my Great-Great Grandfather George Oxley Robinson. Now completely abandoned, the spring house stood with its roof collapsed inside the stone walls. Dad decided that he, brother Dick, and I, would dismantle the walls and salvage the stone. This went on for several years on many Saturday afternoons. The method used was to pull down as much of the wall as possible so that the individual stones would separate from one another on the ground. To accomplish this, we used the cable and the winch on the truck. Dad would back the truck up to the wall, and the cable on the winch would be unwound. We would throw the end of the cable over the top of the exposed sandstone wall. Dad would use a sledge to drive a steel bar into the wall on the inside of the spring house a few courses of stone from the top of the wall. The cable would be attached to the steel bar. Back in the truck, Dick and I took turns cranking the winch until the cable was taut. Once we had achieved a tight cable, we would try to pull the wall down. If this was not accomplished using just the winch, Dad would start the truck and slowly pull forward just a few feet pulling down the stone wall behind the truck. Then, the work of loading the individual sandstone blocks would begin.

On one occasion, both Dick and I were in the truck bed cranking the winch. Dad was standing on the ground outside the bed of the truck. The wall was loose enough for us to pull it down without moving the truck. As the wall collapsed on the ground, a nest of black snakes had tumbled onto the ground by his feet. He could not leap tall buildings like Superman, but Dad leaped into the back of the pickup truck from a standing position at the sight of those snakes. He never liked snakes at all. We all stayed in the bed of the truck as we watched the black snakes crawl away before anyone jumped down on the ground. One by one, we loaded the dislodged stone, which had been their home, into the bed of the truck. These stones were to be for Dad to use in his many building projects.

Eighth Grade Begins

When I began eighth grade, the West Bellaire School that I had known for the past eight years was now history. The eighth grade would be in Bellaire in a building called Central. This building was really the first high school built in Bellaire in the early 1900s to accommodate the overflowing classrooms of those seeking a high school education. When the new Bellaire High School was built in 1925, the old high school building became Central and housed the eighth graders from all over the city. This was a new experience, with many new faces, many new teachers, and many new challenges.

I was assigned to the home room of Mr. James Griffin, who taught history. He was a likeable gentleman, very knowledgeable and interesting. He did not give tests, just a daily quiz. The quiz consisted of just two questions. If you got both right, you were given three points. If you got one right, you got one point. If you got neither right, you got zero points, and the dubious distinction of being a 'double dumbbell,' as Mr. Griffin called it. He was a wonderful teacher who made history easy to learn. I was always interested in history, so his class came easy for me. Mr. Marinelli was our science teacher, and Mr. Roger Toohill taught English. Miss Roth, a tiny little lady who kept her hair in a bun on the back of her head, was our math teacher. She never called me by my first name. It was always 'Frizzi' when she called on me. She was old I thought, and when my father told me that he also had her in school when he was a boy, it occurred to me that she was very old! The one teacher, however, who was absolutely frightening to me was Mrs. Esther Witten who taught Literature. Now literature and reading I really enjoyed, but Mrs. Witten, who was married to a Common Pleas Court Judge, always had a scowl on her face whenever you entered her room. She could yell loudly, but always with a certain dignity. She scared the hell out of me! I must say, however, that the only redeeming thing from her class I recall was the required memorization of the Bellaire Fight Song and Alma Mater. This we had to do for Mrs. Witten before we entered the halls of BHS.

Now, eighth grade was a time for growing up a bit, and exploring things that you could not do in grade school. One thing that I noticed about this time was that girls started to become more interesting than they had been at West Bellaire School. Meeting new girls from all over town provided a realization that there was something mysterious about the new girls that you had not known since Kindergarten. Some had gone to Gravel Hill or First Ward within the city of Bellaire, or Key Ridge and Neffs Elementary from the country. This was a time when all guys my age started to care about how they looked in ways we never had before. I was a shy kid, not very forward, and generally unfamiliar with all things of and concerning the opposite sex. I had learned the basics from Orphy Klempa in grade school but was still curious about things even Orphy did not know.

I had often gone to the Bellaire News Agency, which was along the sidewalk on 32nd Street in the Bellaire City Building, as a boy living on Washington Street. Dick and I would sometimes walk downtown and head to Murphy's where we went downstairs to the toy section. Murphy had a great model collection. I liked airplanes and Dick liked automobiles. Sometimes on the way home, we stopped at this bookstore for comic books. Bellaire News had a great selection of magazines of all types. Well, one Saturday night, I was in town by myself, and I decided that the time had come when I should take that first step that all young men contemplate at about my age. This purchase would be my first 'Playboy' magazine. Unlike some boys who had a father that maintained a secret stash of Playboy magazines, my father did not. So I had to be resourceful, and take things into my own hands, so to speak and acquire one. I decided to adopt the same kind of technique that I had learned from Johnny Beltrondo, which was to wait until the place was not crowded, and then go in and ask for 'one of those in a sack.' I stood on the sidewalk opposite the News Agency and waited until no one was there. Finally, I was able to muster the confidence needed, and I crossed 32nd Street and went inside.

There was an older lady working behind the counter. I had considered and rehearsed what I would say before I even walked across the street. I truly believed that no one was in the place except the clerk. I looked around a minute, and when the clerk came from the back of the store, she asked me if she could get me something. I chose a direct response, well thought out and to the point. "I want to buy a Playboy," I responded. Her next words were equally to the point as she said, "You aren't old enough to buy a Playboy!"

My hopes were dashed. Curses! Foiled I was! Suddenly, and without warning, I heard a big booming voice shout from the back of the store behind the shelving, "Give that boy a Playboy! He is old enough." I recognized this voice immediately even though I had not yet seen the speaker. It was the voice of Harry Sidon, who lived in West Bellaire behind the home of my Grandparents George and Neva Robinson. As a little kid, I used to hang out at his garage watching him make wooden pallets. I also used to play with his little beagle dog that was named "Colonel."

Oh my, the dilemma I was now in! Not only could I not purchase the magazine, I had to worry that Harry would tell my Grandparents George and Neva that I had been there trying to buy a 'nudie book.' But Harry was genuinely sincere that I should have the latest issue of Hugh Hefner's publication of beautiful naked women. I felt like running out of the news stand, but Harry once again told the clerk to "sell that boy the book!" To my astonishment, she did and laid on the counter before me the magazine that I had longed to possess. I plopped my three quarters on the counter and asked her to put the magazine in a sack, just like Johnny would have insisted! So with my 'one of those in a sack,' I offered thanks, and hurriedly left for home. I do not remember the month of the issue, nor do I remember who the centerfold was. I will always remember this incident, and my adult friend, Harry Sidon, who assisted me in my first real adventure in learning about the opposite sex. For seventy five cents I cannot think of a better deal I made during eighth grade.

With my sack in hand, I walked out onto the sidewalk along 32nd Street, walked past the fire station and the new Mellott Library Building toward Brewery Hill. This was where Hamilton Street headed toward West Bellaire at the site of the old Matz Brewery. I stopped here and waited for a passing car to pick me up as I was going to 'thumb' my way home. The Brewery sidewalk was where everyone who needed a ride stood waiting to hitch a ride to West Bellaire, or Neffs, or possibly as far as Key. Usually there were several people waiting here at the same time. When the cars passed, we would hold out our hand with the thumb pointed up to signal that we needed a ride. There were so many people that passed this way during early evening that within ten minutes, you had someone stopping to give you that lift. This was a time when we were not concerned for our safety, and the drivers who stopped never gave a second thought that we would cause them harm. Thumbing today is not seen a lot, because young kids today seem to have cars that back in the 50s and 60s none of us had. Safety, however, is probably the biggest reason. Today, you cannot be sure about the hitchhiker or the driver of the car.

During eighth grade, all the boys seemed to begin to care more about how they dressed. I decided to have my trouser legs pegged. Pegging was a way of tapering the inseam so that at the ankle, the trouser leg was tight. Mom and Dad talked to Aunt Ange DiNardo in Shadyside about making the alterations, and we dropped off my new pants for the purpose of pegging them. Aunt Ange was my Grandmother Philomena's younger sister. As a little boy we used to visit her in Shadyside. Ange and her husband John had a chicken coop in the back yard, and one of the memorable experiences was going out to look at the chickens when we were in grade school. She pegged my pants, and so I began wearing them to school. Another important item of apparel that boys wanted, besides pegged pants, was penny loafers. Once we had them, the next stop was going to be during our lunch hour to have them enhanced a bit. Metal cleats were available at any one of the shoe repair shops in downtown Bellaire, and so I stopped to have my heels equipped with these noise makers. I went to Norman Papola's Shoe Repair on Guernsey Street. Norman was crippled who was friends with my Dad. He put a metal cleat on each heel. We had to be careful in school not to make a lot of noise when walking since they could be loud on a tile floor. They also were damaging to wooden floors making scuffs and scratches. I had mine only for a few days before one of the teachers caught me with them. The routine was to give us a screwdriver and make us go into the hallway to take them off our shoes before we could re-enter the classroom.

I think the most prized item, however, occurred when I got my new pair of Chuck Taylor Converse Tennis Shoes. The best were the ones called All-Stars. These were not your average tennis shoe like Keds, PF Flyers, or Red Ball Jets that you got every summer when in grade school. Converse was a canvas tennis shoe that lasted! We all wanted them, and so Mom took Brother Dick and I down to Mendelson's Clothing Store in Bellaire to get our first pair. We used them in gym class at school where we could wear them indoors.

My hairstyle in grade school was the typical 'butch' or 'flat top.' This required the use of butch wax. Butch wax came in a cylinder stick that was filled with a pink looking wax that you applied to the hair line above your forehead. This wax could prop up your short hair in the front. I did not want this look when I got to the seventh grade. Dad told me that the next time I went to the barber, tell him I wanted a 'full dress cut.' My friend Orphy had a full dress cut style. Now the transition from 'flat top' to 'full dress' took a few cuts to get it looking as it should. Popular at the time was a slicked look, and the most popular hair cream for the full dress man was Brylcreem. Kookie on 77 Sunset Strip was a Brylcreem guy, and so was Dick Clark of American Bandstand. The saying was that a "little dab will do ya," and then "watch out, the girls will all pursue ya!" Brylcreem never seemed to have that effect when I wore it, but hey, it made my hair look like I wanted.

Because we were now in the eighth grade, an announcement was made that boys who wanted to be on the football team should report to practice on a certain day and time. Naturally, I wanted to follow in my father's footsteps after listening to his many stories. I arranged to skip work with my father, since I would be at practice after school instead of coming to the store. Now before eighth grade, I played football and basketball with my friends in West Bellaire for fun. Sometimes we would entertain kids from town who would come to West Bellaire for a game of tackle football, and we would sometimes visit them in town. There was a vacant lot by Elm Street that we used for our football games and I and brother Dick would spend a lot of time engaged in these friendly games. I really enjoyed playing basketball and spent hours down at the West Bellaire School playground for pickup games. I was having fun by participation in the sport. I went to high school football games with my grade school friend Richie Wasko. I watched games on television from the old AFL, had a football card collection of famous players, and knew and understood the basics of the game. The fun of participation seemed to change, however, when I went out for eighth grade football.

All eighth grade boys went to Nelson Field. Under the visitors' bleachers were big boxes containing practice uniforms, and we all pulled out musty-smelling pants and jerseys. My pants were too big, but that was all there was to pick from. We all did best to find something that would fit us. We ran laps and did calisthenics. Because no one really knew who would perform best, we simply tried out for positions. I am not sure why, but I tried out for quarterback. I was not big or strong enough to play a line position. The only thing you had to do was throw a few passes to the coach and be able to run fast. I recall that I came in fourth place in a footrace, so this qualified me to be on the 4th string team. We had tackling drills, we had blocking drills, and we began learning plays, but it seemed like most of the time we were standing around. After a month or so, I came to the realization that I was spending a lot of time after school during practice, when I could be doing other things that I enjoyed. Practice was taking up time that I used for studying or working. I also realized that my modicum of athletic ability, which I possessed, would ultimately doom me to 'ride the wild oak.' Riding the wild oak was a term that simply meant you were going to sit on the bench most of the time. I was young for my class, and I was a smaller, pudgy kid going through puberty while many of my teammates had already passed beyond adolescence. With an understanding of my ability and the knowledge of the time being committed after school for practice, I felt compelled to decide what I should do. At 13 years of age, I decided that I did not want to continue to play football.

Now this would not have been a difficult decision if my father had not played football himself. He did play, and he was good. In my heart, I felt that I would be a disappointment to my Dad by choosing to quit the team. The only way to make the decision would be to talk to my father. This is where my father's rock pile comes back into this story. The early October day that I chose to have this discussion with my father I still remember very well. He was working in our front yard building stone steps with some of the sandstone that we had gathered a few weeks before. I went to him and told him I wanted to quit eighth grade football. He was working with a pick and shovel preparing a resting place for the next stone he was about to place. I felt like he already knew what I was there to discuss with him. He did not stop working, but he told me, "When I was your age, I did not get to play either, but I stuck it out and eventually did play." He continued by saying that, "If you do quit, you won't ever get to play." Dad did not pressure me into making any particular decision, but rather told me that "It is up to you to decide what you want to do." Perhaps he was disappointed with the decision that I ultimately made. I did quit the team, and so perhaps that made me a quitter. Personally, I believed it was just making a choice. The choice was between playing a game, and something that might serve me better in future years. I chose the latter of the two. My Dad never spoke to me about that decision and never tried to pressure me into changing my mind. In fact, we never spoke of it again. I have always felt that I disappointed him.

One Saturday night, I was working at the store with Dad. He needed to do something in the storeroom across the street, and told me he would return when he was finished. I was minding the store by myself. All was quiet except for the radio behind me as I stood at the counter. Suddenly, I remember looking up to find three BHS letterman jackets standing in front of me. I recognized these senior players wearing the jackets which bore their names and that they were football players on the varsity squad. One of them approached the counter, and asked me if we had cold beer, and what kind. Now there were two immediate problems presented. The first was that they were not old enough to purchase beer. The second was that I was not old enough to sell them beer even if they were old enough to drink it. The dilemma became one of acquiescence, or telling them no. Should I call my Dad to come back to wait on them? Should I tell them that I wasn't old enough to sell them beer? Or should I have asked them for ID? What should I do? To this underclassman, it was a difficult decision based entirely on the pressure that can be imposed by one's peers.

My better judgment was clouded. Being in the presence of these 'Gods of the Gridiron' with their Red and Black jackets which appeared like the armor of a knight standing before me, I succumbed to my better judgment. They were seniors in high school, and I was a lowly eighth grader, truly blinded by their presence before me. They wanted a little beer to celebrate a victory earlier in the day, a victory that I had witnessed. I decided to get them twenty four bottles of beer from the cooler, and put them into a cardboard box. They paid me the price of the beer. I think it was Carlings Black Label. The transaction being completed, hurriedly off they went. Their coach Don Ault found out that some of his players had been drinking, and the threat of trouble loomed. Someone must have reported this to my Dad, and the next day he asked me if any football players came into the store, and what they wanted. I confessed to my error in judgment, and Dad reminded me that I should not be selling beer to anyone. Now, in the law we would say that this was 'harmless error.' No one was injured, no one was harmed, everyone got home safely, and therefore, this transaction was somewhat without consequence. The memory today can best be expressed by saying all of us were fortunate to escape any punishment for our youthful errors.

Four years later, I and a few buddies would do the same thing. We drank some beer on a dead end road just talking and making memories of our own. I guess we were not any different than those football players I had sold the beer to that night when I fell prey to the peer pressures of growing up.

"Your Grandfather is a Millionaire"

I resumed working regular hours at the Grocery Store during the eighth grade and as I began High School. My Grandfather Abe maintained the rigorous schedule of opening early morning each day, and my Dad would join him later in the morning. I would take the bus from the high school heading to West Bellaire, but instead of going home, I would get off the bus when it stopped in front of the store. Dad would generally work until about five, and then he would leave me and either Greg or Tom to work until close. I always tried to have my homework done during study hall during the day. This gave me freedom to work without the need to do homework after work had ended.

We were not always busy, so there was time for talking. I remember one time Greg and I were talking about cars, and about how much they would cost. I remember telling Greg that I liked the Chevrolet Chevelle, but it would probably cost too much for me to afford. Greg said to me, "Just get your Grandfather to buy it for you." I responded that I could not ask him to do that, to which Greg told me emphatically, "Shit Danny, your Grandfather is a millionaire!"

Now this came as a shock to me. While it was true that my Grandpa Frizzi drove a Lincoln Continental, and lived in a newer home high on the hill in West Bellaire, I never looked at him that way. He was a respected businessman, serving on the Board of Directors of the Farmer's & Merchant's Bank and Associated Grocers, but he was never looked upon by the family as being anything but a hard working grocer. He had worked all his life very hard, and built whatever wealth he had by the sweat of his own brow, and not others. I decided to ask my father about my Grandpa Frizzi, the reputed 'millionaire.' Dad told me that this was something that people had always told him when he was a boy growing up on

Washington Street. Dad said, "Grandpa isn't poor, but he is far from a millionaire." I never discussed this with Greg again but felt sure that he was wrong about his assessment after speaking with my dad.

My Grandpa Frizzi was frugal. He was not prone to waste something that still had useful life. He was able to make do with less having been through both the Depression and War. He had little as a small boy growing up in Italy, and from these humble roots, he knew the hardships that come from poverty. Once when I was in grade school, on an especially cold morning, my Mom sent me down to the store before it was time to catch the bus. She had told me to get a pair of gloves to wear. There was a rack of gloves in the store, so I went to the rack and took a pair. My Grandfather quickly took the gloves from my hands and put them back on the rack. He did not really give me an explanation, or try to understand why I picked them from the rack. So that morning I went to school without gloves. I guess that my Grandpa was used to doing without when he was my age, and in his eyes, I would survive without the gloves that morning. He was right, I did. But the next morning Mom made sure I had them!

When I worked with Grandpa Frizzi, he enjoyed talking about his family in Italy. He told me many stories about growing up in the farming region of Umbria and growing and harvesting olives and grapes. His family members were not wealthy estate holders. They had chickens, and some farm animals. He related how as a boy, he went to a small school in Piccione, and had chores that he and his brother Artemio had to attend to. He also had an older Sister Olimpia. Michael Presutti, whose grandfather lived next to us on Washington Street, was a grandson of Olimpia. That made Michael and I cousins. One story that Grandpa Frizzi told me was how his family gave eggs to the church they attended because the family had little money or anything else to tithe. A comment was made that 'someone left eggs' at the church. My Grandfather told me it was the priest. Perhaps it was just a harmless comment that had been made in jest, but Grandpa Frizzi told me it was unkind and disrespectful to his family. I do not know if this had anything to do with his disaffection for the Catholic Church, however, he seemed to indicate that it did. Grandpa Frizzi never tried to influence me on religious matters. He avoided talking about his unspoken reasons for his own feelings.

However, I feel so sad as an adult that this will always be a mystery with many questions for which the answers will never be known.

Most of the stories that he told me, however, were about the beauty of the countryside, the history of Italy, and those Italians who brought fame to their immigrant cousins. Naturally, his hero Garibaldi was always a story he liked to tell. But he also enjoyed telling me about other famous Italians. Two whom he often spoke of were men who were his contemporaries. One of those he talked about was the great Italian opera vocalist Enrico Caruso. He was one of the most important tenors in Europe before becoming popular in the United States. I remember perusing my Grandfather's phonograph collection one time and finding a dozen or more 78 rpm Victrola records of his recordings for performances of Caruso. "O Sole Mio," "Santa Lucia" and my Grandfather's favorite, "Vesti la Giubba," the story of the clown who must laugh for the crowd while he cries on the inside. Caruso died in 1921. He told me often that "Caruso was the greatest singer to ever live."

Guglielmo Marconi, credited with being the first to send and receive a radio signal, was another 'great man' according to my Grandfather. In 1909, just two years after Grandpa Frizzi first arrived in America, Marconi shared the Nobel Prize for his work in wireless telegraphy. In 1901, his work to send and receive signals across the Atlantic Ocean set the stage for further development of the radio. Men like my Grandfather felt pride in this discovery, and his countrymen that were credited with it.

Piccione was the small village just outside of Perugia where Grandpa Frizzi was born. Perugia is an ancient town that dates to the Etruscan confederation before the time of Christ, and it became a center for artists and painting. The university at Perugia dates to the middle ages. My Grandfather told me about the buildings by saying, "They are very much older than anything you see here in Bellaire." Piccione is only ten miles from the heart of the city of Perugia, the capital of the Province. Yet, his knowledge of the country was also based upon his points of departure when coming to the United States. He had seen the port cities of Genoa and Naples, and all cities in between. These great cities had massive structures dating hundreds of years old. "Italians," he told me, "are great builders." His oft repeated story about the Leaning Tower of Pisa was his way of saying even that which appeared flawed was really a masterpiece example of great architecture. I think that my own father got that gene for building things through his Italian bloodline. Dad used to like to say that he could just look at a string pulled between two points and determine if it was level. I challenged him once, with a bubble string level, and found he was right, the string was level. Dad always said that, "I have a bubble in my head, so I don't always need that level, I can tell just by looking!" This knack for building was a trait that he credited to his Italian ancestry.

 Grandpa Frizzi suffered from congestive heart failure during the mid-1960s. His second wife, Bernice, passed away in July of 1964. This left him alone in the home he built in West Bellaire. Late one evening, he called our house in distress and was unable to breathe. My Father raced to the house, and Grandpa was rushed to the hospital. He did not seem comfortable living there alone when he recovered. He lived with my aunt Kathryn for several weeks while he was recuperating but he wanted to return to the work he had known since he was a young man. While he was recuperating with aunt Kathryn he returned to nearby Piney Fork where his life in American had begun. When he visited Piney Fork, he led a tour of where the mine had been that he and his brother Artemio had toiled for a coal miner's wage. He found the general store and the old man who had operated it. Although my Grandfather recognized the old man, the feeble old storekeeper did not know my Grandfather. Aunt Kathryn recalled how this trip to where his life as an Italian immigrant began, "was an exciting day for my Dad!"

 As he recuperated, Grandpa Frizzi yearned to be closer to the store in Bellaire. He sold his home on the mystery mound that he had built in 1948. He moved into our home in West Bellaire, and the bedroom that Dick and I occupied was vacated so that Grandpa Frizzi could come to live with us. He funded the cost of constructing the additional bedroom that was added to our home, and when it was completed, Dick and I moved into it. Our Grandfather continued to work, with heart medication taken every day. He would not work the whole day and would come home to our house early for dinner at 5:00 o'clock p.m. Each morning, about five o'clock we would hear him rise to begin the work day. When he returned to our home for dinner, he would spend time with us until bedtime. Most of the afternoon and evening, he would spend in our living room playing solitaire on our coffee table next to the couch. During the summer, he often could be found on our side porch in the shade of the afternoon. He would retire to bed earlier than the rest of us, so that he could rise early in the morning to open the store as he had done since the first store on Hamilton Street was opened half a century before. On Sunday, after we attended church, he would invite us to dinner at the Mayflower Restaurant in Shadyside. On other days, he would visit Aunt Kathryn in Mt. Pleasant, Ohio. Other than this day of rest, the Sabbath, my Grandfather was always working at the store.

My Grandfather was not a deeply religious man in any traditional sense, but he was a good man. His disagreements with the Catholic faith afforded him the opportunity to seek some other faith but he never did. I remember as a young man a discussion regarding Biblical teaching in which my Grandfather participated. One thing that became clear was that he did not accept a literal interpretation of the Bible. Our family always hoped he had some belief in a Deity. His roots in the Masonic Lodge were founded on the principles of equality and freedom, and a place in the great design for life that comes from our Creator. The Masonic Order did not impose any regimen for religious belief, and any member could pursue their own religious beliefs outside the Lodge. Only my Grandfather and God knew if he reconciled his beliefs. My Grandpa Frizzi had many friends, both Catholic and Protestant alike, and even though he shunned any organized religious affiliation, this never prevented his many friendships with others who were a part of them.

Early on August 8, 1967, while getting ready to leave our home to open the store on Washington Street, he suffered a massive heart attack. Efforts by my Dad and Mom to revive him failed. I was thirteen years old at the time, and this sudden death at our home was a difficult one for our family. This came so sudden to all of us. My brother Dick and I had just returned from spending a month away in Houston with my Aunt Sue and Uncle Al. We did not have that time to spend with him before his passing. His funeral was widely attended by many of his customers, fellow grocers, friends and relatives. The Co-Masonic Lodge No. 542 of Bellaire held services. My Dad asked our preacher, Reverend Ralph Hudson, of the West Bellaire Methodist Church, which we attended, to officiate his funeral services. So many people attended his funeral, and all had stories to tell.

One of the old Italian friends of my Grandfather approached my Dad and Aunt Kathryn while standing at the casket. His topic for discussion was about selling my Grandfather's bank stock in the Farmers & Merchants Bank. He told my Father he, "just wanted to be the first to ask, since others probably would too." We wondered if he was there to pay his respects, or to make a 'tender offer' for the stock. Others, however, told my father and Aunt Kathryn many stories about the old days with Abe and Minnie operating the grocery stores on Hamilton Street, on Union Street, and finally at the store on West Washington Street. He was laid to rest in the Greenwood Cemetery Mausoleum beside my Grandmother Philomena, mother of his children. His second wife, Bernice, was also buried here. Grandpa did not die a 'pauper,' but he was far from being that 'millionaire' that Greg Byles had told me about. Grandpa Frizzi, as his Grandchildren called him, and Pabby as my father and Aunt Kathryn called him, gave us something more valuable than his modest estate. He gave us those wonderful stories he told, which we will always remember. He taught us to be proud of our Italian heritage. He gave us his work ethic and demonstrated in life his belief that there is nothing shameful about being successful in business. These are beliefs which strengthened him in life, and that he instilled in us for our own lives.

My Dad was now alone in the operation of the store. I was going to be a freshman in high school at the time. My work schedule at the store increased. My Mom worked at the Farmers & Merchants Bank as a teller, and she would soon transfer to the Morris Plan Bank & Trust in Wheeling. My younger brothers had a paper route that had been handed down through their older brothers. As the oldest of five sons, it was obvious Dad was now more dependent on me to work with him at the store.

Christmas Time At the Store

The holiday season was always a special time at our store on Washington Street. We sold Christmas Trees, and exotic fishes and meats that customers ordered for the holidays. We always sold those Christmas light bulbs that have been replaced by LEDs of today. Some were the little tiny ones used on strings of lights that would all go out if one bulb went bad. The others were the standard incandescent bulbs that you are finding harder to locate these days with each passing year.

We sold several kinds of Christmas trees. One type was the 'Scotch Pine' tree with longer needles and more likely to prick you. We also sold a softer variety that was called 'White Pine.' One of the popular types, however, was the 'Balsam Pine' with shorter needles, and space between the branches that made decorating the tree very easy. Ornaments could be hung easily from the branches of the Balsam without worry that they would fall off. When our delivery of pine trees came, my Dad had them loaded into the garage next to the storeroom. That is where we would normally park the family automobile, but to make room, we vacated the garage to make room for the trees during December.

When Dad had the sidewalk replaced in front of the garage and storeroom, he asked the workmen to put into the cement steel pipes that could be covered with a steel cap when not in use. The caps were flush with the cement grade of the sidewalk. The pipes were spaced about four feet apart, and each pipe was of a different size. Some were three inches, and some were four inches, and others were six inches. His purpose for the pipes was to display the trees more easily at Christmas time. When the trees came in, the steel caps were popped off of the pipes, and a tree trunk could be placed into the pipe. This eliminated the need to build the wooden bases, which were prone to fall over as automobiles whizzed by on their way to town. The sidewalk was somewhat cramped by so many pine trees, but no one ever seemed to complain. After all, it was the Christmas Season! I enjoyed selling the trees for Christmas to the families that stopped by to pick one that they liked. "That one is too bare on this side," some would say. "This one is too tall for the ceiling in the living room," I would often hear. Actually, those with an older home usually had ceilings that were eight to ten feet high, so we made sure that some taller ones were displayed. If we made a sale, the next step was to tie the tree down to the automobile. If the car had a rack on top, it was easy. Many went into the trunk with part of the tree hanging out the back. In the 50s and 60s, automobiles were favored with much larger trunks than are found in automobiles today. Trunk loading required special care, since you did not want the truck lid to damage the tree on the way home. By far the easiest was loading a pickup truck, where the tree was cradled between the side boards.

Now I always had a contest with my father on who could sell the most trees. I can remember riding the school bus home from school and jumping off at the store to go to work. The first question I always asked Dad was, "How many did you sell today, Dad?" We kept a running account of each tree sold, and he was usually able to sell more during the day, so I would have to try to catch up with him that evening. Dad was a carpenter with these trees, and if he found a bare spot, he would take a branch from a similar tree, and drill a hole where the bare spot was, and fill it in with the branch. After all, selling trees is all about 'Presentation' to the customer. Some trees were badly broken in transit, and with those we would cut off the branches to make wreaths, or pine rope. Dad always judged well as to the number of trees to order. I remember many times selling the trees right up until Christmas Eve. Naturally, the price went down the closer it was to Christmas. Some people could not afford much of a tree, and when they brought their little ones to pick one, the price became what they could afford to pay. How could a child not have a tree on Christmas? We sold anywhere between one hundred to one hundred fifty trees each season at this little store on Washington Street.

Back in the store, the excitement of Christmas could be found in the meats and fish that would be sold. While we sold turkeys for Thanksgiving, hams were by far the customer's choice at Christmas. Sugardale would bring us boxes of hams based upon the order that we would turn in. During December, we began taking orders for hams listing each customer, and the size and kind of ham. Some customers preferred a fully-cooked semi-boneless ham. Others preferred those that were boneless. About two or three hams came in each box, and we would need to weigh them so that we could match the ham with the customer's order. Sugardale would make these deliveries and we would need to call the customers to let them know their order was in. Each ham would be identified by the customer's name to make certain that we were delivering to them the ham they had ordered. Dad always ordered extra hams for sale in the store for those walk-in customers who had not already placed their order.

The Italian customers, however, would sometimes order something that was different. 'Pesce', or fish, was often requested. Now the fish was not something that came in a package, it was fresh from the seafood market in Pittsburgh, Bellaire or Wheeling. Now this was not just fish that was sold throughout the year. This fish was special for the holiday. Many Italians prepared fish on Christmas Eve for the traditional "Feast of the

Seven Fishes". I remember one Christmas season when working with my dad and Grandfather, a delivery came into the store. Dad was checking the order, and I joined with him by inspecting the seafood that was delivered. The boxes were filled with crushed ice. One of the first items we inspected was an eel, long, sleek and colored silvery gray. The head and fins were still on the eel. The eel had some teeth along the inside of its mouth and looked somewhat menacing. We had a container filled with liquid and a single octopus. The octopus seemed to have little form when it was removed from the container. The eight legs and head flattened out on the table surface we placed it on. We had baccala, which was dried and salted cod fish. There were waxed boxes of shrimp, and waxed boxes of calamari, or squid. Also contained in the order were sea scallops on the shell. All of this was fresh from the market and the customer placing the order would be required to clean all of the seafood when preparing it for cooking. The squid would require removal of the ink bladder and the head, together with the beak, or mouth. The eel would need cleaned as well, and the octopus looked to me like it would need a lot of work to make it edible. The customer was called, and they promptly came to pick up their order. This would become the family meal on Christmas Eve.

As December and the Christmas season came to a close, we always placed into every customer's paper sack of groceries a color calendar for the following year. These calendars usually had a scene of Americana, much like the Norman Rockwell paintings that everyone seemed familiar with. Scenes of a small boy and his dogs, or a little girl and her kittens, or a family together at dinner were always shown on the face of the calendars. Each calendar had individual pages for the months of the coming year, and the heading was Frizzi's AG Food Center, 2783 Washington Street, Bellaire, Ohio. The older calendars before my father entered the business proclaimed 'Compliments of Abraham Frizzi Groceries of Quality." The telephone number during the 1940s was #217 which appeared on the calendars. During the 1950s, the exchange became OR 6 with the telephone number ending with 6386. This telephone number could be easily found by customers when an order needed to be placed simply by looking at the wall calendar. The calendars were a way of telling our customers that we appreciated their business throughout the year at our little grocery store. We always held the hope that we would continue to see them as customers in the new year to come.

Last-minute orders always came in. Someone always needed something that they had forgotten. We closed the store early so that Dad could be with his own family on Christmas Eve. We always went to our Robinson Grandparent's home on Christmas Eve, which my brothers and I always looked forward to. On Christmas Day, we would open our gifts at home, and then we would go to my Grandfather Frizzi's house. Here we would be joined by my Aunt Kathryn, Uncle Phil and our cousins Steve, Kathi and Gary. We were truly fortunate to be able to have our Christmas with both sets of Grandparents.

Our Delivery Routes

I began driving when I was 15. A driving permit was required, and driver's training school was something that I took during summer to be able to get the permit in September to begin driving. Driver's training school was taught by Reyman Bonar, an elderly teacher at Bellaire High School. The classes were held in Room 225, the large study hall on the second floor of the high school. It was hot and humid in July, and we had to endure the class all day for an entire week. Mr. Bonar had a peculiar characteristic we noticed during these lectures. He would frequently tell us something to remember, and then he would say, "Believe me." For instance, he might tell us that when on a hill you should always put the parking brake on first before you put the car in park. Then he would finish with, "Believe me." We counted how many times he said that during the morning sessions, and I remember it was about eighteen times. In the afternoon, we would count to see if he would top that number. He did teach us many useful things during week, and to be honest, I really did believe him on the driving tips he gave us.

Once the driver training class was completed, I was able to get a driving permit and do some driving. What an experience that was. Rudy Sharkey, the football coach, was the instructor. He had four students in the car at the same time. I don't recall who the others were except for one. Richard Vingia was on the football team, and Coach Sharkey knew him well. When it was his turn to drive, he was really petrified. I remember him driving and coming to a curve in the road, but simply not turning the steering wheel. "Rich, you have to turn the steering to make the car go around the turn" Sharkey yelled out to him. When he didn't turn the steering wheel, the Coach leaned over and with his own hand turned the wheel, and said, "Rich, this car won't steer itself, you have to do it!" When it was my turn, I drove fairly well I think. After all, I had been doing a little driving with my mom and her sister Peggy. Driver's training was fun, and Coach Sharky was demanding but gave us confidence with each lesson. Even Rich was doing better by the time we finished the class.

Now, my dad had purchased a 1960 Chevrolet Bel Air, and this became the car that I started driving. This car was roomy. It did not have power steering. The engine was a V-8 283 cubic inch engine that was such a good engine for the Chevrolet models. There was so much room under the hood that changing a water pump, or fuel pump, or spark plugs was an easy job. I began puttering around with basic maintenance items. My friends and I called this car the 'Six-Oh.' By the time I was scheduled to take my driving test in St. Clairsville, Dad and Mom had purchased a 1968 Chevrolet Caprice Classic station wagon. It was big, but it had power steering. I decided to reject the prevailing philosophy to take a small car to the driving test to make the parking segment easier. I took the Caprice with the power steering and had no problems parking between the posts. After I got my driver's license, I was working at the store with my Dad one evening. My Mom was returning from work at the bank, and she stopped by driving the 1968 Caprice Station Wagon. Dad started out the door with her, and he turned to me and tossed me the car keys to the green Chevy, and said, "You close tonight and bring the car home." Wow! This was exciting! My solo flight, so to speak, in the big 'Six-Oh!'

I used both cars to make grocery deliveries when working at the store on Washington Street. The deliveries were always preceded by an order being phoned in by the customer. The exception was Mrs. Henry who lived in West Bellaire. Every Friday about 9 p.m. and just before closing, Dad would place a call to Mrs. Henry to get her order for Saturday delivery. The phone greeting was always the same. Mrs. Henry would answer the phone, and my Dad would then say, "Mrs. Henry, all right!" She was always expecting his call at the same time every Friday night. He would spend time taking her order which usually filled several pages of the order book. My Grandfather always had regular customers who called, and my Dad picked those up when Grandpa Frizzi passed. When the orders were filled the next day, and boxed up, we carried them to the delivery vehicle which was usually the 1960 Chevy. I learned the routes from Tom Breyer who had replaced Greg Byles. As time progressed, I got to know the routes and the customers.

One of the first customers whom I delivered to was the Murray, Schwartz, and Davis family that lived on North Guernsey Street above Boggs Island in Gravel Hill. I remembered David Murray who was a few years older than me from high school. He was a portly but jolly boy, who played in the band for Mr. Spirk. They lived in one of the old stately homes that lined North Guernsey Street. They had a large vestibule that separated the big wooden front door of the home from the inner door. I would carry the boxes of groceries up the walk, and into the vestibule where I would sit the boxes. I believe they had a dog, so I had to make certain that the boxes were not placed where the dogs could get into them. Many of these homes like the Murray family lived in dated to the early 20th Century, and they were truly the most magnificent anywhere in town.

The deliveries to West Bellaire were on Saturday. Mrs. Henry always had the largest to deliver, usually consisting of two or three large boxes. She lived on Taney Avenue, near her son Bill and his wife Betty. Taney was accessed directly from Bellaire Neffs Road, just before you actually arrived at the West Bellaire School. This narrow road followed along the hillside as it climbed to look down upon West Bellaire. When arriving at her home, I would enter the gate and proceed down the walk to her porch. Some customers wanted you to carry the boxes directly into the kitchen, which we always did when requested. We did not want to enter the house until we were requested to do so. Mrs. Henry did not object, so we always placed her order inside the house.

There were other little grocery stores in West Bellaire during the 1950s and 1960s. Jimmy Greenlee had a small store opposite Klee's Crossing and the B & O Railroad tracks. When I was attending West Bellaire School, Greenlee's store was always a stopping point on the way home. I would stop there with classmates to buy some penny candy on the way home to my Grandparents' house. Jimmy was always a friendly sort, who had a laugh that was infectious. If he thought something was funny, he would belt out a slow but repeated triple laugh of "Heeeh, Heeeh, Heeeh!"

Jimmy's wife had fallen ill, and he put an elevator on the side of the store so that she could get up and down from the second floor residence. Sometimes, we would see her sitting in her wheelchair when we came into the store. She would greet us, and her husband Jimmy, was always friendly.

The other grocery store was owned by Curtis Gooch. He had a small grocery store on Second Avenue at Birch Street. The Gooch family had been in West Bellaire from the days when it was known as Klee Town. His family operated a general store on Bellaire Neffs Road at Third Avenue which catered to the traffic on the highway. We often stopped at this store as kids whenever we walked home with a friend from school who lived along Second Avenue. The penny candy trade was of course what attracted us to this little grocery store. Both Gooch's and Greenlee's catered to the residents of West Bellaire and were within easy walking distance of the many homes that had sprouted up around them.

My most memorable delivery route, however, was along Pinch Run, located at the southern limits of the City of Bellaire. When I would get to the store, Dad would have these orders all ready to go into one of the Chevrolets. If the orders were placed into the 1960 Bel Air, we filled the trunk and the back seat with the boxes of groceries. If the 1968 Caprice Station Wagon was used, we folded down the third row of seats, and everything was loaded from the rear. The first of my stops was at the home of Rita Tiber. Rita was an older lady who I recall had a deeper and somewhat raspy voice. Sometimes she would be waiting for me on her front porch, and other times she would come to the door when I knocked to make her delivery. It was usually one box. She would have the check already written in the amount of the order, and tender that to me before I left.

Up Pinch Run a little further, I would stop at the home of the Chesnick family. They lived in a brick home that was painted fire engine red. The paint must have been an enamel or oil based paint because the house always looked shiny! I would drive around to the side porch, and begin the delivery. Living here was an elderly couple who I only knew as Mr. and Mrs. Chesnick. Also living with them was their adult son. I remember one time I was speaking with the Chesnick's about school, and that my favorite subject was history. The son piped up and told me that his elderly father was a soldier in WWI. The son quickly remarked, "He didn't fight for the United States, he fought for the Kaiser!" I am sure we talked about how he had immigrated to the United States after the war, but such conversations are lost. One thing I remember about this customer was that their favorite beverage was beer. We delivered to this home twice each week, and on each delivery there would be a case of twenty-four long neck bottles of Wiedemann Beer. This was a Bohemian beer that was brewed in Cincinnati, Ohio, and locally distributed. I think it was the old WWI veteran who was drank the beer. Although he had given up his allegiance to the Kaiser, he still liked his 'German Beer.' They would have the empty case of bottles waiting for me to take back to the car for return to the store. The boxes of groceries were next, and after a short chat, and exchange of pleasantries, I would be back in the car to make my final delivery.

Further up Pinch Run was the home of Mrs. Gorshe. Her home was not close to road as were the others. She lived on the opposite side of Pinch Run. To get to her house, there was a foot bridge leading from the road over the Run, and then a flight of wooden steps that led to her home high above on the hillside. This delivery would demand a long hike up to the house. I was great friends with Mrs. Gorshe's Grandchildren Tom and Brenda, both of whom were in my class at high school. The very first time I delivered groceries here, I told Mrs. Gorshe who I was, and she questioned me about whether I knew her Tommy and his older brother Mike. I assured her I did, as well as Brenda. Before I left to go back to the car, Mrs. Gorshe would always tell me the same thing when speaking about her grandchildren. She would always say in broken English, "You look-a just-a like-a my Brucie!" She was telling me that her grandson Bruce and I resembled each other.

I remember telling Tom one time what his grandmother had told me, and after a good laugh, he agreed with her assessment and said, "You do!" Once this delivery was made, I would need to turn the car around on this narrow road called Florence Avenue. My deliveries being completed, I would return to the store with checks from these customers.

I remember other deliveries; however, those were not as memorable as the faces and names that I have recounted. Always happy to see me arrive, in some ways, I felt they did not want me to leave. They offered me cold drinks on a hot day, they made small talk about my school and generally found my delivery a welcome event that they looked forward to. Some enjoyed having company, even if it was just a teenage delivery boy. I enjoyed chatting with these immigrant customers and listening to their stories of how they arrived here in Bellaire.

My Senior Year at Bellaire High School

My senior year of high school was a memorable one. Some of my best memories were made that year. I got my first car, a 1965 VW Beetle. I had begun dating a perky and lively girl named Penny who would later become my wife. I was enjoying school activities, dances, proms, and all those great times from being with a good group of classmates, and a special girl. Yet, there were challenges that I remember.

I wanted, as a senior, to attend the high school football games in which many of my senior classmates were playing. My brother Dick was also playing on the team as a sophomore. Our store was in transition, with a new one being planned in West Bellaire. I could not attend every game, but instead was asked by Dad to work at the store so he could head to Nelson Field to watch my brother Dick play for the Big Reds. I can remember wishing that I were there too. Someone, however, needed to mind the store as Tom Breyer had graduated the previous year, and Dad had not hired a replacement. On one particularly important home football game, I recall hearing the home crowd at Nelson Field roaring with enthusiasm as I was standing on the steps in front of the store. I went to the storeroom across Washington Street and looked out the rear window down at the stadium. The visitors' stands were visible and filled with fans. The crowd roared again. I do not recall what game it was, or who won. All that I can remember is that I had the terrible feeling that I was missing what was an important part of my senior year of high school. I insisted that the game against Martins Ferry, a home game, was one that I would not miss. Dad found a way of arranging for another person to keep the store open, or whether he closed it for the game. We beat Martins Ferry in my senior year, and I was there to see it happen.

I enjoyed playing golf. I had learned from a neighbor, Tom Blake, the art of this game. He patiently worked with me when growing up as a teen to learn the rules and golf etiquette. Tom and I often played at Wheeling Park with some of his friends from the stamping plant in Shadyside. I joined the newly formed golf team at Bellaire during my high school years. I also continued to play basketball at an intramural level with my class of 1970 and for the Hi-Y team. My class of 1970 won the class tournaments both our Junior and Senior years. When the new gymnasium was built on Guernsey Street, my senior class buddies and I, on the Hi-Y Team, played the first game on the dedication of the new gymnasium floor. We played against the faculty. The game was supposed to be part of a celebration for the long-awaited gymnasium to replace the 'cracker box,' which was the stage of the BHS auditorium. The laying of the cornerstone for the new gym went forward as planned, even though the cornerstone had been stolen the night before the dedication. Rumors abounded about who was to blame and where it had been taken. Those rumors blamed my senior class of 1970 as the culprits, and only years later did I ever speak with eyewitnesses who had seen the cornerstone long after we had graduated. The school bought a new one, which was unceremoniously placed, and which remains there today with the date 1969.

These sporting activities that I participated in, at a level that matched my athletic ability, were great fun! I was rewarded during my high school years with a foundation for many long friendships and found happiness in academic endeavors such as working on the yearbook staff, Hi-Y, and the Quill & Scroll Society. I did join the wrestling team and wrestled five matches before being forced to leave the team with mononucleosis. I was still dating Penny, which began during the preceding year, and we were spending a lot of time together. My senior year at Bellaire High School was a wonderful moment in my life.

College and graduation rapidly approached me that year, and I must admit, all of that came so suddenly. I was ready to continue to college, but unlike many of my high school friends who were planning on going away to campus life, I was bound for the regional campus of Ohio University in Belmont County. With a new store being built and with four younger brothers still at home, the time was not right to consider any other option. I had discussed this with my Mom, and she wanted me to attend the local campus of OU at least for the first few years. My grades were good, but scholarships did not come my way for just being above average. Going away to school without financial assistance was not going to be possible with a new store in the works, and the financial stresses that went along with that. Planning to attend school locally would allow me to work and stay at home. Tuition, books and gasoline would be my only expense.

I completed the college preparatory curriculum as a freshman at Bellaire High School and continued throughout the following high school years. I took Freshman English from Mrs. Martha Taylor. She was perhaps the most difficult teacher I ever had in high school. Most students struggled in her classes just to get a grade of B. I usually got C's, and very few classmates got those coveted A's. After a year's reprieve with Miss Steinbicker as a sophomore, American Literature was scheduled for my junior year, once again taught by Mrs. Taylor. High grades from her I found so difficult to come by. To remain in the college prep curriculum, I would have to endure a third year of Mrs. Taylor. Many of my classmates had decided to forego the punishment that we saw her inflict upon our grade point averages, and they opted to take Senior English instead of English Literature.

My first memory with Mrs. Taylor came as a freshman in her English Class. A sentence to be diagrammed was assigned by Mrs. Taylor to about twenty-five sentences from our textbook. We came to class with those completed diagrams for the eighth period class. Mrs. Taylor called upon about six students to go to the chalk board, and she randomly assigned a sentence to diagram to each student. I was one of those students at the board. We all diagrammed our sentences according to subject, predicate, adjectives, adverbs, articles, etc., and then returned to our seats. One by one, Mrs. Taylor reviewed our diagrams with the entire class. I wrote very legibly as a cursive writer as a freshman, and my diagram used my cursive writing. When Mrs. Taylor came to my diagram, she paused and then stated in an inquisitive tone, "And what young lady was assigned this sentence?" Obviously, I had no choice but to raise my hand. The class laughed because Mrs. Taylor had incorrectly associated my cursive writing with one of the girls in my class. She commented that she "believed this was a girl" strictly upon the basis of the neatness of the handwriting. Well, the diagram was not entirely correct, so I listened to Mrs. Taylor's explanations of why it was so. Mrs. Taylor did not seem to understand that my cursive writing being compared to that of a girl was a little embarrassing. Well, I survived her class, and as a junior I took American Literature under her instruction.

One evening in our kitchen, I remember attempting to convince my Mom and Dad that I wanted to take Senior English to avoid Mrs. Taylor. If I did, I would not graduate from the College Preparatory Curriculum. I pleaded with them. My Mom told me, "You have come this far, and no matter what grade you get, you will be better prepared for college." I cried with the frustrating thought of being forced to suffer through my final year of high school with Mrs. Taylor. My Dad entered the conversation and interceded for my Mom. He told me, "We want you to be prepared for college, and although your grade may not be higher than a C, you will be better prepared if you take the course." Similar to the popular news show of the day, 'Point Counter Point,' we went back and forth until I threw in the towel. They won the debate that night. So I took that English Literature class from Mrs. Taylor, continued to get my Cs except for one six-week period when I got a B. I acknowledged in later years, to both my Mom and Dad, that they had been right in their guidance in that kitchen discussion from long ago.

Despite all that I have said of Mrs. Taylor, my life has been better for having taken her class that final year of high school, as well as the earlier two years. I did not realize the betterment at the time. Once when I had already begun college, I saw Mrs. Taylor sitting in her automobile along Market Street in Wheeling, West Virginia. Penny and I were walking to a store to do some shopping. Mrs. Taylor was waiting for her husband to return from a bank.

I went to her car, and she rolled down the window. I said, "Hello Mrs. Taylor." She greeted me warmly, "Hello Danny."

She wanted to know what classes I was taking in college. After telling her, I felt compelled to let her know how important her classes had been for preparing me.

I said to her, "I want to thank you for teaching me during high school so many things that I find useful today. I did not realize how important your classes were."

She smiled and replied, "Danny, I know you didn't realize that, but I am so glad that you realize that now as a college student." She thanked me for stopping to let her know how I felt. I never saw her again after that brief, but so important conversation. She did make a difference in my life. She, and her classes instilled in me a love for the written word.

As a senior, I decided to try out for the wrestling team. I had never wrestled before, but some of my friends who were on the team urged me to give it a go. I did. The team practiced in the new gymnasium until football season ended, and then we moved practice to the field house at Nelson Field. I remember after one practice I had a personal discussion with Rudy Sharkey, the head football coach, who was working in his office. He was my brother Dick's football coach. He was my teacher in health class and for student driving. Sharkey was genuinely interested in the student athlete as a person.

He asked me, "Dan, why as a senior are you only now trying out for the wrestling team."

I told him, "This would be my last chance to earn a letter in a varsity sport, and that my younger brother, Dick, already had earned one of them." Coach Sharkey smiled. I think he understood from my response that I felt pressure in being an older brother, but always in the shadow of Dick because of athletics. He wished me good luck and encouraged me to stick with it. Rudy Sharkey was not just a coach, he was also a mentor. He seemed to know my motivations for seeking a place on the wrestling team without my having to even state them.

As the wrestling season was soon to begin, I was destined to wrestle a heavier weight class than I should. My senior teammate, Jeff Stolz, was already wrestling the 138 lb. weight class, and he was a state tournament-caliber wrestler. Not being able to defeat him in practice, I would have to wrestle heavily at 145 lbs. I could eat lunch while most of my teammates were starving themselves. The first match of the season was against Wheeling Central, and so Mike Presutti, Jeff, and I traveled to Wheeling to watch a match that the Maroon Knights of Wheeling Central had with another team. We hoped to be able to see in action those wrestlers we would be facing later that week. Believe it or not, every wrestler we would wrestle won by forfeit, so we came away with little insight. Now, both Mike and Jeff were Co-Captains and experienced wrestlers. I was not. So not even getting to see my opponent that night was a real letdown for me. I had no idea what to expect later that week.

The night we faced off against Central soon arrived on December 10, 1969. The first match of the night was a victory for our 98 lb. wrestler, Art Jones. Good start! Each succeeding match, however, went to the Knights. When the referee called for the 145 lb. weight class, my heart was beating wildly in my chest, anxious to begin the match. I was so very nervous. The match went forward, each of us trading points, until the third period. I was behind in riding time. Suddenly, I was in that unenviable position of 'looking at the lights.' I was on my back, struggling to avoid being pinned. I can still hear the voice of my friend Tom Gorshe screaming my name from the bleachers, urging me to do something. The partisan Wheeling Central crowd urged my opponent to finish me by pressing my raised shoulder to the mat. My situation was dire. In his attempt to force his weight upon my chest to get the pin, my opponent, a boy named Pelluchette, got too high over my abdomen, and off balance. With my right hand at his pelvis, I was able to throw his legs over his head and flip him on his back. We reversed our positions almost immediately. He was now the one looking at the lights, and I was working to put his back firmly into the mat. After what seemed an eternity, I heard the sound of the referee's hand loudly slap down on the mat close to my right ear. The match was over, and I was the victor. This was the only real contribution that I ever made to the proud athletic history of Bellaire High School. We lost the dual meet that night, with only two match wins, Art Jones at 98 lbs., and me, the unlikely winner at 145.

Few will ever remember this night, but I always will. I will remember the exhaustion when it was over, and the congratulations of my fellow teammates and coach who met me on the mat. But the moment I will remember always is when I saw my father standing by the entrance doors to the gymnasium. He had left the new store in West Bellaire early to see me wrestle, and he arrived just in time to see the referee raise my hand in victory. This was not a moment many others will ever remember. Yet, it is the one I will never forget. My Dad being there to see it happen was as important to me as the victory itself. I felt redeemed in a way and was finally able to erase those feelings that I had disappointed him four years earlier when I had that discussion with him at his rock pile.

The next day after this dual match, the December 11 edition of the Times-Leader reported our team's loss to Wheeling Central. The paper also posted a photo showing the ribbon cutting at our new Frizzi Market which had taken place the day before. Shown in the photo was our Councilman from West Bellaire, Ugo Papola, my Dad and Mom, State Representative A. G. Lancione, Mayor Anthony DeMarco, and Wayne

Taylor from Tusco AG. December 10, 1969 turned out to be big day, for both me and my Dad.

My wrestling career ended with a 3-2 record one month later when I contracted mononucleosis after the Coshocton Invitational. I went to my locker at the field house at Nelson Field when it became clear I would not wrestle again. I went to turn in my equipment, but found my locker had already been raided. My headgear, knee pads, practice gear, and uniform gym bag had already been divided up by my teammates. They were apparently not frightened of the dreaded 'kissing disease' that I had contracted. Later that year, I was given the coveted letter AB@ for my short service that senior year. My dear Mom wanted to buy me a letterman=s jacket, like my brother Dick already had. I told her to just put the letter AB@ on the mirror atop my dresser, and she honored my request. I would get little use out of the jacket, since my graduation was only 4 months away.

As the class of '70' was preparing to graduate, the nation was rocked on May 4 by the killing of unarmed students at Kent State University by Ohio National Guard troops during a protest on Campus. The students rallied in opposition to the Vietnam War after several days of rioting on campus, and four students were now dead. The atmosphere that surrounded our Baccalaureate Service held on May 31, 1970, was tempered as each of us faced an uncertain and tumultuous time and future.

Several days later, on June 5, 1970, I walked down the aisles of the auditorium with fellow classmate Debbie Thoenen to take our place on the stage of the auditorium to receive our diplomas. Everyone was in attendance. My father, Danny, and mother Nancy, my aunts and uncles, and my teachers at Bellaire High School watched us walk across the stage to receive our diplomas from Dr. Creamer. My classmate Sarah's father was on the school board and got that honor. The only Grandmother that I had known in my 17 years, Neva E. Robinson, was also there on this day.

The graduation speaker was a man whose name I do not recall. However, I do remember one story from his graduation address. The story he told was about a young boy. He was a good kid, just not ready to be serious about life. A teacher told him one day that if he didn't change his ways, he would turn out to be as 'worthless as a lump of coal.'

The boy felt terrible because he knew that he was worth much more than a dirty lump of coal. As the story continued, the boy went home, where he found his aging grandmother. She knew something was wrong and asked the boy why he seemed upset. The boy related what the teacher had said to him. The story was concluded with the words of the old Grandmother of the boy. She said, "That teacher is wrong about your grandson. You just aren't ready to shine yet. Your teacher sees a lump of coal, but I see in you as a diamond in the making!"

After my graduation ceremony had ended, my own Grandmother Neva reminded me about that story from the graduation address. She hugged me and offered her congratulations on this momentous day. She told me I should always remember that inspirational story. She presented me with my Grandfather Robinson's cuff links with a single speck of diamond on each one. I have never forgotten that story, that gift, or my own maternal Grandmother's loving words to me on that day. I have often wondered what my Grandmother Philomena would have told me had she been there for my graduation. I bet the same thing!

The new home in West Bellaire became the residence of the Daniel Frizzi family. Additional space including a large yard, full basement, an integral garage, and additional bedrooms were needed by the growing family. One additional bedroom was added to the left side of the home once Abe came to live with the family in his final years. (Frizzi Collection 1963)

The new high school gymnasium was dedicated in 1969 with a basketball game featuring the senior Hi-Y members against the faculty. Left to right, are Robert Biggins, Louis Dossie, Dan Frizzi, Jr., and Tom Mehl, all students, with an attempted block of a shot by teacher Dan Mumma. Observing on the bench from left are Claire Cribbs, long time basketball coach; Walter Mokros, guidance counselor; Richard Games, math teacher; Rudy Sharkey, head football coach; and wrestling coach, Tom LaRoche. (Frizzi Collection 1969)

Leaving for the prom in 1970 from Penny's home at 4647 Noble Street. The vehicle was the 1968 Chevrolet Caprice station wagon which doubled as my father Daniel's family vehicle and also the delivery truck for our grocery store. (Frizzi Collection 1970)

Chapter Eight

The Fourth Store of The Frizzi Family

A New Store in West Bellaire

In the year before my graduation, Dad had made an important decision. He had decided that the little grocery store at 2783 Washington Street would no longer be the best option for the future of the family. Much like the decision that my Grandfather Frizzi had made in 1923 to build a new store on Washington Street, my father decided that a new supermarket in West Bellaire was the future. After much contemplation, he decided to purchase the Spengler homestead along Bellaire Neffs Road at Second Avenue in West Bellaire. On June 12, 1969, Dad became the owner of this property, and immediately proceeded to raze the Spengler family home that was situated on the land.

I turned 17 years of age on September 15, and two days later, Dad and Mom signed a mortgage loan for the construction of the new supermarket. Collateral given to the Buckeye Savings & Loan Company was title to the land for the supermarket and the old store property at 2783 Washington Street. The loan contained a warrant of attorney that allowed the bank to confess judgment without filing suit if timely payments were not made. Dad and Mom were risking much in this endeavor, and they insisted that the loan provide that their home would be excluded from this cognovit provision. Dad would also secure a second loan for equipping the store with a large meat department, a dedicated walk-in cooler, a walk-in dairy cooler, and a walk-in freezer. In addition, the store would be equipped with refrigerated display cases for dairy, meats, and produce. A frozen food display case was also an added feature, so much more accessible to customers than what we had at the old store. The second loan for equipping the store came from the Farmers' & Merchants Bank, where my Grandfather Abe had been a director. This new store was far beyond what we knew on Washington Street and would contain multiple refrigeration compressors and infrastructure at far greater expense. We would continue to operate the old store until the new store had been completed later in 1970, the year of my graduation from high school.

Dad was very busy making plans for the new building during this time. He was concerned about the transfer of the liquor licenses from Washington Street to the new store location. The reason was that the West Bellaire School would sit directly across 2nd Avenue from the new store. A public hearing was held before the school board who could oppose those transfers, which my Dad and Mom attended. They made clear that the transfer was for liquor sales for carry-out and not for on-premises consumption. Albert E. Noice, President of the Farmers and Merchants Bank in Bellaire, was also a school board member. He stood before those at the meeting and said, "This supermarket will be an improvement to the West Bellaire community, and I see no reason why transfer of the licenses should be opposed." It was not, and the approval by the school board was unanimous.

An ad was placed for new employees. Dad and Mom conducted interviews, and the difficult decision of hiring clerks was made. Those I remember from those early days were Trish Trigg, Sally Flowers, Kathy Conroy, and Margaret Tiger. Amelia Papola was the first clerk of the produce section of the store. Dad hired a man named Hudson, who would be the first butcher to work in the meat department.

The plans were designed by Architect J. Davis Wilson, and groundbreaking took place in mid-summer 1969. The new store was to be ready for opening in November, but was delayed until December. When completed, a grand opening was held on December 10, 1969, when Dad and Mom cut the ceremonial ribbon. A photo was taken in early December of our family for use during the opening celebration. I hurried back to the store after wrestling practice, and my brother Dick came after his basketball practice was over. We all assembled so the Times-Leader photographer, Boyd Nelson, could snap a bit of history for the newspaper article announcing the grand opening of Frizzi Market. Dad and Mom looked very happy and proud to be there with their five sons. The only thing remaining was to take one more photograph, and this one had a historic flavor to it also. On a Sunday following church, we all met back on West Washington Street for one final photograph in front of the old family store at 2783 Washington Street. This was a similar family photograph at the place which had been our first home. Looking at the photograph today reminds me of how many wonderful memories were created as a family at this little grocery store and residence above it. The front door behind us had a sign which read, "We're CLOSED."

The new Frizzi Market was advertised the day before the grand opening with a large display ad in the Times-Leader. Registration for door prizes was free to the public. Store hours were listed as 8:00 a.m. to 10:00 p.m. daily, except on Sunday, when you could shop from 9:00 a.m. to 9:00 p.m. One of the best features of the new store was 'Plenty of Free Parking Space,' which was a definite improvement over the lack of parking on Washington Street. Tender loin pork roast was seventy-five cents a pound, and center-cut pork chops were eighty-nine cents a pound. Sugardale all-meat weiners in a 12 oz. package were only forty-nine cents. Under the Shurfine label, customers could buy four cans of apple sauce for only fifty-nine cents, or four cans of yellow cling peaches for $1. Mity Fine bread came in 16 oz. loaves, and you could buy eight of them for just $1. A 10-pound bag of potatoes was priced at forty-nine cents. The newspaper ad stressed 'friendliness, service, and convenience' found in a neighborhood market like the one that had existed previously on Washington Street. So now all we needed were customers to make the new Frizzi Market a success.

After the first few weeks of operation, Dad was surprised that the revenue generated and customer support were less than he had expected. I can remember quiet conversations between my parents about this new venture, and how it was going to affect the family financially unless business and revenues increased. My Dad seemed disappointed, but my Mom gave the reassurance that we were going to do fine, we just needed to give it some time. There were moments, I am sure, when my Dad questioned his judgment about the huge investment he had made. He spent many hours working at the store to generate business for the new store and brainstorming ways to increase traffic. My Mom was always supportive and took a bank job as a teller in Wheeling, and together they found ways to make ends meet when revenue was lower than expected.

Three things were going to be different in the new Frizzi Market, and some of these seemed to be a problem. First, the established history of purchasing on credit was abandoned in favor of a cash operation. Second, we were also limiting our operations so that deliveries were no longer going to be routine, but the exception. The third disadvantage was that without sidewalks from Washington Street to West Bellaire, just a half mile from the old store, our Washington Street customers no longer had easy walking access. The early years of operation were difficult financial ones for my Dad and Mom. In 1972, Dad refinanced his loans to make the payments easier. I had taken a part-time job away from the store at a Pennzoil gasoline station in Bridgeport, Ohio. I had weekend hours and nighttime closing hours. I asked Dad to return to work in the store when I began classes at the regional campus of Ohio University that fall in 1970. He agreed, and I returned to the store on more flexible hours so that my work schedule would permit me to attend daytime classes and still work about twenty-five hours a week. Dad put me in charge of the dairy and frozen food sections of the store, while he concentrated on meat, produce, and all the other responsibilities of running the market. These were difficult years for the store financially, which I soon realized once I had returned.

One job that I recall, in addition to the normal work hours, was to go to the store early on Wednesday morning to meet the Semi-Truck from Tusco Grocers in Uhrichsville, Ohio. The truck would be waiting for me when I arrived about 6 a.m. The driver was a man from rural Tusky County whose name I recall was Ralph Simmons, and he was always there to greet me. Simmons was a good ole boy who liked to harass you at six o'clock in the morning, whether you felt like unloading the truck or not. "Hurry up, I've been here waiting on you for an hour," would be his way of saying good morning. The steel door at the back of the storeroom would be opened, and then Simmons would back his truck up to where he could connect his roller track to our track inside the storeroom. "Hurry up, get a move on," he would yell, just trying to get your goat! Then the fun would begin. Simmons would start throwing boxes one after the other so fast that you could not possibly keep up with him stacking the boxes. He really enjoyed trying to provoke a response, but it was best just to ignore him and go on working. Frizzi Market was his first stop in Belmont County, so he liked to get done quickly, but not because he wanted to get back on the road. No! Simmons wanted to come into the back room, go to the restroom, have a cup of coffee, and shoot the proverbial 'bull!' Only after this ritual had been completed would he be on his way.

Now, once the order was unloaded, our 2-wheel hand dolly would be loaded with boxes of items that were to be on sale. We reserved the third aisle for our specially advertised products that would appear in the newspaper. By placing them in the third aisle, customers would have to pass by the other grocery items on the shelves of the store. 'Cherry Pickers' were known in the retail trade as those who only came into the store to purchase your 'loss leaders.' 'Loss Leaders' were those products you sold in high volume, but sometimes for little or no profit, just to attract customers. Advertised specials were not money makers for the store, but hopefully generated an interest in coming to the store to shop. The third aisle would at least make customers walk past the other grocery items on the shelves. We would build displays stacking the cans, boxes, and other containers of special items, post signs advertising the pricing, and service them during the day as customers shopped.

One of the things my Dad did to promote the store and the specials was to have the WOMP Radio Station call him at a particular time of the day. Joel Savage was the salesman for the radio station, and he would get the information from Dad as to what would be on sale that week. Then, Joel would have Bill Thalman, the on-air talk show host, call and speak to Dad live on the radio. When Dad was not available, I would take the call and give all the special items live over the Ohio Valley airwaves. Sometimes, a customer would comment about my being on the radio. While it was kind of intimidating the first few times, each time thereafter increased my comfort level until taking the call became only a comfortable conversation with Bill Thalman. One of the things Dad always promoted was his Wonder Roast Chickens! Bill Thalman always talked up how tasty they were. We sometimes sold more than a dozen a day and always needed some on hand for dinner time as people were heading home from work.

Now, we ran out of storeroom space almost immediately upon opening the new store. We were still handling pop bottles, and they were taking up space that we needed for an ice machine and other inventory. Dad decided that we should build a pop room extended from the back of the storeroom. One summer during college, Dad, my brother, and I dug out the hillside behind the storeroom to build the new addition. Dad had asked Robert Bandoni, who we all knew as 'Bob,' to lay up the cement block for that building. Now Bob was a big man with a capital AB@. He was barrel-chested, had short, huge, muscular arms, and a large, hard belly. He was a block layer by trade. My Dad asked me to 'mix mud' and carry a block for Bob. I agreed even though I had never mixed mortar or worked on a masonry job before. The closest I had come to this was carrying stone for Dad from the old Spring house on the hill or carrying coal for Bob and Mary Baker.

Bob explained to me the mixture of sand, Portland cement, and water necessary to mix the batch. He told me, "You can carry blocks after the first batch, and then go make the second batch of mortar." Now Bob could carry two 12-inch blocks under each arm; he was that strong. I carried blocks to the scaffold, hoisting them above my head up to him, and mixed his mud for the next two days. I found that you had to work fast to keep up with him. Bob was not only a big man, but he also had a big heart inside that huge barrel chest. He was patient and always kind when I got behind and could not keep up. I was happy to see that the masonry job came to an end, but the time I spent with Bob Bandoni demonstrated what hard work of a laborer was all about. I never forgot that job!

Our dairy products came from Quaker City, Ohio, and the Broughton Dairy Company. The truck would pull up to the back door of the storeroom and unload the milk crates stacked four crates high with a hydraulic lift. My days of getting up early with Dad and driving to Tridelphia for milk had long passed. The delivery driver did that work himself, and all that I was required to do was check his delivery slip against the products in the crates.

Looking for a Car

I had shopped for cars to replace my VW Beetle. One day, I found a 1969 Chevelle SS at Kuchinka Chevrolet in Bellaire on their lot across from the showroom. I remember getting out of my VW and walking into the lot to take a closer look. Mrs. Kuchinka, the owner of the dealership, saw me and walked to greet me. She had sold many vehicles to my Dad, and perhaps she knew who I was. We looked at the car together, and then in the typical Kuchinka way of closing the deal, she said to me, "Can we get this car ready for you tomorrow?"
I replied, "I want my father to look at it before I make any decision."
Her next question was a simple one. "How old are you?"

"I had just turned 17."

Once she learned my age, she told me, "Bring your father the next time," and she abruptly turned and walked away. I never realized that her abruptness was really a legal matter until I took business law in college. Because I was a minor, any contract that she made with me for the sale of an automobile that I did not really need would be revocable, at my option, for any reason and without question. Mrs. Kuchinka did not want to deal with a mere child who could revoke the sale if they changed their mind. She wanted an adult to deal with. I decided that this SuperSport model was too expensive anyway, and opted for the scaled-down Chevelle Malibu.

The Chevelle that I had told Greg Byles about in the 1960s was now becoming a reality, although not the SS model I had envisioned. I purchased a 1969 Chevrolet Chevelle Malibu 2 Dr. Coupe, payments for which I was making from my earnings at the store. It came from Glenn Straub's Auto in Wheeling, sold to me by a salesman named Carl 'Lefty' George. The cost was about $1,895.00. The Malibu had a black vinyl roof, a pin stripe on gold paint, and a black interior with astro-ventilation. It was a dependable ride, and it was a similar style to the car that I had wanted. Just like my Dad, however, I wondered if I had purchased more car than I could pay for on my wages working at the store. Gasoline was going to cost more, even if it was only twenty-nine cents a gallon. The 18-month loan was at the Morris Plan, where Mom worked. Penny and I enjoyed just driving around in this car, and passing the time we spent together, as I completed college and she completed X-ray training at Wheeling Hospital.

One day, the Broughton's driver came into the store and asked me to go outside with him. When I walked through the back door of the store, I saw the broken bracket on the Broughton hydraulic lift, and saw my Chevelle Malibu. Metal crates of gallon jugs of milk had tipped off the lift and onto the side of my car. My driver's side window was broken, and my door was smashed. I was crushed, just like my car! The Broughton's driver said he was sorry, but there was nothing he could really do to prevent the accident. I had to go back to driving the big 'Six-Oh' until it was repaired.

The first butcher that Dad hired was a man named Hudson. He was not there very long before he left to work somewhere else. No butcher required Dad to take over the meat department until a replacement could be found. Dad hired a little guy from Paden City, West Virginia. I think his name was Roy. He dressed somewhat like a cowboy, and he talked with a southern West Virginia drawl. He would always greet the ladies who walked by the meat case in a pleasant way, which was appropriate. He liked to joke with them but was always helpful in explaining the various cuts of meat in the case. He left one day and did not return. The next butcher I worked with during college was Bud Lendon. Bud was a little less friendly and less helpful than the cowboy from Paden City. He did a good job, however, which allowed my Father to focus on other aspects of the business. Bud had a favorite word that he used quite often. When meat had spoiled and had to be thrown away, or when the cheesecloth which covered the sides of beef was left standing too long in water, they began to smell. Bud liked to say the word "rancid!" Bud was using a term that has a specific application to foods such as meat and oils. I learned that word from Bud, and every time I hear it spoken, it brings me back in time to when Bud the Butcher was behind the meat case at our store.

After I went off to law school, I learned about a mishap that occurred in the meat cooler. Bud had apparently been hanging up a hind quarter of beef in the cooler when he accidentally placed his hand behind the meat. He impaled his hand with the steel hook through the palm. The meat was holding his hand against the hook so that he was unable to get free. My Dad had to go and pull the meat down from the hook for Bud to break free. Dad took him to the hospital, and he recovered in time and then returned to work. This was an example of how dangerous the meat room could be with meat saws, grinders, slicers, and those steel hooks! I only cut myself with a knife once when I worked at the old store on Washington Street. I still carry the scar on the thumb of my left hand. I was using a banana knife, which has a curved blade at the tip. We used to sell frozen ground beef patties, and sometimes they would stick together. I was using the banana knife to separate them. The blade slipped and went into my thumb and nail. The cut could have been worse, but the blade was slowed by the thumb nail. It was a painful cut that healed after some time. The scar remains as a reminder of how quickly a sharp knife handled improperly can cause injury.

College and the Draft

During my first year of college, I entered what was called the University College for undeclared majors. At the time, I wanted to learn to fly and become an airline pilot. My plan was to graduate from college and, with my degree, apply for OCS, or Officer Candidate School. The Vietnam War was winding down in the early 1970's, but we still had a draft system operated by the Selective Service Commission. I was eligible to be drafted when I turned eighteen, as I entered my first year of college. My buddies and I remember well the day of the draft selection on August 5, 1971, which determined our draft number. The selection would determine whether it was likely that young men my age would be required to enter military service and likely be sent to Vietnam. Each day of the year, representing a birth date, was pulled at random. My birth date, September 15, 1952, was the 291st number pulled. My chances of being drafted were now almost impossible based on the previous year's experience, and I could now concentrate on school without the uncertainty of military interruption.

This was a tumultuous time in the life of a young man. The Vietnam War sparked great protests throughout the nation. This was especially so on college campuses. Young men could not drink legally, but were old enough to carry a gun in Vietnam to kill the Viet-Cong. Penny's brother was in Vietnam, was wounded twice, and returned with two Purple Hearts. Part of him was left in Vietnam because he returned as a different person. He had witnessed the horrors of a war that most young people, like me, could not imagine. Anger and emotion on both sides of the issue of whether the war was for a legitimate purpose at such a high cost became part of the social discussion. Many young men, and their own fathers, found themselves in lifelong conflict over this war. The divisions it caused left individuals and the nation with long-lasting scars. Bobby Kelly was a boy whom I knew from high school. He worked at Isaly's on Belmont Street during high school, and always dipped those 'skyscraper' ice cream cones that resembled the Chrysler Building in New York City. Bobby became the first casualty that I knew in high school to die in Vietnam.

On March 8, 1971, Dick and I convinced Dad to go with us to the Mohammed Ali and Joe Frazier heavyweight fight being shown by closed-circuit TV at the Capitol Music Hall in Wheeling. Ali had been stripped of his unblemished heavyweight title in 1967 when he refused to be inducted into military service. He was prosecuted for draft evasion and convicted, but appealed his conviction to the Supreme Court. He was eventually permitted to return to boxing to regain his crown that had been wrongfully taken away. He was brash, mouthy, and claimed to be the AGreatest@ fighter who ever lived. He was a living symbol of opposition to the Vietnam War. To most older men who had served in Vietnam, and to veterans of WWII and Korea, Ali was considered a traitor. These men came to the Capitol Theater that night to see Ali get a thumping from 'Smokin Joe' Frazier.

A young Cassius Clay, now called Mohammed Ali, had earned the heavyweight title from Sonny Liston with a 7th round TKO in 1964. In 1965, I listened to fight two on the car radio in our green 1960 Chevrolet with my dad in the garage. Clay knocked out Sonny Liston in their second meeting in the very first round. My Dad wanted to see Clay defeated, most likely because of his loud and outspoken manner. My Dad seemed upset that the knockout of Liston prevented that from happening, and especially so early in the fight.

My brother Dick and I admired Ali for his great ability as a boxer, and so on this night, we hoped he could take the title back. My Dad was not strongly committed to either side, but he hoped for a memorable fight night with his two oldest sons. I had believed that Ali had been stripped of his title unfairly. He became a symbol of the resistance to the Vietnam conflict, and therefore, was widely supported by college students and those who opposed the War in general. This boxing match was staged in New York City at Madison Square Garden, where so many boxing matches had occurred when my Dad was a boy. This would truly be an epic battle between two factions of Americans, each with opposing viewpoints on the Southeast Asian conflict. This boxing match was in many ways a non-lethal, but political extension, of that conflict.

The scene was unforgettable. At the sold-out Capitol Theater was a loud and raucous crowd, mixed between men of all ages. Combined with the closed-circuit feed from New York City in the Garden, the atmosphere was so exciting as we entered the theater. We climbed to the balcony to take our seats, which were nearly in the last row. The Capitol was electric that night! Ali looked statuesque as this fight was about to begin. Frazier was smaller and compact, but bulged with muscle. Chants by the older crowd were 'Frazier, Frazier, Frazier,' while my brother Dick and I joined our contemporaries with chants of 'Ali, Ali, Ali!' The noise level with each blow delivered was as loud as any sporting event I had ever attended. My Dad had always told us that Cassius Clay, the name Ali held before converting to the Muslim faith, made a mistake by just not going along with his induction orders. Dad recalled how former athletes like Joe DiMaggio and Elvis Presley went into the military when called, and were mostly used in public relations positions. Dad told us that Ali would have been a promoter of the military and would never have seen Vietnam. While true, Ali conscientiously objected to being a promoter of this conflict, which he did not support, and suffered the fate of losing his title.

Ali was knocked down in the fifteenth round, which significantly impacted the outcome of the match. Frazier was awarded a unanimous decision. Joe Frazier, however, had taken a tremendous beating in victory. There was no doubt in our minds, as we left the theater that night, and walked back to our car parked at the wharf garage, that we had seen perhaps the greatest heavyweight fight of all time. My Dad, who had seen fights of Joe Louis and Rocky Marciano, agreed. Frazier's unanimous decision did not change anyone's mind about Ali. He was, and still is, in my mind, the 'Greatest' fighter to ever have lived! He proved this in later fights by regaining his title. This boxing match in 1971 was just one public example demonstrating how torn the nation was over the Vietnam conflict. Protests abounded on college campuses, and the war would affect my plans as I continued my education at Ohio University.

It became clear that my future as a pilot in Officer Candidate School would not be certain with the Vietnam War winding down. A glut of pilots was returning from the military. My chances of becoming a pilot in a Navy flying program were slim. President Nixon's plan of Vietnamization was slowly ending the war, but with continued casualties to young men my age. I discussed this with Michael McTeague, my history professor and advisor at Ohio University, and he suggested that I consider going to law school. He told me that a business degree was offered at the regional campus level and would be good training for entering law school. I made the decision to accept his advice and apply to the College of Business at OU.

Mom arranged for me to meet the family attorney, Joseph McGraw, to find out what classes would best prepare me to enter law school. I went to his office in the First National Bank Building. I was greeted by his Secretary, Mrs. Breyer, who was Tom Breyer's mother. Mr. McGraw was kind enough to meet with me and told me this. "The most valuable classes that I took in college that prepared me to be an attorney were accounting. I use accounting principles every day in my practice," he said. So I followed Joe's advice and took as many accounting classes as I could. Accounting 101 through 103, and Intermediate Accounting 303 through 305 were all available at the local campus. Kenneth Poulton, a retired full-bird Colonel, was the instructor of those classes. I still use those accounting principles he taught me then in my work today.

Working at the store throughout college required a balance between work, class, and study. I found that college work was much more difficult than high school. I was not alone in this dilemma, since most of my classmates in college were also employed while taking classes at the regional campus as non-traditional students. I was a full-time student, always taking a full load, so that I could finish in 4 years. The balancing of my time became more difficult since study time had to be factored into the equation.

Dad began to give me more responsibility at the store. I began to write checks for suppliers and make deposits when asked by Dad to do so. I was able to see the financial side of things in the grocery business through these administrative tasks. Ordering was divided up. I ordered the dairy and frozen food items in a booklet that was designed for that purpose. Once I was finished, Dad would take the booklet, check my order, and finish ordering the rest of the products in the store. He always ordered special items. At first, we began to mail the order to the warehouse in Uhrichsville, and later, we went to an early system of ordering by running coded order strips through a machine attached to our telephone, which sent tones to a similar machine in Uhrichsville. I am not sure how well it worked, and I remember it had some early problems. Later that week, our order would arrive by truck. My Dad and I were never in conflict at work in the store over things relating to the business. We each worked on our own tasks, and he seemed happy with my work. Were it not for my schooling, I do believe he would have given me even more responsibility at the store.

We still had some of the same tools that we used at the old store, but many were now upgraded. Our new cash registers made the work of clerks much easier. Our coffee all came ground in cans, and so we no longer had the electric coffee grinder in operation. The old produce and meat scales were replaced with more modern ones. Our meat slicer was still the same, but now we had a band saw in the meat department for cutting meat. These new tools became integral to the operation of the new Frizzi Market.

While at Ohio University, a business communications class was one of my required courses. The course studied various ordering and other business communication systems. A class paper was required to be turned in near the end of the quarter detailing a business communication system that each student chose from existing Ohio Valley businesses. I asked Dad if he could contact someone at the Tusco Warehouse in Uhrichsville and arrange for me to get a tour of the operations. Dad's call put me in touch with one of the VPs there. I drove to Uhrichsville and spent half a day learning the warehouse system, beginning with the rail and truck deliveries of groceries to the warehouse. The tour also included an explanation of how orders were received into the warehouse by grocery stores, just like Frizzi Market. My notebook was full of information I had learned that day during the tour. Notes about my observation of freight being unloaded from rail cars, mail and telephone orders, warehouse pneumatic tubes used for processing orders, assembly of orders, loading of trucks for delivery, billing and payment for orders, were all a part of the notebook. I completed my paper for my class and handed it in to the professor. I also sent a copy to Tusco and gave one to my Dad. The professor, Joan Warner, who was from the business department in Athens, called me at the local campus and asked for permission to use my report for a paper of her own on which she was working. She must have found the paper helpful. I did not learn about what she had published, but I got an "A" on my paper and in the course.

One of those things that always plagued a retail business was pilferage, more commonly known as shoplifting. Now this should be distinguished from a grocer's son 'eating the profits' with a maple creme or two! In our prior location, the store was small, and shoplifting was easier to detect. In a larger store, like Frizzi Market, with four separate aisles to monitor, the petty thief had more space within which to operate. We would often find someone who was taking cigarettes, or bottles of beer, or meat from the meat case, and concealing the items in their jacket or pants. I remember once confronting a man who I observed taking a package of cheese from aisle one. He then walked past the meat case to aisle two. He no longer had the package of cheese in his hands, so I confronted him at aisle three. I later learned what the word 'asportation' means in criminal law when I went to law school. It is defined as the 'taking and carrying away' of another person's property without their consent. To sustain a criminal conviction, the perpetrator must usually pass the checkout counter to have committed that element of petty theft. Only then would his clear intent be evidence of asportation to take what did not belong to him. We never prosecuted anyone for stealing, however, and what we really wanted was to get the stolen item back on our shelf and the petty thief out of the store. When I confronted this man, I asked him, "What did you do with the cheese?" He opened his jacket and reached into his pocket to retrieve it, and when he did, he pulled out a package of Polish sausage from our meat case by mistake! This kind of petty theft had a huge effect on profits in a grocery store that operates on the narrowest of profit margins.

To combat this problem, my Dad decided to contact a security company about installing cameras in the store. The company sent installers who arrived and worked on the installation with the utmost secrecy. Dad had cameras installed to be able to view the checkout counters and each aisle. The installers then posted signs stating that the store was monitored by cameras and that shoplifters would be prosecuted. When the installation was completed, the installers said, "We have to check to make sure that the cameras are working correctly." They told Dad to make a telephone call to the number of the company, and someone answered, identifying themselves as the remote monitoring station. The installer then directed one of the employees to stand in certain places in the store so that they could be viewed through the cameras. The employee was told to hold up a pre-determined number of fingers, which could be viewed through the camera at the remote security station. Unknown to the employee, each number of fingers they were told to hold up to the camera was actually a script known by the security company. The person on the other end would then tell Dad over the phone how many fingers were being held up by the employee. Dad would then repeat that number, which was always identical to the number of fingers held up by the employee. The installer then would ask another employee to try out a different camera, and sure enough, the remote security station always repeated to Dad the exact number of fingers on the employee's hand. Employees were impressed with the new system.

The cameras were all dummy cameras, and the ritual of calling out the number of fingers was just a scheme by the installer with the company official on the other end of the call. My Dad was in on this scheme. The system was a deterrent, at best, but not actually functional. This may have worked for a time, but once it was discovered that the cameras were not actually recording or transmitting any video, their effectiveness was gone. Dad left them up anyway!

During the early 1970s, there was a sudden rash of burglaries in Bellaire. The target was local businesses. Dad and Mom had gone away for a week or so and left me in charge at the store. One day, after a burglary of a business in town was reported in the newspaper, a Bellaire Police Officer came to the store and asked to speak to Dad. I explained that Dad was away and that I was working in his place. Upon further inquiry, I asked, "What are you wanting to discuss with Dad?" The officer replied, "We have information that your store is going to be the next business that gets burglarized." Geesh! What a time for Dad to be away, I thought.

The officer then continued his inquiry, which left me stunned. He asked me, "Where do you keep the money at night?" He specifically wanted to know, "Where is your safe?"

I thought to myself, why would the police need to know where we keep the money? So I said to the officer, "Why do you need to know that?" He got a little incensed that this young kid was going to ask him questions. He responded by saying, "This isn't like what you see on TV, this is real, and someone could get hurt!" Well, that night, I made sure to leave the store with a bag of checks and cash money when I went home after closing. If we were burglarized, all they could get was some item from our shelves.

A few days later, a report came out in the newspaper that a police officer was injured when he fell from a fire escape on the back of the Murphy building. The storyline was that the officers were apprehending a burglar. Most of the business community became skeptical. The general belief of retail merchants was that the burglars were really wearing uniforms. Before long, the rash of burglaries ended, and rumors were the subject of an investigation by county law enforcement. Bellaire's finest were the suspects in the rash of burglaries. No one ever went to jail. The best evidence that it was a handful of local officers lies in the fact that the burglaries suddenly stopped. Looking back on this incident, I really think that our store was going to be the next target, as the officer had told me. But I think he knew who the burglars were going to be! Whether he was trying to warn me or he wanted the information to pass along, I will never know.

My Dad was always looking for projects that his boys could use to occupy their time. One of the best projects that he came up with was selling firewood. Property that had been in my mother's family was being strip-mined, and a haul road needed to be built for the trucks to pass from the pit to the State Highway. This road had gone through wooded land, and many large trees had been bulldozed to make way for the road. They were just lying around, and Dad and Mom suggested that we cut them up for firewood to be sold by the cord.

One of the best memories of our home in West Bellaire was the big living room and fireplace. We used that fireplace all winter long. A friendly fire in a fireplace makes an atmosphere like no other. We spent hours during fall and winter enjoying the fruity smell and crackling embers of burning firewood, and the warmth that filled the room. We found the living room a romantic place to sit and talk with a favorite girl, or a place to gather on Christmas Eve. Near the warmth of our fireplace, we enjoyed a place where our family created wonderful memories together. Our new venture would hopefully provide the fuel for creating those memories for others while providing us with exercise and a little extra income.

We began to cut up the fallen trees that lined the haul road. Much of it was wild cherry, which was an especially favorite fruitwood for burning indoors. We also had some locust trees that were better for making posts than for burning in a fireplace. Locust tended to 'pop' when burned and did not produce the same aroma as wild cherry. Locust logs also presented another problem. They were full of knots and were difficult to split. My Dad had a favorite saying when facing a difficult piece of wood to split. He would say with each blow of the axe against the stubborn log, "Do you think you're gonna win!" He would repeat that phrase with each blow of the axe until finally, he had succeeded in the task at hand. That would be when the log split apart, and my Dad had finally won!

All summer long, we harvested these trees. We bought a McCulloch chainsaw, which worked well, but soon became too small for the size of trees we were cutting. We made an investment in a Homelite with a bigger cutting bar. Some of the trees had been pushed over the hillside when the road was constructed, so Dad suggested that we use a block and tackle to pull them up to the road. We used the Chevrolet truck belonging to Dad as the power source for pulling the trees out of the ravine. The wood was cut into lengths of about 14 inches, and then was split with an axe. We loaded the truck and stacked the wood at the store in West Bellaire, letting it season in the summer heat. I placed an ad in the local newspapers in September, and soon calls started coming in. I kept a list of the names, addresses, and telephone numbers of those wanting a load of wood, and arranged a date for delivery. We advertised 'by the truckload' since there were different ways of interpreting a 'cord of wood.' A full cord is supposed to be 128 cubic feet of stacked wood. Our truck would not hold that much. We simply made clear that what we were delivering was what we could pile in the bed of our truck. That first year, we delivered to all communities on both sides of the Ohio River and had extra cash at Christmas time.

The next season, we began again in the summer. This year, I recall that I had a lot of my spare time invested in the cutting side. Sometimes my younger brothers would go along to help load the wood and stack it at the store. My goal this year would be to purchase an engagement ring and propose an engagement to Penny in early fall. I had gone to my Uncle Stanley Ostasiewski of Stanley's Jewelers in Bellaire to pick out a diamond ring. Stanley was married to my Grandmother Philomena's younger sister, Aunt Virginia. When I was a small boy, Dad and Mom used to stop in the jewelry store where Dad would talk with his Aunt Virginia. They were businesspeople just like my Grandfather and Grandmother, Minnie. In fact, Aunt Virginia worked for my Grandfather, Abe, and Grandmother, Minnie, at the store on Washington Street when she was just a young girl.

Stanley's Jewelers in Bellaire was widely known. When you looked at a diamond at Stanley's, you were looking at quality diamonds. He advised me to buy a special diamond, which was a little more expensive than what I thought I could afford to spend. Stanley was a trusted jeweler, however, and I did as he told me. This diamond was 55 points, and about $900.00, and the perfection of the diamond was what Stanley stressed to me. When I had enough money to put the down payment on his counter, he placed it into a setting and gave me the diamond ring. On October 5, 1973, when Penny had turned twenty-one, I proposed to her. She had been out with my parents and had just returned from a football game at John Marshall High School in Moundsville, West Virginia. She accepted my proposal, and we planned a June wedding after I had completed my first year of law school. We selected June 28, 1975. This would be my Dad's 49th birthday.

The LSAT Exam was required for admission to law school. I never liked the kind of tests that were based solely on aptitude and for which you could not really study. They reminded me of those darned time tests in grade school. I elected to find a testing site that was close to home so that I would be more relaxed and familiar with my surroundings. I took the first test in Washington, Pennsylvania, at Washington & Jefferson College. The test was scheduled in Old Main on the campus. I arrived early and still recall the large busts of both George Washington and Thomas Jefferson that adorned the hall. The test was one that drains you and gives you little insight as to how well you did. When my results came back, I had done poorly. My only recourse was to take the test a second time, and for that I would have to go to Athens, the main campus of Ohio University. The test in Athens was given in McCracken Hall. This time, I improved my score by 100 points, but it was still not high enough to be considered acceptable at a state-supported law school like Ohio State. I wanted to remain in Ohio after law school, so I was particularly interested in Ohio schools. I received an acceptance from Ohio Northern University in Ada, Ohio. Ohio Northern was an old school and had a good reputation among lawyers I had spoken with. This was a Methodist-affiliated school, and since I attended the Methodist Church, their admissions office must have felt that I was a good fit for their program. The major problem was the tuition cost. Back then, we were on the quarter system. My tuition for just the first quarter would be triple the cost at a state school like Ohio

State. So student loans were going to be necessary to help finance the cost.

I finished my undergraduate degree in Business Administration by attending classes during the summer of 1974 in Athens, Ohio. My classes were in Copeland Hall. I had a small apartment on State Street and walked the alley each morning to Mill Street to meet my fellow classmates for a ride up town to Copeland. We went back home every weekend during the summer and then drove back to Athens on Sunday. Classwork seemed so much easier without the routine of work.   During the hot summer days, Duane Gill, Jimmie Bizzari, and I would go fishing for carp under the Mill Street Bridge to pass the afternoon, before heading home to our apartments. During the afternoons when I was not fishing, I watched television and was consumed by the Watergate hearings. They were in full swing, and before I would leave for Law School, the nation would be rocked with the resignation of President Richard Nixon.

Leaving for Law School

Upon being accepted into law school at Ohio Northern University, my time working with my father in the grocery store was coming to an end. Beginning in the 4th grade during the early 60s, 14 years later, I would begin a new direction for my life's work. In my final week that summer of 1974, there were many people whom I saw for the last time. The staff of the Market with whom I worked was bidden farewell with hugs and well wishes. Many of the truck drivers of our suppliers, including Ralph Simmons, related to me that my college education was taking me down a different road, hopefully leading to a career in law. This would be a new venture for me that I embarked on with great trepidation. I was, once again, questioning in my own mind if I was up to the task of competing with a large class of students from major colleges back east, as well as here in Ohio. My future progress was uncertain. I was leaving home to join 200 other freshmen law students with varied backgrounds and degrees. I asked myself the important question: would I be able to compete with them? I finished in the top thirty students at the end of my first year, which convinced me that my undergraduate preparation was more than adequate.

On completion of my first year of law school, I returned during the summer of 1975 to take a clerking position at the Lancione Office in Bellaire. This was an opportunity to gain experience working with lawyers on real cases. I enjoyed this summer work and found it challenging, but interesting. Penny and I were married on June 28, 1975, and we began our life together in Ada, Ohio, for the completion of my final two years of law school. Two summers later, I took the Ohio Bar examination in July of 1977, and then took a job back in Bellaire with another established law firm. My first employment as a graduate was at the law firm of Malik, Malik & Knapp, located in my hometown of Bellaire. The Malik firm offered me the opportunity to work while I awaited notification that I had passed the Bar Exam. In early fall, I received notification that I had passed and was sworn in to the Ohio Bar at a ceremony conducted at the Ohio Theater in Columbus, Ohio. I have been engaged in that practice of law for the past 43 years, and since 1991 as a solo practitioner.

When I moved back to Bellaire in 1977, there were approximately 20 attorneys with offices in town. Today, I am a single member of that vanishing breed of small-town attorney with a general practice. I am now just a general practice attorney at law here in Bellaire, Ohio. Much like the disappearance of the small neighborhood grocery stores that dotted all communities half a century ago, careers in law as a small-town attorney are also disappearing from our main streets. With the passing of those years, I now better appreciate the feelings of Chingachgook of James Fenimore Cooper fame, who uttered those unforgettable words acknowledging that he was the last of a vanishing breed. I think that this was perhaps a reason why my father did not want to see Frizzi Market end upon his retirement. He, too, realized that small-town grocery stores were vanishing from communities and little neighborhoods all over the country.

Grocer's Development Corporation and Convenience Stores

Many changes contributed to the loss of so many neighborhood grocery stores. It actually started to occur even before Dad decided to build the new store in West Bellaire. Two of the most important factors that caused this disappearance were mobility and franchising. Progress always is at the expense of someone when the old way of doing things changes into something new. Just like my Grandfather Abe and his 'REO Speedwagon,' you had to be able to 'Roll with the Changes!'

The Interstate Highway System, begun in the 1950s opened the entire country to motor vehicle travel. A trip that used to take hours traveling on the National Road to Columbus, Ohio, or to Pittsburgh, Pennsylvania, was now much quicker. This same type of phenomenon occurred in the 19th century with the invention of the iron horse that connected small-town America to all parts of the country by rail. Steam travel by river, packet boat by canal, and land passage by coach were all abandoned in favor of the railroad. This occurred throughout America once again when President Eisenhower obtained the passage of the Interstate Highway Act in 1956, which created 41,000 miles of projected Interstate highways. Automobile manufacturing boomed. You were urged to 'See the USA, in your Chevrolet' as just one advertising slogan. We as kids can remember Sunday afternoon drives to places that we had never visited before, yet we could still be home for bed and school on Monday. This would not have been possible without improved mobility on land. Just as railroads had sounded the death knell for canals, overland coaches, and steamboat travel, the Interstate Highways and the automobiles using them would now erode the railroad passenger train.

This new mobility of the nation had the effect of spawning the growth of franchising. Because we could go further from home, we needed restaurants, gasoline stations, and a variety of places to visit while on the road. This was made possible because mobility had created a demand for marketing of products and services to a traveling public. 'Blue Laws' were designed to prohibit sales contracts on Sunday, which was considered the Lord's Day to be a day of rest. This mobility brought about the unpopularity of such laws as the traveling public was demanding places to go and things to do on those Sunday afternoon drives. Over time, these laws were eroded, and all that is left today are certain prohibitions on the sale of liquor on Sunday. Even these laws are eroding.

Franchising is perhaps the reason that this occurred. The new demand for a meal while away from home created the Burger Chefs, Wendy's, and Kentucky Fried Chicken of the world. The rest is history. As we look at the exits along any Interstate Highway, we find restaurants that serve meals, although not the kind Grandma made, while we are on the road to some distant place.

My father, and many of the grocers who were associated with the AG warehouse in Wheeling, West Virginia, met to decide the fate of their store businesses and the warehouse that served them. Many of the grocers were getting older, and many were retiring and closing their doors. A decision was made to form a new corporation known as Grocer's Development Corporation in the latter part of the 1950s. This company would acquire a franchise that would be able to build, own, and lease convenience stores selling a limited inventory of grocery staples. The franchiser was from Chicago, Illinois. The concept for the franchise was to provide 'convenience' stores to local communities and the traveling public. The stores were to be scaled-down versions of the neighborhood grocery stores with limited grocery items, while providing the convenience of hot and cold deli food products, along with bakery items. The name of these stores was 'Convenient Food Mart.' With the Grocer's Development Corporation acquisition of the local franchise, these convenience stores sprang up everywhere throughout the Ohio Valley. They would eventually replace those little grocery stores that had been operated by my Grandfather Abe, in neighborhoods all across the nation.

Now the AG member grocers had to raise the money to acquire this franchise. My Father went to the local banker to get a loan of $5,000.00 to be able to invest in the capital stock of the new company. The banker did not want to give Dad the loan, stating he thought this venture was much too risky. Dad did not take this response for a final answer and instead secured the necessary funding to be able to purchase stock in the new company elsewhere. This was the best investment my father ever made. The new company flourished. His investment in this new company, which the banker told him was too risky, turned out to be my Dad's retirement plan. The company was run by many of the same familiar faces that were members of the AG Warehouse, and my Dad enjoyed so many great memories with this group of friends, as he continued to operate his own grocery business in West Bellaire.

When Grocer's Development Corporation finally dissolved and sold the franchise business, my Dad's retirement plan was in place. He would never have been able to retire but for investing in this franchise known as Convenient Food Mart. Fortunately, he did not listen to that banker who opposed his loan to make the initial investment. This was one of my Dad's proudest moments in merchandising.

The change in landscape, however, has been caused by the new mobility and franchising, which has led to a serious erosion of the small neighborhood grocery stores across America. In the 1950s, Bellaire alone, a community of 12,000 people, had forty small neighborhood grocery stores. The two largest were A & P and Kroger. All the rest were just small stores like Frizzi & Son Grocery on Washington Street. They could be found in every part of the community, stretching from South Bellaire, Rose Hill, Indian Run, to Gravel Hill. All were family-owned grocery stores. Some of the best memories of growing up in these neighborhoods as kids will always be those little stores. Who can forget ice cream cones at Frizzi's, or pizza at Tony's Quality Market across from the high school? Who can forget Keller's Grocery on Belmont Street, or Stadium AG after a football game? Who remembers the Sanitary Food Market of Sam Cicogna near Crescent Street, which he established after that first job with Frizzi Brothers grocery store in the 1920s? Will anyone ever forget Bill and Ted Fry at their market in Gravel Hill? What about Busack Brothers located on Hamilton Street near where my Grandfather Abe, and his brother Artemio opened their first grocery store 100 years ago. Just as the Boccabella Grocery Store was associated with the First Ward, White's Grocery was a part of Gravel Hill. These are just a few of the many neighborhood grocery stores of my youth. The many children in the community who grew up as my boyhood friends in the 1950s and 60s will fondly remember them.

Groundbreaking for the new Frizzi Market in West Bellaire in the summer of 1969. Left to right are architect J. Davis Wilson; Bellaire Safety Director Johnny Myers; Councilman Ugo Papola; Gene Hershberger, Tusco Grocers Sales Manager; Daniel Frizzi, the grocer; Ed Miller, Jerome Miller General Contractor; Clarence Ramsay, Ramsay Electric; and Benny Battistelli, Power City Plumbing and Heating. (Frizzi Collection 1969)

Frizzi Market soon after opening in 1970. The old 1960 Chevrolet (the Six-Oh) is in the parking lot along with other vehicles. Shopping carts await customers under the mansard roof outside the entrance to the market. (Frizzi Collection 1970)

The grand opening photograph taken in December 1969 which appeared in the local paper advertising the opening of Frizzi Market. From left, Daniel Jr.; David; Daniel Frizzi Sr. holding Dean; Doug; Nancy Frizzi, and Dick. (Frizzi Collection 1969)

Dad poses for a photograph in the new produce department which appeared in the high school yearbook for 1971. The large produce case was such an improvement over the open air rack at the Washington Street store. Behind is the deli meat case. (Frizzi Collection 1971)

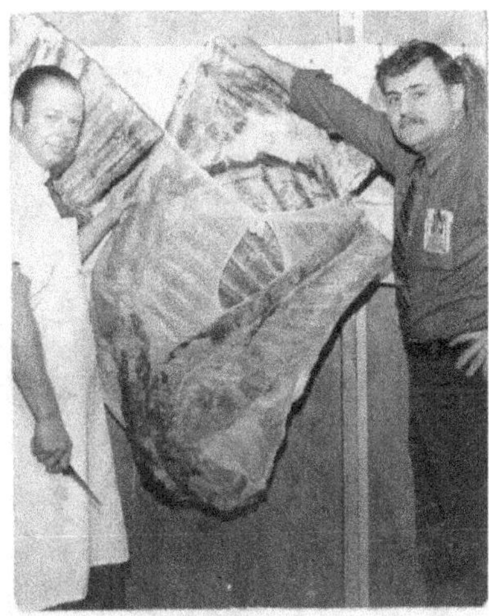

The dedicated walk in meat cooler was directly accessible from the meat department which eliminated the walk across Washington Street for beef. "Bud" Lendon, butcher, stands with my Dad, showing off the Sugardale meats from Canton that will soon be cut into steaks and roasts for the display case. (Frizzi Collection 1973)

A Frizzi Market party after closing with family and employees. From left are Joe Buti, stock boy; David Frizzi; Dick holding Dean; Danny Jr.; Danny Sr.; Doug Frizzi; Amelia Papola; Jimmy Steele; Lana Pasz; Jane Robson; Rae Klempa; and Christine Protiva. (Frizzi Collection 1973)

A farewell photograph was taken at 2783 Washington Street on a Sunday afternoon following church.   Abe Frizzi built the store as the third of the Frizzi family, and was now empty.   It was used by the family for storage. The upstairs apartment where my father began his life, and later I began mine, was now just for rent. This place where grandparents Abe and Minnie began their lives together in the 1920's, and my father Dan and mother Nancy did the same in the 1950's, was now a part of history. (Frizzi Collection 1970)

Chapter Nine

A Century in Time

A Striking Resemblance

Many have said that my Dad and I look so much alike. Looking at photographs of my father, and comparing them to my own through the years, there is no denying our relationship as father and son. Many clients have remarked to me those words, "You look so much like your dad!" Some, however, have mistaken me for my Dad with the passing of time. One client whose legal matters I had completed was waiting in my office for copies of her documents to be photocopied by a secretary. While we waited, she told me about all the good times she had in high school, and she began to relate a memory of going to Wheeling on a streetcar. She was certain that I had been on that streetcar with her and other friends. When I told her that I didn't think we had, she said, "Oh yes we did. Don't you remember that you were with Frank Ragni?"

I was immediately struck by the realization that she truly believed she was speaking with my father. I explained to her that she was mistaken and that she was remembering my Dad, who was also named Danny. She apologized for the mistake and said, "But you do look so much like him!" She seemed embarrassed by the mistake. So I gratefully employed my standard response in such situations and said, "Thank you so much for the compliment". I will never grow tired of hearing others remind me of that resemblance I bear to my father, nor will I grow weary of giving that sincere response. The comparison will always be a true compliment. As the years passed, however, those who remember my Dad Danny will go on ahead, as did he, passing on June 20, 2012, leaving fewer people who remember him. I receive that compliment now less as I grow older, simply fewer people who knew us both.

Throughout my years of living in the same family household growing up, my mail and my dad's mail were often confused unless we distinguished our names. Dad always used 'Sr.,' and I started to use 'Jr.' to make sure we weren't going to open letters, cards, and bills sent to the wrong person. This was a practice that we started and continued when I lived with the family on Birch Street. Even as adults, we still get each other's mail. Dad would get my bills, and sometimes I would get his. I would sometimes get a call from Dad asking me if I had 'bought something' where he also shopped. We both had accounts at many of the same stores. Bellaire Tire, Mendelson's Clothing Store, and DeVendra's Gulf were all places where we had established credit accounts. We could always straighten out the confusion, and if the account was insignificant, we just paid it along with our own charges.

A Century in Time

After leaving the store in 1974 to go to law school, each of my brothers graduated from Bellaire High School. We all went off to employment opportunities away from the grocery business, still operated by our father. My brother Doug returned briefly to work in Frizzi Market in the early 1980s. Dad agreed to send him to butcher school in Toledo to learn the art of cutting meat. He came back to work in Frizzi Market for several years as a butcher and manager of the meat department. This allowed Dad some freedom away from the Market. After several years, however, Doug also moved on to other employment.

Each of us, at one time or another, helped Dad when he needed some assistance. We brought our trades and talents to the store business to lend assistance when Dad needed help. Whether it was legal, electrical, construction, or just labor, we always tried to lend a hand, but our regular employment did not permit us to pursue a work career in the store. Dad continued to operate the Market by himself until he reached retirement age in 1991. He was anxious to retire and wanted to begin traveling and enjoying retirement with Mom. He was now on the School Board and found this work rewarding. Mom was especially hopeful that Dad would be able to spend less time at the store so that they could spend more time at Epworth Park in Bethesda, where they had purchased a cottage. Traveling, which is one thing that running a small family business often prevents, was also on their agenda.

Dad considered what he should do with the market. He contemplated a sale of the Market. He spoke to representatives of Grocer's Development Corporation in Wheeling about possibly purchasing the Market and operating it as a Convenient Food Mart. He also considered leasing the store. Dad asked me to check with another company in Wheeling that was in the wholesale grocery business to determine if they might have an interest. While these discussions were positive, they never fully developed to a seamless completion. Dad told me he hoped to find a way to continue the Market under the Frizzi name. This is why he approached my brother Dick to determine if he had an interest in running the store with his wife, Kim. Dick was a full-time steelworker, but with his wife's help, he was Dad's pick to take over the store. Dick and Kim agreed, and paperwork was drawn up for Dick to continue the operation of Frizzi Market.

During that time, he learned of those many challenges that faced the business, and the realization that a small grocery store was rapidly evolving into a different kind of business. Operating a grocery store as my Grandfather had known it was not going to return, despite the most diligent effort exerted. The store had to become a convenience-driven store, and not a fully functional grocery store. The meat department was converted to a deli and bakery operation. Fruit, vegetables, and produce were continued on a very limited basis. Catering to the public became difficult with competition from the large Kroger Superstore that was built in Bellaire in the 1990's. When Walmart and Sam's Club entered the grocery business, Frizzi Market could no longer be operated as a grocery store. This was becoming increasingly more difficult. Dick operated Frizzi Market until his own retirement in 2019. In that year, a century after our Grandfather Abramo married our Grandmother Philomena, the grocery business of Frizzi Market was transferred to new ownership. The Market was re-purposed as a wholesale food manufacturing operation, with a continuation of retail deli and bakery service. After more than 100 years under the Frizzi name in Bellaire, Ohio, our family sadly ended our grocery connections. Frizzi Market became the last of the small neighborhood grocery stores to survive in Bellaire, Ohio, a community where dozens had existed just 50 years before.

This was a bittersweet time for our family. We were proud of the century-old business that had been started by our Grandparents, Abe and Minnie, and continued by our father, Danny. We were happy that a new life for the business would keep the store open and permit it to continue at the Frizzi Market location. Yet, there was a sad reflection that came along, realizing that only our wonderful memories of growing up in a store business would be left to sustain us. Our parents were now gone, and the small grocery store business had passed on as well.

Just a Grocer's Son from Bellaire

In 2005, I received notification from the Ohio University Alumni Association and local campus officials that I was to receive the Austin C. Furbee Award. Austin Furbee was an attorney and member of the Belmont County Bar long before I was admitted in 1977. At his death, his family established an Award in his honor, to be given annually to a graduate of Ohio University who had begun their education at the local campus. Mr. Furbee was a visionary who helped to establish this local campus where my college work began. My Father attended this banquet where I was to receive the award. Mom could not attend due to illness. He was positioned alongside the Furbee family in front of the dais.

Concluding my remarks, accepting the award that evening, I spoke directly to the Furbee family members gathered there. I told them that I had never met their husband and father, Austin. Yet, I was sure he knew me even though our paths had not crossed. I wanted them to know that were it not for his vision and his belief that a young man like me would one day seek a college education, I might not have been addressing them that evening to receive the award.

My father sat with them when I offered this final thought: "So let me say thank you, for Austin's vision, that one day, a young man he had never met would choose the local campus Austin helped to found. No one in any respect remarkable, only an average kid seeking an education, I am *'just a grocer's son'* from Bellaire."

In giving thanks, I wanted my father to also feel some pride in all that he had done to get me to that moment. I believe with all sincerity this had been possible only because I grew up in that grocery business, just as he had. The early training in that little store on Washington Street made such a difference in my life. While our life's work took us in different directions, I continue to believe that our upbringing in that family business was the foundation for all things we may have achieved as adults. So just as my father was, so too am I, so proud to be "just a grocer's son" from Bellaire.

A photograph from the early 1980's of my father and I at a high school awards assembly where we each presented awards to graduating students. (Frizzi Collection)

Epilogue

Of the four grocery stores discussed in this book, only two are still standing in Bellaire, Ohio. The first store of Frizzi Brothers, located on the east side of Hamilton Street, was a residence until it was demolished and acquired by the Great Stone Viaduct Society as part of a rail-to-trail project. The second store, located on Union Street, was also established by the Frizzi Brothers and currently houses the Bellaire spaghetti house known as the 'Roosevelt.' The fourth store is located at 112 Second Avenue in West Bellaire, and currently houses the new business of 'Around the World Gourmet," which is a food processing and manufacturing company of gluten-free products. It also contains the deli and bakery utilized by Frizzi Market before closing. The third location of 2783 Washington Street is where both my father and I became Grocer's Sons.

Just as people do, places and things also grow old with the passing of time. The West Washington Street that I have described in these pages is not what one visiting there today will find. Sadly, this small section of town has deteriorated and decayed over time. Many of the homes are not occupied by those friends and customers whom I have known growing up. Many other homes are simply vacant. Just a few of the families mentioned in this book have descendants still residing here. I would be remiss in not explaining this to those who read these pages. What I have painted through my words is a mental picture and a view of the way West Washington Street used to be.

The little neighborhood grocery store of Abraham Frizzi and the storeroom across the street still stand, but both are boarded up by the current owners and are not occupied. When I pass along the street that I knew as a boy, I feel sadness in seeing West Washington Street as it has changed. When I speak with others who share similar memories, they also regret how time has changed the street where we grew up. We do share one common sentiment. Each of us feels grateful that our lives began here many years ago, creating all those friendships, experiences, and moments included within these pages. The successes of so many fine children who are now adults, but who came from humble beginnings, should make all proud. Those successes are a credit to the families and that time and place from long ago. We can take pride that we are the children of all those wonderful families who resided on West Washington Street and hold memories of my Grandfather's neighborhood grocery store.

Proud veterans from the "Greatest Generation", like my father Danny, pose at a final celebration of the Veterans of West Washington Street. Pictured from left front are Julie Rusciolelli; unknown; Armand Massa; Joe Nardo; Evan Nardone; Dominic DeFelice. Back from left are unknown; Daniel Frizzi Sr.; Dominic Presutti; Dean Giacometti; Marion DePaulis; George Cowen; and Pete Tuccio. Thank You For Your Service! (Frizzi Collection 2006)